To Wayne:
May this ~
some fond ~
Good luck to you in all
your ventures. Sincerely,
Ginger Wadsworth

February 8, 1997

MW01057022

$35^{00}

Good Luck

Jimmy the Greek

Photograph taken in the late sixties.

— Jimmy Snyder

Farewell

Jimmy the Greek

The Wizard of Odds

by **GINGER WADSWORTH** *and*
JIMMY SNYDER

EAKIN PRESS ★ Austin, Texas

FIRST EDITION

Copyright © 1996
By Ginger Wadsworth

Published in the United States of America
By Eakin Press
An Imprint of Sunbelt Media, Inc.
P.O. Drawer 90159   H   Austin, TX 78709-0159

ISBN 1-57168-144-2

Library of Congress Cataloging-in-Publication Data

Wadsworth, Ginger
    Farewell Jimmy the Greek: wizard of odds / by Ginger Wadsworth and Jimmy Snyder — 1st ed.
        p.   cm.
    Includes index.
      ISBN 1-57168-144-2
      1. Jimmy the Greek. 2. Gamblers — United States — Biography. I. Jimmy the Greek. II. Title.
    HV6710.3.J56W33   1997
    795'.092 – dc21
      [B]   96-51764
                                                              CIP

To all the fans who believed in
Jimmy and loved him.

*Rare family picture. Order from left to right: Jimmy's birth mother, Sultania;
his aunt, Maria Andriotis; his sister, Mary; and Jimmy.*

— Synodinos family picture

Contents

Jimmy's father, George, and stepmother, Agnes,
attending Jimmy and Joan's wedding on June 14, 1952.
— Synodinos family picture

Preface

Tommy Manakides approached me in 1992 with the idea of writing this book. He had met Jimmy the Greek in 1988, shortly after Jimmy's expulsion from CBS, and had grown quite fond of him.

Tommy elaborated on the importance of the truth being told concerning Jimmy the Greek's disappearance from the public eye. He also shared an observation that Jimmy the Greek was quite different from the hardened, crusty image portrayed by the media. My curiosity was aroused, but I set out to write this book objectively. The more I researched, the more I became convinced that there was truth to his claim.

He arranged for Jimmy and me to meet for the first time, and within minutes of our introduction Jimmy the Greek had already inquired about my age and place of birth. I told him I was from Birmingham, Alabama, and he immediately nicknamed me "Birmingham" and never again called me by any other name. When I told him my age, his face lost expression and he stared blankly at the wall. Then he said, "I had a daughter, a beautiful girl, who would have been the same age as you." He told me that she died of cystic fibrosis.

Our bond was immediate and it was not long before he began recounting stories of his past. He told them almost word for word, time and again, in the same way a parent recites a fairy tale as if it were the first time the child ever heard it.

I corroborated with Tommy, who knew him better than anyone during his final years. This proved beneficial in revealing the other side of Jimmy the Greek. Jimmy's love for Tommy was evident to anyone who saw them together. I once heard him tell

Tommy, "You're a good man and the best of friends. Thank God you're here with me. I love you." That softer, warmer side of Jimmy the Greek unfolded as the years drifted by. I believe he wanted Tommy to know who he really was because he knew that the book would ultimately allow the world that same advantage.

During one of their conversations, Jimmy expressed his fear of being remembered as a racist. Tommy made a vow to him that he would do everything in his power to erase that fallacy.

I did not know it at the time, but it was only hours after he made that promise to Jimmy that Tommy asked me to undertake this project. This book is the fulfillment of his promise. If Tommy had not shared the intimate conversations and experiences he had with Jimmy, perhaps none of us would have had the opportunity to know the "real" Jimmy the Greek, Wizard of Odds.

— GINGER WADSWORTH

Chapter 1

Vital Lessons

THERE WOULD BE NO Jimmy the Greek — oddsmaker, gambler, and commentator for CBS-TV's *NFL Today* show — had he not undergone the tragedy of his childhood. In fact, his entourage of friends, family, and colleagues probably would have known him as a reverent priest in a prominent Greek Orthodox church, a famous attorney, or a talented concert violinist.

That was where Demetrios Synodinos was headed under the careful guidance of his mother, who pushed him in his studies, ingrained in him religious beliefs, and insisted on his taking violin lessons. Those aspirations abruptly ended in Steubenville, Ohio, on March 28, 1928, when Jimmy was ten years old.

He was playing sidewalk "tennis" with his friend, Johnny, in front of his father's grocery store, the White Star Meat Market, when his mother called to him.

"Jimmy . . . Come on, my boy. Let's go home." Jimmy's mother, Sultania, was walking with her sister, Theano. Theano was separated from her husband and had come to live with Jimmy's family for a while.

"Hey, Mom," Jimmy said. "Can I stay and go home with Pop?"

"No dear," his mother chided, "you must get home and study. After all —"

"After all, I have to make good grades if I'm going to be a lawyer, I know," interrupted Jimmy. He rolled his eyes at Johnny.

1

"Okay," Jimmy said.

They began to walk the five-block stretch that led to his home. Jimmy walked ahead, moping and looking back at his mother with his piercing brown eyes that tugged at her heart. After they completed a block and a half, his mother said, "All right, Jimmy, you can stay but when you get home —"

"I know," Jimmy said, his eyes lit up, "I'll study."

Jimmy ran back to the store and Johnny and he resumed their game, even though it was 8:30 P.M. They played by the street lights. He had been losing and was just beginning to catch up when he heard the clang of a paddy wagon leaving the police station down the block.

They stopped playing, watching to see where it went. It passed them, headed in the direction of his home, and then Brooksie, the neighborhood cop, drove up. Jimmy froze. He was young, but intuitive.

Brooksie entered the store, and almost immediately Pop and he scurried back out. Pop yelled, "Demetrios, come with me!"

They went to the police station. As they walked inside, Jimmy saw his mother's red pocketbook lying on the desk.

"Where is she?" Jimmy screamed. "Where's my mother? Where's my mother?"

Brooksie was biting his twitching bottom lip.

Jimmy impatiently said, "She's dead, isn't she?"

Brooksie's eyes swelled with tears. "Yes, son, your mother and Aunt Theano are dead."

Jimmy swallowed hard, fighting to hold back the tears.

"Dead?" His voice quivered.

"It was your Uncle Pete. He killed them and then shot himself."

Immediately, Pop grabbed Jimmy into his arms and they firmly embraced, collapsing into a chair. Pop screamed, "I knew he'd do it. I knew it!"

Jimmy's uncle, Pete Galanos, was a war hero with a chest full of medals. He suffered battle fatigue. When Theano, a great beauty at age twenty-six, left him, it pushed him over the edge.

Jimmy learned that after he left them, his mother, aunt, and two younger sisters had continued down the street. His mother held hands with his sister, Mary, while his Aunt Theano pushed

Marika in the baby carriage. When they got in front of the house, Pete, equipped with an arsenal of weapons he had saved from the war, appeared out of a secluded dark area near the house. He fired once, hitting Jimmy's mother. As she fell to the ground, she told Mary, "Let go of my hand and run!"

Mary released hands and grabbed the stroller that was now free. She was fearful that her uncle might kill baby Marika or that the carriage might roll down the street and hurt her. She pushed the carriage and ran as fast as her little legs allowed. Then she heard more shots and looked back to see her aunt collapsing to the ground. There was another shot. It was directed at Marika and her, but missed. She ran in between her house and her neighbor's and hid.

Then, there was the final shot, the bullet that entered the right side of Pete's head and exited the left. His body slumped onto his wife's lifeless body. He was still alive.

Almost immediately the streets filled with hundreds of bystanders who gasped, shrieked, and wept at the ghastly scene. Women and young girls wailed in horror. Within minutes of the tragedy, the police arrived and had the bodies of Jimmy's mother and aunt rushed to the morgue. His Uncle Pete was taken to Ohio Valley Hospital, where he died two hours later. People lingered at the crime scene for more than an hour after the tragedy, comforting one another and exchanging versions of what happened.

When Pete died, they found a letter of explanation in his pocket, written before he left Donora, Pennsylvania, where he lived. In it he said he killed his wife because he loved her and he killed his sister-in-law because she and other family members were jealous of him, persuaded Theano to leave him, and wanted her to marry another man. He wrote that he, alone, was responsible for their deaths as well as his own, and urged law enforcement to charge no one else with the crime.

The letter further explained that he provided a good living for Theano in Donora but she refused to live there under the influence of relatives.

Then it said: "If any of my friends get into trouble, I hope they will settle their affairs so they will not have this kind of trouble which has befallen me."

He offered words of strength to his brother, Christopher: "I do not want you to feel bad when you hear about my death." He asked Christopher to take care of his financial matters.

When Pop screamed at police headquarters that he knew Pete was going to do something tragic, he had just cause for his intuition. During the summer, Theano had visited Greece with relatives. Upon returning in November, she decided to live with Jimmy's family in Steubenville, instead of joining her husband in Donora.

Late one evening, Pete and his brother, Christopher, showed up at their house and captured Theano at gunpoint, forcing her into the automobile. They took her back to Donora. Two days later, they were arrested and authorities were unsure whether a man could be accused of kidnapping his own wife. They held the two of them in jail pending an investigation before the grand jury. During that investigation, Pete consented to Theano living with her sister in Steubenville and said he would do no harm to her or Jimmy's family.

Officials asked the Synodinos family whether or not they would press charges. Fearful of what Pete might do, they declined. At that point, the case was dropped, but their fears escalated.

Theano had married Pete when she was young. She had been unhappily married for four years and did not love Pete anymore; yet, she respected the sacredness of their marriage vows. Throughout their marriage, Pete gave her no money, was extremely possessive and jealous, and spent money on other women in his unfaithful ventures. Theano had lived with Jimmy's family for four months when Pete could no longer accept their separation. In his letter, he said he would join his wife in another life.

That night, when Jimmy's father and he returned home, people were everywhere even though it was late. He went to bed and almost instinctively waited for his mother to tuck him in. Jimmy always thought it was silly when she came in and kissed him on his cheek, but if she came now, he would not feel the same.

He finally dozed off and awoke to the sound of children playing outside. He looked out the window and saw his friends, Pete and Johnny, whittling away with their pocket knives at the telephone pole in front of his house.

He pulled on a pair of pants and grabbed his shirt from the floor, buttoning it as he ran out the front door.

"What are you *haftas* (a Greek term for idiots) doing?" Jimmy asked.

The two boys turned and jumped, startled by his presence. Johnny mumbled, seemingly caught without words. Jimmy snatched the knife from him and looked at the pole. Suddenly, he turned white, and his knees began to tremble. He felt weak and almost faint. A bullet was embedded in the telephone pole. The realization of what happened struck him. It was not a nightmare. His mother was dead.

"Jimmy, are you all right?" Johnny asked. "You don't look so good."

Jimmy felt a big lump in his throat. He swallowed hard. He felt like crying, but could not let the boys see him cry.

After they left, Jimmy stood there alone, looking at the bullet-pierced telephone pole. He stuck his index finger into the hole and touched the bullet. He wondered if that bullet was the one that was intended for himself, had he not begged to stay. For the first time, he realized how close he had been to death. He thought about the shot aimed at Mary and Marika. He knew he would not have been so lucky had he been there. He probably would have put up a fight when he saw his mother killed. Maybe he would have run away, but he was sure that he would have been killed. He was confused, feeling grateful that his life was spared and guilty at the same time.

In a way, he felt a little responsible for his mother's death. Maybe if he had been there, he could have protected her. He wanted to run straight to her arms, the one safe place to go, when he was frightened and sad. He longed to be held just one more time. Where was she now that he needed her more than ever?

He could never forget that numb, hollow feeling that thundered in his heart and wrenched the center of his soul. Festering feelings of fear and loneliness plagued him to the point that he felt like exploding.

A part of Jimmy was gone forever: the innocence and trust of childhood, the love and nurturing of a mother and an entire family structure to which he was accustomed.

Shortly after his mother's death, his father, Uncle Stanley

(actually it was Pop's cousin who seemed like an uncle), his two sisters, and he left Steubenville and returned to Greece.

"Why do we have to leave Steubenville?" Jimmy asked.

"Because we're going home," Pop said.

Jimmy remembered hearing his relatives talk about Kios, the magical island. Grandpa was always "going to the island" and coming back. He started this pattern in 1904. They all moved to Steubenville because the other Kios villagers went there. No one remembered who were the first Kions to live in Steubenville, but everyone else from the island followed. Grandpa opened the biggest food store in town, the White Star Meat Market.

One time when everyone was talking about Kios, Jimmy asked Uncle Stanley why everyone loved the island. "If they like it so much, why do they come here?"

"Because," he answered, "the living is good there, but the money is good here. Blessed is the man who has both."

Jimmy knew that the home village was Kalamote, or "the good eye," and the island's language was his language. He was never allowed to speak English in the house.

"You will learn to talk American in school," Pop said, "and you'll learn from your playmates. But here you will speak the language of your people."

The journey to Greece was endless. As the waves tossed and rolled, Jimmy found himself leaning over the side of the ship to throw up.

"Throw up on the deck," Pop said, "or you'll throw yourself up and over to feed the fish."

Jimmy held tight to the stanchion as he threw up on the deck. Then he saw the first sight of land, which he figured was Kios, but it turned out to be Portugal.

"Poor-too-gal," they told him. Then there was Naples, and Pireaus, with a trip to Athens, where Pop bought him a .25 rifle. Finally, the island of Kios rose out of the blue-green Aegean Sea.

When they finally stepped ashore, he could not understand why the island kept moving. Uncle Stanley teased him about walking bow-legged, but Jimmy only thought about jumping into the first bed he saw. When he found one, he slept around the clock.

In the morning, he went downstairs and found Grandpa alone in the house.

"Grandpa," Jimmy said, "where's Pop and Uncle Stanley?"

"Men rise early while children sleep in bed," Grandpa said. "You're father is in the field with his gun, where the quail flutter, just as he was when he was your age."

Jimmy hurried back upstairs to get his treasured .25 rifle and ran back down.

"How do I get there?" he asked.

"Your car awaits you at the front of the house," Grandpa said.

All right, Jimmy thought, *I can handle that – a real car.* He was rudely awakened when all he saw was a jackass. Then he remembered coming from the boat the night before through streets too narrow for a car or even a good-sized wagon. He went back inside the house.

"What am I supposed to do with that?" he asked.

"Well, if you want to get anywhere," Grandpa said, "and you don't want to walk, that is what you'll ride."

Jimmy never found his father that morning. The jackass had its own idea. A jaunt through the fig trees. When the animal stopped on its own accord, and the young rider sampled the ripest fruit from the low-hanging branches, a deputy appeared from nowhere, shouting, "You, boy! What are you doing here stealing fruit? Little bastard, you'll come with me." He grabbed the rope bridle and led them through the orchard and into town, past laughing villagers, to the office of the constable.

"I've got a serious case of theft here," the deputy said. "He's been stealing figs."

The constable laughed, and for the first time, Jimmy ceased being afraid.

"Well," the constable said, "if he's stealing, he's stealing from himself. This is Demetrios, grandson of Synodinos. And that acreage is what his grandfather means for him to have."

For the first time in his life, little Demetrios Synodinos (he later legally changed his name to James Snyder for the sake of convenience) understood the pride of his family's heritage.

Grandma ruled the island women. The well was drawn at 7:00 A.M. and at 5:00 P.M., and the women stood around waiting for her to make her appearance. She drew the first water. Woe be to the woman who stepped in front of her. The same procedure was followed at Sunday mass. Grandma was the first to en-

ter the church. If she was a moment late, the women waited for
her. Her name was Kyriaki, or "Sunday," and she was as peace-
ful as her name, until she was crossed. This was true of all the
Synodinos family.

Pride carried Jimmy through the next few weeks, miserable
every one. There was no electricity; he lighted a match to a lamp.
There was no radio or telephone to talk to his buddies. Actually,
there were no buddies. He went to the bathroom through a hole
in the backyard, like the outhouses of early America. Gradually,
however, Kios began to take hold of him.

Jimmy learned the rituals of the island. He saw how Turkish
tobacco was grown, dried, packed, and auctioned. "Turkish tobacco?" he had asked, and was informed that Kios was only a
quarter mile off the coast of Turkey. He always assumed that the
land mass over there was Mother Greece.

Eventually, he made friends with the village boys and
learned to gamble drachmas on the toss of a stone. The boys
enjoyed setting their game on a bridge that spanned a creek near
Kios, each putting a coin on top of a stone and tossing at the
other's. Jimmy spent three days searching for the right stone, a
small one, easier to control. He won most of the drachmas, and
his friends said he won because he did not need the money. He
was rich; that is why he could throw easily. The truth was, he
loved the game and did not think about the drachmas.

There was a school in town for all the children, but this
would not do for the son of George Synodinos, grandson of
John Synodinos. This heir, this paragon, had to have a private
tutor. The daughter of Dalma was hired to instruct him. That
was the only name Jimmy ever knew. The family name was
enough, and the affiliation was identity. Dalma was an old lady,
by Jimmy's standards, in her late twenties, and was strict in her
demands for completed assignments in Greek, mathematics, and
English. They took long walks, rode jackasses, and had their lessons under olive trees.

In the spring of 1930, Dalma packed a fine lunch with an
emphasis on desserts for the sweet tooth of her student. They
were high in the Kios hills and looked down at the coast of
Turkey. For the first time, the world seemed right to Jimmy. It
was not difficult to see why. Here he was being nurtured and

cared for by a Greek woman who was the same age as his mother when she died. Dalma was gentle and kind, but she also pushed him to excel at his studies. They were surrounded by beauty and serenity. Finally he had found someone who made him feel secure enough to confide in.

For the first time since his mother's death, he revealed to Dalma the tragic details of that evening in March when his life changed forever. After he spilled his pain, he trembled with emotion. The daughter of Dalma hugged him in her arms as they sobbed. Her embrace helped quiet his fears and eased some of the pain that was bottled up inside him. They stayed together for a long time, looking at the calm water. Jimmy breathed a deep sigh of relief.

Following his mother's death, he grew up quickly. He began looking for things to fill the void in his life. Pop and Uncle Stanley had a cold yet soft regard for him. They saw nothing wrong as he gravitated to the company of older friends. One night he joined a pair of eighteen-year-olds from Kios. Jimmy asked, "Hey, isn't there anything to do in this place?"

"Yeah," one of them answered, "but only if you've got the money."

Jimmy waved $10 and they headed for Smyrna. Smyrna is the largest Turkish town within the purview of Kios, across a narrow band of water and inland a few miles.

When they arrived, Jimmy followed behind his pals as they entered a brothel. Each was introduced by the madam to his lady of the evening. When Jimmy laid eyes on his maiden, he felt numb. She was the most beautiful woman he had ever seen. Scantily clad in a red, lacy negligee, his eyes could not help glaring at the fleshy breasts that protruded from her bodice.

She led Jimmy to an alcove of delight and gently seduced him. He remembered this woman as a *Turkala*, meaning a Turkish beauty. This experience immediately gave him a sense of importance and temporarily filled in his emptiness. As he strutted out the door, he told the madam, "Put the other two guys on my bill." For two U.S. dollars, his friends and he were treated to the mysteries of the Smyrna night.

Jimmy's illusion of being a man was greater than the reality. Shortly after his sexual introduction to manhood, he was introduced to his future stepmother.

Pop decided to remarry. All the eligible girls of Kios were after George Synodinos. They knew that whoever married him would go to America, which offset the burden of raising his three small children. Pop selected Agnes — the brightest, the prettiest, and the one who showed the most interest in his children.

Agnes reminded Jimmy of his real mother. She was warm, and Pop seemed happier with her around. She eased some of the tension around home and provided nurturing for Mary and Marika. Like his mother, Agnes was a hard worker who prioritized family before anything else.

Soon, the Synodinos family returned to Steubenville, Ohio. It was 1932, and thirteen-year-old Jimmy was not little anymore. Pop had fared well, selling his big store before leaving for Kios — just months before the Black Friday of the stock market. Now the Depression had set in Steubenville.

To Jimmy, the Depression meant there were no more handouts from Pop. His father had taught him, "Go first class or don't go." They had dined in the finest restaurants and stayed in the best hotels, with money that cashed in four-for-one. Now he was broke in Steubenville without even a jackass for transportation.

He began doing business at the junkyard, scrounging around the back alleys for old newspapers and bottles and anything else he could lay his hands on. When the junk man let him have an old discarded bicycle frame, Jimmy offered a proposition: "Help me get the pieces for this thing and I'll go all over town getting stuff for you." The junk man laughed and sold him two wheels at half price. Piece by piece, Jimmy put the bike together, then spent the last of his capital on a paint job, in his colors, the Greek colors: blue trimmed in white. Every kid in the neighborhood wanted to borrow it. After a few loan-outs, he stopped the free rides.

"You can have it all day for twenty cents," he said. Four months later, he had seven more bikes and was netting $1.60 a day.

Jimmy's bike business began to crumble after a while because customers kept disappearing with the rental property. Ironically, at that same time, there was a sales meeting at the Eastman Kodak Company that directed him toward a more interesting way to earn money: gambling.

Chapter 2

Steubenville:
A Gambler's Observatory

JIMMY THE GREEK WOULD never have gotten his start in gambling if his mother had not been killed when he was so young. He would never have had the freedom to roam, much less the time, because he would have been too busy studying, participating in church activities, and practicing violin. Somehow after she died, he developed an independent spirit — it was he against the world.

Now he could have gotten involved in a number of activities that would have been more destructive for a youth, but Steubenville hosted what might be termed as the finest of gambler's observatories — a place for a gambler to learn the "ins and outs" of the gaming world.

The wide-open town of Steubenville had 40,000 citizens and eleven bookmaking establishments. On Water Street, Boy's Town, a boy could have the top-of-the-line prostitute for $2. Every candy and cigar store had a pinball machine that paid off and punchboards with a big gold seal.

Steubenville produced great casino operators in the boom years after World War II. The Facinto boy, Mokie, ran the casino at Caesar's Palace. Paradise Island in the Bahamas imported Bob Sasso. Joey Tamburo wound up in Reno. Pre-Castro Cuba belonged to Dino Cellini. There was another kid, Dino Crosetti, who was the Romeo dealer at the Rex, an Italian joint. He later

11

changed his name to Dean Martin and never made it as a gambler.

Shortly after Jimmy's bicycle business failed, he saw another opportunity. A salesman had complained about box camera sales when an idea hit him. He decided to give every seventh grader in Steubenville a free box camera, post a $25 prize for the best photograph, and see what happened to film sales.

Jimmy set out to win that $25. He sought professional advice at Miller's Camera Store. Mr. Miller told him that in his experience, all photo contests were won by "nature studies," and then explained. Jimmy took fifty-five pictures of the big tree in his front yard during the morning, noon, and twilight. One day, Mr. Miller said, "You go home for lunch every day, don't you? So that means you pass the Ace newsstand. Do me a favor, on your way home tomorrow, pick up a racing form for me."

After that, Mr. Miller showed him how to use a darkroom and charged him nothing for the prints he made of the big tree. Jimmy won the $25. By now he was hooked on photography and was good friends with Dan Miller. On his way home for lunch he delivered the racing forms, and on the way back to school he delivered Miller's bets to the back door of Money O'Brien's Academy Pool Room, where the gambling was. His Uncle Mike had a barber's chair in the front of the poolroom, so Jimmy used the back door. What the family did not know would not hurt *him*.

To Jimmy, Money O'Brien's place was just a bigger punchboard.

It did not take him long to realize that Dan Miller's action usually went one way — into O'Brien's pocket. Miller loved parlays and horses listed at 20-to-1 in the morning line. By now, Jimmy read the form himself and lingered at O'Brien's to see what the other bettors did. He started holding out some of Miller's bets. Now and then, he slipped in a $1-show parlay of his own. He was fourteen, almost six feet tall, and did not dress like a school kid or ask a lot of dumb questions. He listened, at least until he found out what was going on.

All the talk was about the Kentucky Derby. Two days before the race, Jimmy picked his horse and decided to make his first "real" bet. He had $62 of Miller's and O'Brien's money, and another $18 in the school savings account. He forged Pop's name to withdraw the savings and bet everything — $80 — on the nose.

Jimmy's horse, Calvalcade, won easily. That Saturday night Jimmy knew he was the smartest fourteen-year-old horseplayer that ever lived. It caused quite a stir in the back room of the Academy when O'Brien congratulated Dan Miller on his Derby score and Miller said, "Whaddya mean? I had the horse that ran second, Vanderbilt's horse, Discovery."

That summer Jimmy started running O'Brien's bets against other bookmakers. The tall Irishman with sandy hair raked in the money with his own book, a craps table, some poker, and a Big Six Wheel at the Academy. He wanted to beat the horses, too, but never could. When O'Brien tried to tip him $5, Jimmy turned it down.

"I don't want a tip," he said. "I'll just take two and a half per-cent of what I carry."

He was soon running bets from one book to another all over town. Some months he was the only winner.

O'Brien had two partners at the Academy, Tom Griffin and Harry Cooper. Griffin and Cooper also owned a nightclub ca-sino on the edge of town called the Half Moon. It was a popular place, and Jimmy invented a new business for himself there, parking the customers' cars. The Half Moon paid him ten cents a car. He soon had four helpers doing all the work. They got the dime and he collected the tips.

During the day at the Academy, Jimmy began watching the dealer at the Big Six Wheel, an ancient geezer named Paul Dun-kel. Most of the time, when Dunkel raked in the losers, he missed the bets on the number under his left elbow and the money rode free. Jimmy started playing that number. O'Brien had never seen Jimmy show interest in the Big Six and was curious. After a few plays, O'Brien's face lit up with a grin and he came over. "Dun-kel," he said, "go help on craps . . . And you," he pointed at Jim-my, "you get behind there and handle the wheel." Within a few weeks, Jimmy was dealing craps and learning to stack chips. He kept stacks of chips on his dresser at home to practice cutting one stack even with another, developing a smooth, fast "feel" for the chips necessary for a dice dealer to keep the game flowing.

One night the next spring, Jimmy came home late and

found Pop waiting up for him. Pop thought he was still parking cars at the Half Moon.

"Where have you been, you bum?" Pop asked.

"Working," Jimmy said.

"Working what?"

Jimmy took out his bankroll — $1,400 — and fanned it. He knew he was making more money than Pop. Pop slapped him across the face, convinced Jimmy had stolen it.

A month later, Pop needed $1,000 to buy a freezer to store a new product on the market, Bird's Eye frozen foods. Jimmy gave him the money. There was a tear in Pop's eye. It was about this time that Jimmy stopped calling him Pop and began calling him George.

By the time he started high school that fall, he was dealing craps at the Half Moon. He went out for football as a sophomore, but a bungling juvenile stepped on his hand and he decided he could not afford the sport. After all, he was raking in $7 to $15 a night with those hands.

He attended high school during the day, and worked the tables at night, where the action was designed to move faster than the player's eyes. He learned about percentage dice shaved to favor an ace-six and a plenitude of snake eyes and boxcars. He discovered that a "marked wheel" was a roulette table rigged to activate a pin under a heavy number. He could not prove it, but he sensed that all the bastards who ran the games that way would stay forever in the minor leagues.

Everyone at the Half Moon thought Jimmy was twenty-one. He wore triple G suits and Kuppenheimer's at $70, from the Hub or Denmark's clothing store. He wore special-ordered Bostonian shoes, $30 a pair, but never wore a hat. There was still a depression on, but not if you picked fast horses and played for the house.

With all this going on, Jimmy was content to work with Money O'Brien at the Academy and deal for Cooper and Griffin at the Half Moon. Griffin, the quiet Irishman, was fascinated by the way Jimmy handled the chips — "checks" in dealer's jargon.

"Let me see you take twenty, Greek," he would say, and Jimmy lifted twenty off the top every time, never nineteen and definitely never twenty-one. Little Cooper was Griffin's opposite —

talking with his hands and jabbing fingers, lapsing into Jewish dialect. He was an old banter sure of his turf.

It was Cooper who first called on Jimmy when high rollers crowded at the craps table. "We need your speed, kid. Give us a fast two furlongs." When the money is on the line, the faster play increases the house percentage. Cooper liked Jimmy and often challenged him.

Cooper said, "Greek, O'Brien tells me you think you can read a form."

"I can read it a little," Jimmy said.

"What? What? Speak up, Greek, you're not in church. I notice you always talk softly until somebody tells you that you're wrong. I got a proposition for you."

"I'm listening."

"You pick a horse the night before, any goddamn horse in the list, and I'll lay you two-to-one."

"You were born dead," Jimmy said.

He looked at Cooper's bet as a license to steal. He had to pick the horse out of the overnight entries and before any odds were listed, but even so, within a month he had $700 of Cooper's money.

"Gr . . . ee . . . k." Somehow Cooper stretched that word into three syllables. "Greek, you are nickel and diming me to death. When are you going to make a bet?"

"I got one for you at Saratoga," Jimmy said. "Merry Lassie in the feature. I like her for $700."

"Let me remind you, keed, if Merry Lassie is scratched, you lose."

"I don't bet scratched horses," Jimmy said. He knew the filly would be around 1-to-2 in the morning line.

The next day Jimmy was at the Academy listening to the call. "At the quarter, it's Merry Lassie by three . . . at the half it's Merry Lassie by two . . . in the stretch Merry Lassie's on top by one. . . . There is a photo in the seventh at Saratoga. . . . The winner is Clodian." That call remained with Jimmy forever. It was one of many instances that eventually led him to give up horse racing as a serious betting proposition.

Until the night Johnny Tatos came down with his people from Little Washington, Pennsylvania, Cooper never knew Jimmy had a temper to match his own. Tato's group was what the Half Moon regarded as "good players," that is, both sharp and heavy. Cooper took a look at the action and said, "Pay them off in $25 checks."

Jimmy did not say anything. Cooper thought the bigger chips would increase their play. Jimmy knew differently. People have a tendency to hold on to $25 checks and cash them in at the cashier's cage. They continue to buck ones and fives against the house. Besides, Jimmy felt he could keep the game flowing with the smaller checks.

In fifteen minutes, Cooper was back at his elbow. "What are you, deaf?" he asked. "I told you to use the 25s."

Jimmy turned and faced him nose to nose. "Stick the 25s up your ass!" he yelled. "Deal 'em yourself," he said as he walked out. That was the last time Jimmy wanted to work for someone else.

He was in greater downtown Steubenville before he realized how bad his timing was. It was pay night at the Half Moon. He was tapped out — fillies that fade in the stretch will do that. Too angry to go home, he went to the Fort Steubenville Club on Market Street, a walk-up after-hours sanctuary with private membership. He only had some pocket change, but he could sign the tab and play the slots. His first nickel hit two cherries and a bell. He moved to the quarter machine, and hit a $10 jackpot. He put the $10 on a "lucky number" he had been playing for weeks: 807. The next day 807 was the final number in the stock exchange volume, and he collected $6,000. *To hell with the Half Moon,* Jimmy thought.

That winter he quit high school. He had a brand new $750 Plymouth and about $500 left in reserve. Cecil (Skeeter) Gallagher was a horseplayer he knew from around the Academy, and he said to Jimmy, "You know why we're not cashing any bets. It's because we're not on the scene. You've got to look those babies in the eyes, move around at night and pick up inside information."

"Not only that," Jimmy said, "but we are up to our asses in snow." Gallagher and he headed for Florida. They had $900 between them and were going to devote all of January and February to bringing Tropical Park to its knees. This was the beginning of a ritual for Jimmy: hitting Miami Beach for the winter.

There was more than fun involved. It was also a badge of "the big time" for the fellow who bet money. During the winter at Steubenville, when a guy was busted, his friends needled him, "Hey, Jake, when are you going to Florida?" He would say, "Oh, in a week or two, after the slow players get cleared out."

Gallagher and he took a suite at the Causeway Apartments. That was the way they liked to put it. What they really did was rent two rooms at $14 a week that shared a connecting bath and rearranged the furniture so the beds were in one room and the sofas and chairs were in the other.

In three weeks, they were busted. Jimmy had $22 and Gallagher had a few dimes. He gave Gallagher $20 for bus fare and sent him north, 1,026 miles back to Steubenville. Gallagher promised to raise the money to bring him home. That night Jimmy met Cornelius Jones, another dealer from Steubenville, outside the Hickory House Restaurant on Twenty-third Street where all the gamblers hung out. Jonesy later ran the most exclusive casino in Cleveland and the Desert Inn in Las Vegas, but that night he did not look like a winner either.

"How's it going?" he asked.

"My rent's paid," Jimmy said, "and I just sent a rescue party north." They added it up and they had $6 between them. Jonesy poked a thumb at the restaurant. "We can go for the beef ragout for $2.50," he said. "If we don't have dessert, that leaves a buck tip for the waiter."

The Hickory House had a Greek busboy who enjoyed swapping the old language with Jimmy. He came over and said, "Tomorrow I go to the track. Have you got a horse for a fellow Greek?" Jimmy told him he liked a horse named Red Rain and he made Jimmy repeat it three times and then write it down.

Things were slow at the Causeway Apartments, sitting around all day reading old racing forms. That night Jimmy met Jonesy at the restaurant again. He had promoted $10 for the big beef ragout dinner, this time with dessert. As soon as they went inside, Popkin, the owner, rushed over and said, "A guy's been in here asking for you. He didn't know your name, just said, 'the tall Greek.'"

"That's okay," Jimmy said. "When he comes in, send him over. If he doesn't know my name, he isn't a bill collector."

Before they made it to the table, the busboy came over and embraced Jimmy. "Ah, my friend," he said. "The horse you gave me I bet him six across and I win $84.50." This fellow Greek assumed Jimmy had the horse too. What Jimmy really had was indigestion.

When they began eating their cheesecake, an expensively dressed midwestern-looking guy walked up and introduced himself. It turned out he owned a meat-packing company in Pennsylvania, F. W. Alexander, Inc. "I want you to know," he said, "I couldn't help overhearing you last night when you gave that horse to the busboy. When the race came up today I was down $3,000 . . ." Jonesy gave a little twitch in his chair. In 1938, that was a ton of money for an average meat packer to be betting. "I bet $500 across on Red Rain," Alexander went on, "and I feel I owe you something. Please take this." He pointed a sheaf of bills at Jimmy.

Jimmy said, "Oh, no, I can't do that." Jonesy nearly broke Jimmy's shinbone with a kick under the table. Alexander insisted and Jimmy got kicked again. On the third offer Alexander took the bills and shoved them into Jimmy's coat pocket. Later, when he looked, he counted five $100 bills. His first thought was, *Now I can play.*

Alexander insisted that Jimmy join him at the track the next day. This was Tropical Park, Jimmy's favorite racetrack up to the day they stopped racing there. Alexander, along with his wife and mother-in-law, was staying at the new Vanderbilt Hotel on Collins Avenue, and he offered to pick up Jimmy in his car. Jimmy did not want him to know he was staying in the Causeway Apartments, so he arranged to meet him outside the Vanderbilt.

Alexander had brought his own limousine and driver, and before Jimmy settled back in the cushioned seat, Alexander wanted to know who he liked in the first race. "I don't like anything in that one," Jimmy said, "so you're on your own. I like a horse in the fifth race and another in the eighth. Other than that, I don't like a thing."

When the fifth race came up, Alexander bet $600 across — win, place, and show — and Jimmy bet $50 the same way. That $50 was a third of his bankroll. The horse ran second, so Alexander netted $1,200 and Jimmy netted $100.

Jimmy's pick in the eighth race was the morning-line favorite at 2-to-1, a horse named Flag Unfurled, who was known to finish late. Tropical Park had a short home stretch, and Jimmy's only concern was that the horse might be unable to make up ground before getting to the wire. Alexander asked, "How strong are you on this?" Jimmy told him it was a stronger bet than the one in the fifth. He bet $1,000 across and Jimmy went $100 across.

Flag Unfurled broke out of the starting gate last and Alexander yelled, "He's left at the post!"

Jimmy said, "No, that's the way he runs. When he hits the turn at the backstretch, he'll be in stride and when they come for home, he'll be passing horses." The script went just the way he wrote it. Flag Unfurled was eighth, then seventh, then sixth, running past horses like they were sixteenth poles, and Alexander was going crazy. The horse was drawing three lengths away. Alexander was slapping Jimmy on the back. "You're a genius!" he yelled. "Nobody . . . nobody knows more about racing than you do."

On the way back to the hotel, Alexander added up the day's winnings and said, "Here, partner, this is yours." Of his $4,800, he wanted Jimmy to take half. Jimmy told him that was not how it worked. He advised that he keep the $4,800 and they would go at it again tomorrow. He pressed $200 on Jimmy for his "daily expenses." This was an overlay of $194, but Jimmy took it.

Jimmy went by the Vanderbilt the next day to meet Alexander, but there was no answer in his room. He was stunned. He had him paged in the dining room. No answer. Finally, he asked if there were any messages, and there was one. "My mother-in-law wanted to go to Cuba today and there are some things a married man has to do. This is one of them. Will see you when I get back. — Alex"

That day the three horses Jimmy liked all ran out of the money. On top of that, he had to listen to Jonesy tell him what an idiot he was not to grab the $2,400 when he had the opportunity. He said, "It's a long price you will never see the guy again." Jimmy was thinking that if Alexander had not gone to Cuba, this day would have been a disaster with the horses he had picked.

Every night they ate at the Hickory House, the only place where Alexander knew to reach him, and for a while it looked like Jonesy was right. On the fourth night, Jimmy received a message to meet him Saturday at the Vanderbilt in time for the races, but when he arrived he learned Alexander had not checked in. He figured it was another missed connection, probably the last one, so he went back to the Hickory House to pick up Jonesy. He was standing in front of the place when the limousine pulled up and Alexander yelled, "Come on, let's go! We're late."

Jimmy only had one horse in the Saturday races, a horse named Middle Watch. Again Alexander asked, "How strong?"

"As strong as we can go," Jimmy said. "The whole $4,800." Then he had second thoughts and told him to hold out $2,000 until they saw what the place-and-show pools did. There was not anything there, so they had $2,800 to win on Middle Watch when he was leading by five lengths in the stretch. It was an overcast day, and suddenly a shaft of sunlight hit the track right in front of the horse. Middle Watch jumped the rail.

Jimmy wondered whatever happened to the horse, whether or not they destroyed it. If he had owned a gun at that time, he would have helped. Alexander surprised Jimmy. He put an arm around Jimmy's shoulder, and said, "That's the way life is, Jimmy, but that's what makes it so interesting."

Alexander had to return to Pennsylvania on business the next day. He split what was left of the pot, $1,000 each, and they said goodbye.

Jimmy would never forget his episode with Middle Watch, but by the following Tuesday he was betting again. He was interested in a horse named Many Stings, who figured to be the favorite in the Tropical Park handicap that Saturday. His ex-boss, Harry Cooper, was coming down with Jack Nolan, the political boss of Steubenville, and Nolan bet big. On Tuesday, Many Stings got away badly, then put on a tremendous rush to win a match race. It reminded Jimmy of Flag Unfurled, but that was not this horse's style. He turned to Jonesy and said, "This horse is absolutely dead now. He won't do a thing in the handicap and he'll be a heavy favorite, at least three-to-five."

"I hope not," Jonesy said. "Nolan will be here and he'll probably make a big bet on him."

"If he does," Jimmy said, "whatever he bets, I want part of it."

On Saturday they were all together — Cooper, Jimmy, Jonesy, and Nolan — in the box seats with the Tropical Park operators, Charles Wolf and Joe Tobin, who were old friends of Nolan. Nolan was such a big bettor, especially for 1938, that he could not put his money into the mutuels. It would have driven the price down to nothing, and he was always betting short-priced horses anyway. Cooper and Jonesy were there to "take him off," book his bets. Wolf and Tobin knew what was happening, but they did not mind — Cooper or Jonesy would put a token $500 or $1,000 into the machines on each of Nolan's bets.

When they posted the numbers for the big race, Many Stings was put up 1-to-2, and right away Nolan told Cooper, "I want $10,000 to win and $20,000 to place." Cooper nodded, accepting the bet. Then he started fidgeting. The little guy was naturally nervous anyway, and now he was anguishing.

"I can't refuse Jack," he said, "but I'm in a jam. This horse is a cinch."

"Don't worry about it," Jimmy said. "Let me lay some of this horse, any part you don't want — or what you'll trust me with over the money I've got." Jimmy was riding a streak. He had $1,600 when Alexander left town, and in a few days, had built it to $6,000. He felt he could do no wrong. He said, "Go tell Nolan you want him to press his bet," and Cooper almost jumped out of his skin.

Five minutes later, Nolan came back to Cooper and said, "I want $5,000 more to win and $10,000 more to place on the favorite." Jimmy could not help laughing at the look on Cooper's face. A bookmaker named Jockey Lightning came over and relieved some of the pressure.

"You got anything you want to lay off, Coop?" he asked.

"Yeah, I'm giving you two and four on the four horse." Many Stings was four on the program.

When the ex-jockey walked away, Jimmy said, "Whatever you're giving away, cut it down. I want some of it."

Cooper said, "How much money have you got?"

Jimmy told him how much he had. "And I want to lose every penny of it, plus. I got some ability to make money. Trust me."

"All right, Greek," he said, "you got $3,000 to win and $6,000 to place."

Jimmy told him again to stop worrying, that Many Stings was guaranteed to run out of the money. He hated to see a man suffer.

"If you don't like the favorite," Cooper said, "who *do* you like?"

"The eight horse," Jimmy said. "Dolly Vall."

Cooper said, "Okay, let's you and me bet $10 on Dolly Vall." He was a strange guy. He would take a horse for a lot of money, but he would never bet more than $10. He had a simple explanation for it: "I don't believe any of them can win."

Many Stings ran a staggering fifth, and Dolly Vall won and paid $84.

Five years later, when Jimmy's name began to mean something — he was "Mr. Greek" and living high, seated in the boxes at Aqueduct — a slender fellow in a gray suit walked over to him and said, "Jimmy, do you remember me?"

Jimmy said, "Do I remember you! Come on, Mr. Alexander, let's you and me go have a drink together."

He said, "Fine, Jimmy, but first — who do you like in the third race?"

Chapter 3

B & F Commissioner

JIMMY WAS STILL A KID, not even nineteen, but had seen enough to decide a guy could not juggle the dice, cards, horses, and ball games simultaneously. To have an edge, he had to focus on one and stick to it. For dice and roulette, he had to be on the house side of the table, and Jimmy was tired of casinos.

Cards were out of the question too. Playing poker on a big scale demanded a lot of physical stamina when a game went twice around the clock. He noticed all the poker players he knew looked a little worn out.

Except for the big races, he discarded horses. There were too many intangibles. He could not feel in control of a bet, and a bettor who thinks he is, is a fool. Racetracks were relaxing and entertaining, but not if you planned to stake your financial future on it. Besides, you have to wait all day for an overlay in the place-and-show pools.

That left one thing: sports, minus the king of sports, mainly the team games. This was an area he could research, form an opinion, then stake his judgment against another's. Besides, at least he would be betting on people.

His bankroll had slipped since he got home from Florida. He had taken $6,000 — which he still thought of as a separate bundle from the time he hit the number 807 at the Fort Steubenville Club. With his lucky-number money, he bought Reynolds

Metal stock at 14⅞. Years later, when he got a divorce, he had to sell it at 35. Reynolds later went to 250.

Now he had less than $3,000 in the bank and only $450 in his pocket on the night of the second Louis-Schmeling fight. He went up to Bob Sasso's place and asked him, "What have you got on the fight?"

"It's nine-to-five," he said. Jimmy thought it would be a lot more than that. In fact, he thought Louis was a cinch. Schmeling had knocked him out in the first fight, but the German had put in two hard years since then, and was now thirty-three. Louis was in his prime.

"I want to lay it," Jimmy said.

"If you want Louis, you got to lay two-to-one," Sasso said. They went round and round until Jimmy got it back to $900-to-$500. He gave Sasso his $450 and said he would go get the other half. His sister, Mary, was holding $500 for him.

Sasso said, "Don't worry about it. Bring it up after you lose."

"I'll bring it up before I lose," Jimmy said, "because I ain't going to lose."

Jimmy never made it home because he ran into Tom Griffin at the corner of the Green Mill Restaurant, where everyone loafed around and drank coffee all night. He said, "I just bet Sasso $900 to $500 on the fight. You want half of it?"

Griffin said, "If you like it, why not?" He reached into his back pocket and gave him five $100 bills. Then someone yelled that the fight was on and they went into the Green Mill to hear it. Clem McCarthy was screaming, "He's out! It's all over!" Louis had stopped him in two minutes.

Jimmy turned to Griffin and said, "Tom, we win it!"

Griffin said, "Naw, I can't take that. You never got my half down."

Jimmy went back and collected from Sasso, and Griffin still would not take his $250. Finally, he said, "Tell you what, I'm going down to Hot Springs for a few weeks. Keep our money together and go ahead and play with it, whatever you like."

When he came back about thirty days later, Jimmy went in to see his friend at the Academy. Jimmy handed him $2,200. Griffin said, "What's this?"

"That's our Schmeling money," Jimmy said. "I ran it up to $4,400."

"My God," Griffin said. "You gotta be kidding. Nobody ever gave me money back. Why do you want to give it back? Just keep going with it, play better, play higher."

Jimmy said, "You know what I'd like to do? I'd like to rent an office." Griffin said he was thrilled with anything that suited Jimmy. He took the smallest space in the National Exchange Bank Building, right across the hall from Jack Watson's stockbroker office. There were days in the years ahead when he moved more money than Watson did. The sign on his door read "B&F Commissioner," as in Baseball and Football. Griffin and Jimmy remained partners for ten years, with all Jimmy's expenses, living, and everything coming off the top. Later he took a salary. The bankroll eventually reached into six figures. Griffin never said anything about what Jimmy bet. This was all gravy to him.

From Jimmy's new office, with a filing cabinet and a desk and two phones, he decided he had outgrown Steubenville. Around town you could bet good money on big events, but in day-to-day betting it was hard to get down more than $200 or $300. At the Imperial Restaurant on Sixth Street, he met a guy named Natie Farber who bet in Pittsburgh, and he introduced Jimmy to his bookmakers, Aces and Kelski. They were the first big bookmakers with whom he did business. He could bet them $1,000 on the phone on anything.

They also contributed to his continuing education. They were laying what you call "a wide line." If the odds were 8-to-5 and Jimmy liked the favorite, he had to lay 2-to-1. That was a twenty percent spread, and it would grind you down if you stayed with it.

The first bet Jimmy made with them, Pittsburgh was a 3-2 favorite over Nebraska, and he won $1,500 on Nebraska. In those days, football was all odds. The bookmakers did not start posting point spreads until 1941 and 1942, and even then, a lot of people stuck with the odds or played both. After Jimmy built a favorable reputation with Aces and Kelski, he got an okay to phone bets into the Amorita Club, where two bookmakers named Tucker and Brown took the calls. In a few weeks he was $2,500 ahead and drove to Pittsburgh to collect.

The Amorita was on the iron mountain overlooking Pitts-

burgh and had a peephole in the front door. A few moments
after Jimmy punched the button, a voice came through, "Get
away, kid!"

Jimmy said, "I want to see Mr. Tucker."

"I told you," the guy said, "we don't let kids in here."

"Tell Mr. Tucker that Jimmy from Steubenville wants to see
him."

After a long wait, the door opened and a tall, handsome guy
stared at Jimmy. "For Christ's sake," he said, "are you the one we
owe money?" It turned out Jimmy might have looked old in Steubenville, but he was still young in Pittsburgh. Tucker took him inside and introduced him around. Milton Jaffe, who then owned
the Bachelor's Club a few blocks away, and later a piece of the
Stardust in Las Vegas, was a patron of the Amorita. He also met
another partner, Slim Silverheart, and that made it his lucky day.
He learned that Slim had a national reputation for integrity. He
was the final arbiter for any gambling dispute that developed.

For instance, when Leo Durocher came along and began
the strategy of starting a left-handed pitcher and replacing him
right away with a right-handed one, it caused a big controversy
all over the country. A lot of people made their bets specifying
"if so-and-so starts" because a change in pitchers could make a
big change in the odds. Durocher, of course, made the opposition load its lineup with right-handed hitters. Gamblers argued
about who was the actual starting pitcher in that situation. The
appeal went to Slim. "If the man throws one pitch," he declared,
"he is the starting pitcher." That was that, as if it came down
from the U.S. Supreme Court.

When the guys at the Amorita Club noticed how Jimmy was
winning, they paid him the compliment of favoring the side he
liked. That is, they moved the line — early.

The next winter when he was in Florida, Slim introduced
Jimmy to the big bookmakers: Mel Clark in Chicago and Billy
Hecht in Minneapolis. He intended to bet big money someday,
and these were the people he needed to know. Hecht created
the Gorham Press and became the first to sell a betting service
around the country for $25 a week — the famous "Minneapolis
Line." Hecht and his partners were the forerunners in assem-
bling executive ability into bookmaking. Hecht had three full-

time handicappers working for him. They learned early that if a guy was a continuous winner they had to move toward his number. Big bets did not faze them. It was *who* bet that mattered. When a guy they respected took six, they dropped the line to five or five and a half. In later years, they gave Jimmy the line on Monday and let him bet into even more money. Then they adjusted it.

The B&F Commissioner's office was making steady progress when the first Joe Louis-Billy Conn fight came up in 1941. This almost split up his partnership with Griffin, which by that time showed a net of $90,000. Conn was from Pittsburgh, right in their own backyard, and was Irish. Naturally, Griffin liked him. Jimmy liked Louis, especially when he could beat the odds in Steubenville and Pittsburgh, where there was a lot of money on Conn. In New York it was 18-to-5, but Jimmy was giving only 5-to-2, and in some cases 2-to-1.

The week of the fight, Griffin appeared at the office. He asked, "Who do you like in the fight?" When Jimmy told him Louis, his face reddened and Jimmy thought steam was going to come out of his ears. "By how much?" he asked.

"The whole thing," Jimmy said.

"Well, I hope you lose your ass!" He slammed the door on his way out.

This was the biggest bet Jimmy ever made and he felt it the night of the fight. Cornelius Jones, "Jonesy," the fellow who shared his beef ragout with Jimmy in Miami, was running the casino in the Mounds Club at Cleveland, the most fabulous place in the country at the time. He kept his home in Steubenville and had two beautiful daughters, Betty and Babe. Jimmy was dating Betty but liked Babe, and that was why he kept coming around the house. Finally, Jonesy told him, "I know you're kind of soft on Babe, but one gambler in the family is enough." Jimmy went out to listen to the broadcast with the girls and they were going crazy rooting for Conn because he was winning the fight. It sounded like he would take a decision. For the first time, Jimmy actually felt a pull in his stomach over a bet. He said to himself, "My God, am I going to lose this, lose two years of work in just one night?" He promised himself he would never put up the whole bankroll again.

It must have shown on his face. "You're white as a sheet," Betty said. Suddenly, in the thirteenth round, Louis caught Conn and knocked him out, and color came back into Jimmy's cheeks. "You were pulling for Louis," Betty said. "How much did you have bet on the fight?"

"Four hundred."

"Well, I was rooting for the other guy, because that wouldn't hurt you."

Griffin would not speak to Jimmy for a month.

Betting a championship fight comes down to a matter of opinion, because everything about the fight is laid out for you in the papers every day. Betting college football was a different proposition, especially in the days when communication and publicity were comparatively primitive. Jimmy hit on an idea that gave him an edge. He went to the Penn Station in Steubenville, where the railroads came through east-west and north-south, and he talked to the porters on the trains. He told them to collect every newspaper they could get their hands on along the line. He tipped them fifty cents or a dollar per paper. Soon he had papers from all over the country only a day after publication most of the time. The *St. Louis Post-Dispatch*, the *Nashville Banner*, the *Atlanta Journal, The New York Times* — all were loaded with college football stories by solid writers. Fred Russell in Nashville, Furman Bisher in Atlanta, Dave Condon in Chicago, Allison Danzig for *The New York Times*, Shirly Povich of *The Washington Post,* and Al Abrams in Pittsburgh were writers who gave the information needed when evaluating a team's chances.

The important advantage was to know more than anybody else *before* the season started. It took several weeks every season before the handicappers got their lines adjusted to shade down false favorites and upgrade surprise teams.

There was a Steubenville kid, a cousin of Jimmy's, Mike Paidousis, whose way Jimmy helped pay to the University of Tennessee. Mike was the first of a series of great athletes — the number would eventually reach seventeen — that he helped steer to colleges across the country. Jimmy called him every now and then to talk about the Southeastern Conference. One September, Jimmy received good information about Wake Forest. He asked Mike if he knew anyone there and he said no, but he had a cousin playing football for Virginia Tech. Jimmy called the cousin and asked him what he thought about Wake Forest playing North Carolina the following week, not revealing which side he liked.

The kid said, "We played them both in practice games."

Jimmy said, "You did?"

"Yeah. We beat North Carolina by four or five touchdowns, not keeping score, but like you do in practice scrimmage. Wake Forest kicked the hell out of us."

Jimmy could hardly wait for Monday to get the number. He called Billy Hecht in Minneapolis. He was doing business there and in New York, Chicago, and Pittsburgh. They gave him 8-to-5. Wake Forest was the underdog because North Carolina won the year before. His limit at the time was $1,000 per bet, and he took it at every spot. He went back later and they had it at 7-to-5 and he bet them all again. He bet them each seven times for a total of $28,000 — the bankroll again. So much for the promise made while listening to Conn and Louis.

He had put out a football card around Steubenville which ended up being distributed in four different states. There were seven cards around, and six of them were the same because they used the Minneapolis line. Jimmy's was different because he thought his numbers were better. When Cornell opened the season against Ohio State, all the cards had one side favored by six and he put it six the other way. Common sense told him he should have made it even and been all right, but he was arrogant. His team won by three and he lost about $9,000. (The player had to pick at least three teams on those cards, giving or taking points. The listed payoff of 5-to-1 was actually 4-to-1 because it included the player's original bet. The correct odds on a three-team parlay are 7-to-1.)

Now when Jimmy came out with Wake Forest a six-point favorite over North Carolina, everybody thought he made another mistake, and they jumped on it.

It came up a muddy day in Carolina with atrocious conditions, a rainstorm for four quarters. A Wake Forest player tried to field a punt and it went through his hands into the end zone, where North Carolina fell on it and won the game, 6-0.

Jimmy was totally busted. His bankroll was gone, and he still had to pay off the cards. He called Slim Silverheart and told him what happened. He said, "Well, Greek, it happens to everybody. You have got to show what kind of man you are now."

Jimmy knew exactly what he meant. Your credibility and word are all you have as a gambler.

Slim said, "I'm going to help you. What you owe here, I'll let you carry. You don't have to worry about this one. Pay $500 a month or something. Call Billy Hecht and tell him how much business you're doing on the cards."

Billy reacted the same. "Tell you what," he said. "I'm going to let you play, but you got to promise me that whatever you do, you'll pay as you go along. I'll leave this $13,000 balance and you pay $1,000 a month until it is paid."

Jimmy paid off New York and Chicago. He did not even bother to call. He paid off the card, which turned out to be a bonanza the rest of the season. Because he had everybody paid off, the next week they did $18,000. His was the pink sheet, and everybody looked for it.

He made a killing on more than cards. The next week Wake Forest was playing Duke and was a fourteen-point underdog. He had to go easy because he was low on cash, but he did call back and bet $2,000. Wake Forest won the game straight up, and never failed to beat the point spread the rest of the year. North Carolina bettors never cashed another ticket. He paid Slim and Billy off within three weeks and ended up having a great season. Wake Forest was an example of why gamblers hate bad-weather games.

A mud-bath day in New Orleans made him do something he had never done before or since: pray for a win. It was the 1942 Sugar Bowl between Fordham and Missouri. Fordham opened at 9-to-5 and he laid $1,800 to $1,000. When it dropped to 8-to-5, he laid another $1,600. Then a story broke that one of Fordham's top backs, Jim Blumenstock, had a bad ankle. Helen O'Connell, the blonde singer with Jimmy Dorsey's band who made "Green Eyes" famous, had been dating Blumenstock. The Greek knew O'Connell, as she was a Steubenville girl. He phoned her, and she started laughing. "There's nothing wrong with his ankle," she said. "He chased me all over the room last night."

When Jimmy phoned Pittsburgh, he found out the Blumenstock rumor knocked the odds down to 7-to-5, so he pressed his bet. He ended up with $8,000 on the game.

It rained in New Orleans. Fordham went ahead 2-0 when Alex Santilli blocked a punt through the end zone. Blumenstock played every down. A kid named Harry Ice gained 102 yards for Missouri but never got into the end zone. In the final minutes Missouri got close enough for a field goal. Jimmy was listening to the game on the radio. He looked up at the ceiling of his room. "If You're up there," he prayed, "now is the time to come to the rescue of Your boy, Jim."

The field goal was short and his $8,000 was safe, but he did not like the feeling that remained. That was one promise he kept: no more prayers on bets.

Chapter 4

Grantland Rice Disagreed

GEORGE'S MARRIAGE TO AGNES produced another brother and sister for Jimmy, John, and Angela. Since Jimmy was at least fourteen years older than them, the kids thought he was only a half step behind the Almighty. Agnes had always treated Jimmy as her own. He still called her Agnes, but in his mind he thought of her as "mother." John and Angela were not a half brother or a half sister; they were all one close family with never a conflict, once George understood Jimmy was going his own way.

Everything was centered around Jimmy's schedule. They would call him at the office to find out what he wanted for dinner and what time to have it ready. It was always there, on the minute. The clothes he was going to wear that night were laid out on his bed, the shirt freshly ironed, and a suit just back from the cleaners. Anything Jimmy owned was sacred. It was difficult to describe the way his little brother and sister would say, "That's *Jimmm-meee's.*" It was like a prayer.

Jimmy thought of his life as typical of the Greek family life. He figured that if he had stayed in that environment — gone home to Kios, claimed an old-country bride, apprenticed at the grocery store — he could be sure to live to a ripe old age. His family history confirmed that. His other Uncle Tom went back to Kios when he retired and died there at the age of 90. His great-grandmother lived to be 116, his grandmother, 103, and grandfather, 96. Jimmy once laid odds 6-to-5 that he would live until he was 85. Unfortunately, he went to the grave eight years early, missing that final call.

Because he had this feeling for his family, a series of small bets he made in 1943 meant more to him than a dozen big scores that followed. He cleaned out Meyer Pearlman and Slim Neal, who were making book together in Steubenville.

As he got more and more into studying college football, he learned that the odds posted by bookmakers were not necessarily correct. In fact, there were many times when he thought his numbers were more accurate. Pearlman and Neal would take no more than $500 on a football game from him. Nevertheless, that season he hit them for $20,000, which was their whole bankroll. Pearlman quit and opened a men's clothing store. He made a fortune and was eternally grateful for the assistance: "If it hadn't been for you, Greek, I wouldn't be so successful."

Slim Neal should have opened a clothing store too. He wanted to keep booking his bets, even though he was out of cash. "I got my house," he said. "You want to play against my house on Sunset Boulevard, up on the hill? It's worth $12,500."

"I don't want to take your house, Slim."

"Goddamnit, you tap me out and you're gonna stop betting? Give me a chance."

"If you insist."

In two months, he turned over the deed. Jimmy gave the house to George. He and Agnes lived downstairs and rented the upstairs. It gave them a little income, and they had a nice place to live.

One of the games that sank Slim and really made Jimmy's season successful was Notre Dame versus Great Lakes Naval Training Station. Notre Dame was unbeaten and had outscored opponents 326 to 50. The Irish had a great team, with five All Americans: John Yonakor, Jim White, and Pat Filley in the line, quarterback Angelo Bertelli, and halfback Creighton Miller. Johnny Lujack was backing up Bertelli. They were knocking off college kids like they were running through a picket fence.

They were not going up against college kids this time. In the war years, service teams were often an even match to play the collegians. Notre Dame opened as a seventeen-point favorite, and the odds straight up were tremendous. What the bookmakers did not realize was Great Lakes had some great players too: Steve Lach, Steve Juznik, Emil ("Six Yard") Sitko, who was All American for Notre Dame in 1949, Dewey Procter, Lou Saban. They were coached that year by Tony Hinkle out of Chicago, later the coach and athletic director at Butler. That game would be the biggest thing in his life. Later, Paul Brown succeeded Hinkle and took many of those Great Lakes sailors with him when he started the Cleveland Browns.

For some reason, if you really liked an underdog, you went to Philadelphia. You could always get a half point more on the long side. Jimmy figured Philadelphia just liked favorites. The top bookmakers in Philly were Sam Litt and Slame Glassman. Jimmy called and said, "Slame, if a guy liked a seventeen-point underdog, what price would you give?"

"Oh, hell," he said, "that's a 10-to-1 shot."

They both knew it was really 15-to-1.

"Well, maybe it is," he said, "if it's Notre Dame playing or something."

This was a bartering situation. They settled on 13, but he would not book $2,000. Jimmy settled for $500 at 13 and $500 at 12. Then he called Litt and got the same bet. He finished up around the country betting $3,500 with odds and $18,000 with points. Notre Dame was leading 14–13 until the last 33 seconds, when Lach hit a 46-yard touchdown pass.

Suddenly, Jimmy was famous. Walter Winchell had a note in his column: "The smart bookies are singing the blues in Philly. A young Greek in Steubenville, Ohio, hit them for half a mill backing Great Lakes over the Irish." What happened was Slame told a guy in Atlantic City, who told a guy in Pittsburgh, and the score inflated at every stop.

It was this game, and Winchell's publicity, that forced Jimmy to start keeping records for the IRS. He had a guy in his office mark down every transaction, wins against losses. On his income tax form he listed his profession as "speculator," and he paid off the net.

He was doing other things for Uncle Sam in those years, too, promoting war bond raffles and rallies everywhere he could. It helped alleviate pressure. When he reported for his induction physical, he learned of a congenital defect in his stomach wall. The doctor said, "You've got to have it taken care of. You can't lift anything heavier than ten pounds." Jimmy told him he never lifted anything heavier than a telephone. Years later in Las Vegas, it almost killed him.

So there he was, a tall, large guy out of uniform. From time to time he got an anonymous letter from somebody he figured had a son in the service. Jimmy wondered what he was supposed to do, so he helped sell war bonds.

Jimmy did another bit to boost America about this time, and also to help his good friend, Harold Salvey, in Miami Beach. Among the top gamblers there were some beautiful men, and Salvey was his favorite. He was a little guy, 5'8, pug-nosed, and a good dresser originally from Detroit. He was one of six in a syndicate that handled bookmaking up and down the beach, including the top hotels. You could lay in a cabana and bet every track running. That was where the term *syndicate* originated, though it came to mean something more ominous than what Salvey and his partners were doing. Salvey was the political man in the group, communicating with the councilmen. He was the ambassador to the politicians, and that kept the whole thing going.

He kept Jimmy going on occasion too. Once Jimmy called him from Steubenville and said, "Harold, I need some money."

Harold said, "I'll get a package off to you today." He meant he was sending it by registered mail. A couple of days later it arrived, a cigar box wrapped in brown paper. Inside the box was $50,000 in cash. He was a beautiful man.

He called one day complaining about the blackouts along the Florida coast. "Damn," he said, "I'm getting the hell out of here. All these stories about German submarines lining up on our lampposts. I don't need this aggravation. I'm getting the hell out."

"Harold, I'm going to give you some advice." Here was Jimmy, at twenty-two, counseling his elders. To Jimmy, it was strictly an odds proposition, and he was never shy about declaring his odds. "You're nuts, just point-blank nuts."

"Shut up, Greek. What the hell do you know about it?"

"I know this — you had a bet on the U.S. and now you want to get off."

"What are you talking about?"

"Everybody down there is selling at a distressed price right now and if I had the money, I'd buy up every piece of property I could get my hands on. It's a no-lose proposition. If we lose the war, what is it, anyway? If we win it, you're rich. All you're doing is betting on the U.S. to win the war. What bet can top that?"

"I'll be goddamned," Salvey said. That is what he did, with every dime he could raise. After the war, he became a millionaire over and over. If Jimmy had told Salvey that pepper was white and salt was black, he would have bet on it.

In the years right after the war, Jimmy started building his own investments — because college recruiting suddenly became the cutthroat business we all know and love today. Jimmy's section of the Ohio River Valley included southern Pennsylvania and rock-hard West Virginia and was a mother lode for great high-school football players. He knew most of these kids personally. A lot of them got summer jobs, at a strip mine he had an interest in, or through friends who owned companies. Penn Station began to look like a coaches' convention, and most of the coaches ended up seeing Jimmy.

"Tha's a boy up in Pennsylvania who is a monster — ah mean, a monster tackle — and that boy tells me ah got to see Mr. Snyder about him coming to Yale." This was Herman Hickman, and the start of an enduring and loving friendship.

Jimmy sent the kids $50 or $100 from time to time. At Christmas he helped them get train fare home. There was one kid who was 5'4 that Jimmy helped out the whole way through Georgia Tech because he liked him. The kid went on to become the mayor of Steubenville. When there was a game Jimmy liked, he knew who was injured and what kind of player the backup man was.

One week during the basketball season, Jimmy called Mike Paidousis at Tennessee to chat and ask how things were in general. Tennessee was going to play Dayton the next night, and Jimmy believed Dayton was severely underrated at the start of the season. Mike said the kids at the dormitory were laughing about the basketball captain: "His girl gave him the shaft today, and they've been steady for three years." This kid was Tennessee's leading scorer. Naturally, Jimmy took Dayton strong and cashed a big bet.

That time Jimmy's followers picked it up, and the number on Tennessee, an eleven-point favorite, dropped to seven by game time. Dayton won, 57–38. The next day, when Jimmy called the Gorham Press for the line on the games that night, Leo Hirshfield got on the phone. Billy Hecht's office took the bets, but Hirschfield sent out the line. "Greek," he said, "after last night, Tennessee has been barred. No more Tennessee in this office." If Leo made a mistake, he blamed someone else. Tennessee remained barred.

Jimmy's contacts worked in other wondrous and innocent ways. When Hickman was coach at Yale, Jimmy visited him early one summer at his Connecticut cabin. Hickman lived in New Haven, but had a shack in the mountains. Jimmy loved the mountains; he had a cabin home in the backwoods of Carolina too. While Jimmy was with him, Granny Rice came up to visit. Rice was enthusiastic about Vandy, his alma mater, coming off a great year. He told Hickman and Jimmy that Vanderbilt might even be a national champion in the upcoming season.

Jimmy began pointing out some things to him— such as the fact that Vanderbilt had lost its coach (Red Sanders had moved to UCLA) and that the new coach, Bill Edwards, was coming off the Cleveland Browns staff to change Vandy from single-wing to T-formation. Rice would not hear a word of it. He was convinced that Vandy would be the greatest. Then Jimmy caught himself. *What am I doing, arguing with this guy?* he wondered. *He's going to tout Vandy as a world-beater when he writes that big preseason piece in Collier's.* Rice's syndicated column was the most respected in sports. He decided to leave him alone.

Later that summer, Hickman invited Jimmy to the annual college coaches' convention at Evanston, Illinois. Edwards was there, and he started rattling on about how he was going to teach the Southeastern Conference all about the "T."

Bobby Dodd of Georgia Tech was standing nearby, not with Edwards, but close enough to hear what he said. Dodd was sort of tossing a football from hand to hand, and in his slow southern drawl, he said, "Yeuhs, and he gits to teach uhhs first."

Jimmy rushed to the phone to see if anyone had a line on the game yet.

The week of the game, Vanderbilt opened a fourteen-point favorite. Jimmy did not use the phone. Instead, he flew to Chicago and went to Mel Clark's office to see Charley McNeil, his top handicapper. He said, "Mac, I've got a proposition for you."

"I knew you would, Greek boy," McNeil replied.

"Vandy is playing Georgia Tech and I want a straight price on the game, and we both know what it figures."

Mac said, "A fourteen-point favorite in other games is one thing, but at Grant Field against Bobby Dodd is another."

Jimmy thought to himself, *Well, why the hell don't you make it seven then?* Aloud Jimmy said, "Professor, I agree with you, but you got to give me a fair price." Jimmy thought this was a lock-mortal cinch, so he did not mind taking his offer of 5-to-1. He bet him $4,000 at that price, and took the fourteen points for $22,000.

Georgia Tech did not need any points. Dodd's team won, 12–7.

The next week Jimmy bet again. The following week he bet again. That year he did nothing other than bet against Vandy. Those twenty-nine returning seniors Grantland Rice idolized never learned the new formation. Jimmy won a packet, and Edwards did not last long.

Jimmy enjoyed his contacts with college coaches, and he benefited from the friendships by acquiring information that influenced his handicapping. He rarely got anything that he could surely take to the bank. One exception was a conversation he had with Herman Hickman.

Hickman had a giant of a personality. Latin scholar, poet, bon vivant—even in the unlikely event he became a hardware merchant down the block, Hickman was a lovable guy. Jimmy was thrilled for him one season when he went out to Wisconsin, and his team, Yale, defeated the Big 10. That was the team that had Levi Jackson. Jimmy called to congratulate him. "Save your breath," he said. "I haven't had those bums out of the clouds in two days. They're still celebrating. The goddamn band met the train, and there's been nothing but parties ever since. And we're playing Vanderbilt this week. Nobody knows this hardly, but Vanderbilt is probably the number-one football team in the United States."

Jimmy had the same notion. This was the season before Edwards came in, and Red Sanders was loaded. He could not resist picking Herman a little more. "Vandy is a strong team," Jimmy said, "but you'll hold your own with them, won't you?"

Hickman said, "I would if they'd practice. But they don't give a damn about Vanderbilt, some chicken-shit school down south. They're thinking about playing Harvard and Dartmouth and all these other pushovers up here."

Jimmy commiserated some more with his friend and then made his first $100,000 wager. He won it easily, with a score of something like 35–0.

Jimmy had just about stopped betting on anything except the Southeastern Conference. On Saturday afternoons in Steubenville, all anyone could get were broadcasts of Notre Dame and Ohio State games. Since Jimmy had all his money down south, he went to the movies every Saturday to get his mind off of it. He saw some lousy movies, but he made a lot of money.

Only once did his friendship and counseling with young athletes cause him embarrassment. This developed from accepting bets on high school games. Steubenville High had a fine team and everybody in town wanted to bet on them. Jimmy always had an opinion, and when the big game came up against Canton McKinley, he said it was by six. Some $2,000 in bets was forced on him, against Steubenville. There was no sentiment in this town.

A bartender at the Fort Steubenville Club was the only loyalist. He backed the home team for $200. This "book" was overloaded.

Steubenville had a great athlete on its team, a kid named Gilliam, who was already getting offers from colleges all over the country. He came up to see Jimmy, because he heard about all the other kids he helped. They talked for about half an hour. Jimmy recommended him to Bo McMillin at Indiana, where he became a standout, one of the first black athletes he helped get to college.

Gilliam had a bad moment against Canton. He was running for a touchdown when the strap on his pants broke. When he grabbed the strap, he fumbled the ball, and Steubenville lost the game. Jimmy lost $1,800. The next day, Jack Watson, the stockbroker across the hall, walked in to see Jimmy. He was sent by the editor of the *Herald Star*, Steubenville's daily newspaper. The editor and he were on the school board together. He got to the point right away. "Did you have Gilliam in the game?" he asked.

"Did I *have* Gilliam?" Jimmy responded.

"It's all over town that Gilliam was up here the other day, talking to you. I saw him. Did you do anything wrong with him?"

Jimmy's first inclination was to lose his cool. Here he was betting thousands of dollars around the country every weekend, and he was going to be scrutinized over a few hundred on a high school game. Jimmy took a deep breath, getting control of his temper. "Jack," Jimmy said, "look at these slips — I lost eight bets and won one."

"Who did you win from?" he asked.

Jimmy mentioned the guy's name.

"That's the guy who's screaming," Jack said.

Jimmy learned his lesson. He never again made a number on a high school team or got involved in a hometown game. That is why he never made a number on the University of Nevada at Las Vegas for football or basketball. They had great teams, but were too close to home.

There was a time, however, when he recalled having been a force for good. It was the case of the most highly sought prospect in the annals of the Steubenville Valley. This was a raw hunk of a great person named Bob Gain who played for Weirton (West Virginia) High School not far from his town. Jimmy knew he was a prize, a "can't miss," but he had not realized until then how pressurized college recruiting had become.

One night his front doorbell rang. It was 11:30, and that startled him. He had a glass door on his front porch that a visitor had to enter before reaching his front door. Then there was an intercom hookup to talk to guests.

Jimmy had never seen the guy on his doorstep. He said, "You don't know me. My name is Mike Balitsaris. I'm an assistant coach at Kentucky."

Jimmy said, "Well, you got the right kind of name." Balitsaris is as Greek as Socrates.

"I'm from Pittsburgh," he said, "and I got a favor to ask of you."

Jimmy let his fellow Greek in and furnished him with some Scotch. He said, "I have got to get Bob Gain or I'm fired. I went to Bob and he told me he wouldn't go anywhere unless you okayed it."

Jimmy already knew this. Bob Gain was one of his strip miners in his off season. He said, "Mike, you know there are a hundred schools after Bob."

"I don't give a damn if there's a thousand. You got to help me. Bear Bryant says I get him or my ass is out."

Mike stayed at Jimmy's place that night. Jimmy knew Kentucky was one of the schools Gain should consider. He had to go to either Kentucky or Georgia, because he knew he was only going to major in football. Jimmy did not make any deal with Mike that night, but a couple of weeks later, he came back with another Bryant assistant, Carnie Laslie. Laslie had a mountain of snow-white hair. He looked like a Roman senator, and had a warm personality. After a half hour with Laslie and Mike, Jimmy wanted to send the whole Weirton team to Kentucky.

There was a problem, however. Gain's mother was a widow, and the family had no money. Another school had offered to give Mrs. Gain a whopping bonus if her boy went their way. Bob told Jimmy about this.

Now this was a terrific kid, straight shooter all the way, and Jimmy cared about him. He said, "Bob, put the money deal out of your mind. Whatever it is, I want you to remember this — the school is not giving you any money. This is a friendship situation between you and me, not because you're going to Kentucky. I'll give you the money, anyway, no matter where you go. You don't have to be obligated to anybody."

Jimmy honestly believed the boy's career would be in the best hands with Bryant, Balitsaris, and Laslie. Gain signed with Kentucky.

Jimmy was not about to miss the next spring practice at Kentucky, when Bob Gain first started with the varsity. It so happened that a prominent bookmaker he knew from Lexington, Ed Kurd, was also present. They watched the boys in their annual Blue-White scrimmage.

Jimmy said, "Ed, what kind of odds would you give me that I could pick out one of those freshmen and bet you he was going to make All America by his junior year?"

Kurd was a big, heavyset fellow with a voice that sounded like it came up from his ankles. "Oh, hell," he said. "That's a prohibitive price, you know that. A million things can happen to him. He could get hurt; he could flunk out; he could get killed. Shit, Bryant might kill him if he looks at him wrong. It would have to be a real big price."

"Fine, just for $100, give me the real big price."

"I'd have to say 25-to-1 on that, Greek, 25-to-1."

Jimmy thought, *How many times have I been through this? These sons-of-bitches are all alike.* He said, "Wait a minute, you said a *big* price. Don't insult my intelligence."

"All right, you get 50-to-1 for $100, but it's got to be a legit All-America team. I want either the AP or UP. If he's not picked on either one, I win it. First team only," he said.

"Absolutely, but one more proviso. If he makes it as a sophomore, I win it too."

"All right. Which kid do you want?"

"His name is Bob Gain — and remember that name because it's $5,000 if you lose it."

Jimmy would always remember it too. Bob made second team All America as a sophomore, then he made Associated Press, United Press, and Football Writer's All America as a junior.

The $5,000 from Kurd got Jimmy even on his recruitment, or so he thought. After he retired from his eleven-year career with the Cleveland Browns in the early sixties, Bob got word from home that Jimmy was in financial trouble. He did not call. He did not write. He just sent a check for $2,500.

Chapter 5

A Costly Reputation

FROM THE TIME JIMMY was a teen, he lived where the fast money flowed. This atmosphere attracted people who wanted some money for themselves with minimum work — such as pulling a trigger or swinging a baseball bat. He learned early to spot these types when he started working nights at the Half Moon.

There was a guy named Shannon, built like a linebacker, yellow hair clipped to a half inch. He had muscles bunched on the back of his neck like ridges on a washboard. One night Jimmy noticed he was throwing money around at the bar, buying drinks for everybody.

Jimmy said to Harry Cooper, "Shannon musta had a lucky day. What'd he bet on?"

Cooper said, "He doesn't bet. He charges people to live."

Thereafter, Jimmy cultivated Shannon and many of his friends. He would ask, "How are you holding?" The friend would say, "I ain't." Jimmy would say, "Let me lay a hundred on you until you turn it around." He sometimes even offered a couple of hundred if he had heard any recent bulletins about broken teeth or fractured jaws. He counted on the word getting around that he was an okay kid. It was his own program of crime prevention.

This worked fairly well until the 1940s, when he began getting a reputation far and wide as a man of big transactions that usually went from somebody else's bankroll to his own. That was when he learned a fellow could get tossed into the Ohio River if he was not careful.

When Jimmy flew into the Pittsburgh airport from Florida one night, two guys he knew happened to be there. At least, he *thought* they happened to be there. He returned to Steubenville to attend the funeral of a good friend. Later he wondered if they had learned when he was coming and set him up. They offered him a ride home and he accepted. When he got close to Steubenville, the driver pulled over to the side of the road over-looking the Ohio River. It was a scenic view, when the moon was out. The other guy in the front seat turned around and pointed a gun at Jimmy.

"What's this all about?" Jimmy asked.

"We want you to give us some money, Greek. We know you got a big roll and we want some — like all of it."

"I don't have that kind of money," Jimmy said. He did not, at least not that day. That was his first mistake. Getting into the car was the second one.

The driver was smoking a cigar. He grabbed Jimmy's arm and put out the cigar on the back of his hand. "I got $300 on me," Jimmy said. "Take it."

"We want $10,000, Greek."

Jimmy told them the $300 was it. The driver got out and walked to the trunk. He came back with a big brown blanket. He said, "Come up with the money or you go in the river."

Jimmy knew the guys were serious. He could see it in their eyes. A strong-arm guy who gets in motion is like a train on rails. His eyes were glazed and Jimmy could see he was disconnected from the real world. That kind of sight could make a man lose control of his bladder. The next thing Jimmy knew, he was wrapped in the blanket and could hardly breathe.

"You gonna give it up?" one of them asked.

"What the hell can I give up?" he said, trying to get his message through the blanket. "I'll give you anything I can get my hands on."

"We want $10,000."

"That's out. Go ahead, throw me in. If I could get $10,000, I'd use it myself." Jimmy knew if he said he could get any kind of big money quickly, they would think he had more. "I'll try to get $1,000 for you, but that's all I can promise. If you want me to try that, I will. I'm not going to the law, I'll guarantee you that."

They untied the blanket and dumped Jimmy on the slope leading down the river. It was *that* close. "All right," the gunner said, "we'll call you tomorrow." They knew he would be staying at the Fort Steuben Hotel. "And we don't want any more talk." They charged him $300 for his ride into town.

Jimmy knew they had no respect for anything, especially his life, but he also knew he had to take a stand or he would have a welcoming committee every time he returned to Steubenville. He made them come up and get the money: $500. "Not only is that all," Jimmy said, "but I'll never give you guys a dime after this. If you needed $500 you could've got it by asking, you know that. You didn't have to take me to the river."

"We thought you were in real good shape."

"Even if I was, you wouldn't have got it."

"We should've thrown you in the river."

"Yeah, and get nothing."

Jimmy was always a target. The trick was not to have all his money on him. When he was in Steubenville, he often bet with Billy Griffith in Barberton, Ohio, outside Akron. He was a great bookmaker for two reasons: If you hit him you got paid, and he gave a price on anything. They always checked out at $10,000, whoever owed whom. Jimmy usually had it coming. He would drive up there to collect and would take a big manila envelope with him. He had a smaller envelope inside the big one. He would slip his money into the smaller envelope, put it inside the big one, and address it to himself. Outside Billy's poolroom was a mailbox. He would drop the package in the slot. At that time, the U.S. mail was better than a team of bodyguards.

One day when Jimmy drove up to Barberton with a kid who worked for him, Paul Marsh, he forgot the envelopes. He collected his money, $8,300 this time, and told Paul, "Let's go to the men's room."

Paul had a wooden leg from the knee down and Jimmy was one of the few people who knew about it. In the men's room, Jimmy locked the door. "Unstrap your leg," he said, keeping his voice down.

Paul looked at Jimmy like he had made an indecent proposition. "What the hell for?" he asked.

"Because I forgot the damn envelopes," Jimmy said, "and
we got to stash this money." Jimmy kept out $300 and put the
$8,000 inside his leg. He did not want to leave right away, so he
shot some nine-ball with Billy's son, Jackie, and as usual,
dropped $100. When Paul and Jimmy walked outside, Jimmy
pretended to put something in the mailbox outside.

A few miles outside of town, a car drew alongside them and
forced them to the side of the road. "Keep quiet," Jimmy told
Paul. "They don't know where the money is."

"All right, Greek," one of the guys said. "We know you
picked up a big package from Billy. Let's have it."

"I got $200 on me," Jimmy said. "I dropped the package in
the mailbox like I always do."

"The hell you did. Out." They searched Jimmy and Paul,
digging in all pockets, but they did not go near Paul's leg. Then
they searched the car, slashing the upholstery, looking in the
trunk and under the hood, inside the visors, every place.

"Do you believe me now?" Jimmy said.

"I guess you did mail it, Greek."

When heisted, it is the worst thing not to have any money
on you. This happened to Jimmy one winter in Miami Beach. He
stopped by the Cavendish Club, a bridge club, on his way to a
dinner dance at the Surf Club. He went there to collect $2,000
he won from Jule Weiss, a bookmaker, earlier that day at the
racetrack. He was all dressed up in his white tie and tails with not
even $20 in his pocket.

Jimmy played at the Cavendish himself, though he was not
really good. He was just learning to play, but some of the best
bridge players in the world were there, and he always believed if
you want to learn a game, you should play with the best. Tommy
Abdu, another gambler, liked to play bridge. He would take a
master player and Jimmy would take one, sort of like a bridge
pro-am, and they would play for fifty cents a point.

That night, Jimmy stood around waiting for Weiss when
four guys with stockings over their heads came in carrying
sawed-off shotguns. "Everybody up against the wall!" One of
them ordered. It was like someone stirred a tank of minnows

with a stick. There were fifty people on the main floor, and another couple of dozen on the balcony level watching a television fight. In the confusion, everyone attempted to stash their cash. Midgey, a little gambler Jimmy knew, stuck his roll in a water pitcher. Moe Manus slid his money into a sandwich. Slim Silverheart crammed $5,000 into an air conditioner. In the middle of the room, one of the robbers spread out a white tablecloth. "All your money," he exclaimed. "No jewelry, just cash. Walk up single file."

Jimmy was behind a bridge player named Harry Harkaby, one of the best. Since Jimmy did not want to stiff anybody who was carrying a sawed-off shotgun, he whispered, "Harry, can you loan me something?"

Harkaby looked around at Jimmy, dumbfounded. He held out his money clip. "Take what you want, Jimmy. What difference is it?"

Jimmy took two $100 bills from him, and when he got to the tablecloth, he threw it on the floor.

"Is that all you got?" the guy said.

Jimmy pulled his pockets out. He took off his coat. "I was waiting for a guy to bring money he owed me," Jimmy said. "That's all I got on me."

"You sure?"

"I'm sure."

He stared through the stocking mask for a full ten seconds. Then he made Jimmy drop his pants. Finally, he waved Jimmy away. "All right, go ahead."

Meanwhile, one of his confederates watched the clock, calling out the time. It was a regular countdown. He sang it out: "It's 11:40 . . . 11:41 . . . 11:42 . . . 11:43. . ."

Finally, he said, "Okay, it's 11:44 and a half. Let's go!" With that, they were gone, backing out of the room and through the door. No more than forty seconds had passed, literally. Jimmy was still buckling his belt and zipping his fly when Jule Weiss breezed in, as if nothing happened. Jimmy told him he had just missed a hell of a floor show. Weiss handed Jimmy the $2,000 he owed him, and Jimmy decided it was a good time to leave.

As he headed for the front door, he heard a voice yell, "Hey, Greek, where are you going? Didn't you forget something?"

Jimmy stopped and turned around and saw Harkaby. Jimmy laughed. "I sure did, Harry," Jimmy said, and he handed him two $100 bills.

This was just another gun-to-head confrontation, but when a fellow bets money like Jimmy did, there were more subtle dangers involved. Jimmy was in Miami in 1948 for the Orange Bowl game between Georgia Tech and Kansas. By then, he had followers around the country. People were waiting to find out who the Greek was betting on, including some people who made Jimmy's Ohio River rollers look like choirboys.

This time Jimmy liked Georgia Tech, a seven-point favorite. He thought they should be up by thirteen. Maybe this was because he admired Bobby Dodd, the coach. From the time he started gathering out-of-town papers through his railroad porters in Steubenville, he learned that Dodd told it like it was. He said things like: "I'd rather be lucky than good" and "I don't see why we shouldn't be favored over Georgia. We've got a better team." Dodd was noted for creating a razzle-dazzle offense, but when he had the material he forgot all about that and just stuck it to them. This year he had the material. Jimmy made a sizable wager on Georgia Tech and gave the points. When pressed, he confided the opinion to a few select inquisitors.

The line started going up, to eight and twelve and finally thirteen. As New Year's got closer, somebody mentioned the game dropped to eight. Jimmy could not understand it. Tech had not come up with any injuries in practice.

That is when one of his special friends came to see him and Jimmy discovered that he himself was the man in the middle. "The word out of Chicago," he said, "is that you talked Tech down here and bet Kansas up there."

"My bet's on Tech," Jimmy said. "I never touched Kansas."

He said, "I hope so, Greek."

The next day Jimmy had a follow-up contact from some of his friend's soldiers, but he did not convince them either. He knew he had to straighten this out or he would really be in trouble. He found out the big bet in Chicago was placed in Mel Clark's office by a gambler out of St. Louis who was trying to build himself up as Jimmy the Greek too. His name was Jimmy Karras.

Jimmy called Mel. "I didn't bet you on the Orange Bowl," he reminded him. "I'm getting a bad rap from the other kid's bet. I'm going to have some people call you. Do me a favor and tell them what happened."

Mel did, and it was straightened out before game time. Georgia Tech won by thirteen. Jimmy won his bet, of course, but if Tech had lost, and certain people thought he had a wad on Kansas, he could have lost his hide.

Jimmy never denied there were occasions when his contacts with the wrong side of life paid dividends. This happened in Miami, too, when he was on vacation at the Cadillac Hotel. He went to the track every day. When he returned to the hotel, he enjoyed taking a nap, then a shower, and would go out to dinner late, around 9:00. He always left the light on in his room. One night when he came back from dinner, the room was dark. The next thing he knew, there was a gun in his ribs and the door was closed. The lights came on. There were two of them.

"Your money, your watch, and your ring," one said.

"You got it," Jimmy said, as softly as he could. "Don't worry. I'm not going to say anything."

"You got the right attitude, Jack."

One of them took a sheet off the bed, tied Jimmy up with it, and stuck him in the closet. It was not too tight, and after a few minutes he was free. As far as he was concerned, that was it. They got about $3,000, plus a nice gold watch and his diamond ring, but he was not going to the cops about it.

The next day, looking for a loan, he went to Twenty-third Street, where all the gamblers loafed, and some of the tough guys too. A godfather type named Mikey and a few fellows of vague reputation used to call Jimmy to find out which teams he liked. He never tipped too many people, but he did Mikey. They had a cup of coffee together. "I got a story for you," Jimmy said, and told him what happened.

"What'd they look like?" Mikey asked.

"Forget it. I'm not looking to get even. It's over."

"Jimmy, what'd they look like?"

The way he said it, Jimmy knew he had to tell him now, so he described the two heisters the best he could. Two days later, his telephone rang. It was Mikey. "Stop down by the Hickory

House before you go to the racetrack," he said. "I got something for you."

He had Jimmy's watch, ring, and $2,500. "They were broke," he said. "I let 'em keep $500."

"Hell, here's $500 more to give 'em. On me."

When you moved around in Miami and New York in gambling clubs and certain restaurants, you saw people from that other world. Jimmy avoided them. A friend of his would say, "You see that gray-haired guy over there, with the black-rimmed glasses? He's in the mob. He's —"

"Don't tell me," Jimmy said. "I don't want to know." He did not want to know anything more than was in the newspapers, and not all of that. He knew a few gamblers who thought they were getting into easy money, handling betting operations for the wrong people. It turned out to be the hardest money they ever saw. They could never shake loose. He was asked ten times to work as a handicapper, and was always careful in the way he begged off. He created sound excuses why he could not and kept everything friendly. They knew they could call him any time and he would give them an opinion on a game they liked.

The one time he did get involved was no fault of his own. In retrospect, he was not sure of what he could have done differently. He got into a slow-pay situation with two bookmakers in Ohio — they did not have the money, and he had to square other bets he lost. He called a friend in New York, a gambler, and tracked him down at Gallagher's Restaurant on Fifty-second Street. He told him he needed $40,000 for a couple of weeks. He did not have it, but he said he would see what he could do the next morning. The next day a stranger drove down from Pittsburgh and handed Jimmy an envelope with the money. Jimmy paid off his bets, then called the guy in New York to thank him. He got the shock of his life. He had not sent any money, but it took them only a few minutes to figure it out.

He said, "Jimmy, you know ——— ?"

"I don't know him," Jimmy said, "but he calls me now and then about the teams I bet on."

"Well, he was in the place last night when you called. I was having an after-dinner drink. I mean, he asks me to the table, you know?"

"Go on."

"When I got back from talking to you, I mentioned I felt bad because I don't have the $40,000, after all the times you —"

"Never mind. What else?"

"Nothing else. All he said was, 'I hate to hear that. The Greek is good to people.' And I finished my drink and left."

"Oh, Christ."

"Maybe it wasn't him that sent the money."

"Who the hell you think it was?" Jimmy said. "The tooth fairy?"

A couple of days later, Jimmy's friend in New York confirmed it was that man, all right, and told him of Jimmy's plans for immediate repayment. In a week Jimmy had that $40,000 paid back. Then he held his breath.

Years passed. Jimmy pushed the incident to the back of his mind. Then one fall he was in New York, busted again. By then he was married and Joan was pregnant. Jimmy was in the Hickory House when his long-ago benefactor walked over to him. "Greek," he said, "I need a favor."

"What do you need?" Jimmy asked.

"We've got a big joint up in Montreal, but we need a little help on the sports. Can you go up and straighten out the sports for us? If everything works out, we'll take care of you."

In this man's language, "take care of you" was a weighty promise, like six figures preceded by a dollar sign. Jimmy had to do it. He figured he owed him. At least he would be compensated. "I'll fly up there tomorrow," Jimmy said.

At the time, some of the big bookmakers left the United States following the Kefauver hearings and went to Montreal to operate. Gil Beckley was the big man in the Montreal operation. He had been a horse bookmaker in Cincinnati, and needed someone who knew sports. Jimmy knew he could not go up there with all these bookmakers and not have any money to play, so he borrowed $2,000 from Pops Popkin and $3,000 from Oscar Chason, a furrier. Jimmy left $400 with Joannie and caught a flight the following day.

Three hours after he walked into Gil's joint, he realized what was wrong. There is a difference in bookmaking that even some people in the business do not realize. If Joe Blow bets

$10,000 on a football game, you do not change the price. Joe
Blow is Joe Blow, and his opinion does not mean a thing; however, if a professional bets $1,500, a guy with a successful track
record, you change it fast. In Montreal, Gil had been changing
the price no matter who bet.

In a few weeks, Jimmy straightened it out, and in the meantime ran his $4,000 up to $33,000 betting on college football. He
did not have the bankroll in his hand. It was in the book, on
paper. Now the bowl games were coming up with Mississippi —
Navy in the Sugar Bowl, the big one, because Navy was the Lam-
bert Trophy team, champions of the East; and the East was
where they got their biggest play. Jimmy's price on the game was
Mississippi favored, but everybody else in the joint wanted to
make Navy the favorite by three or four points.

"I'm not talking about which team is better," Jimmy said.
"The price that'll get the most action is pick 'em, not Navy by
three or four."

By now, Gil Beckley was doing well. Where he had been a
million loser, he was a million winner. He figured he did not
need Jimmy the Greek anymore to tell him about sports.

"I'm opening it Navy by four," Gil said.

"I'll tell you what," Jimmy said. "Bet my thirty-three on Mississippi plus four."

"You're on," he said.

Right away, he cut the number to three, and then he
dropped it to two. A few days before the game, it was pick 'em,
and then it was Mississippi by one. The only reason Jimmy had
played the game was to get points with Mississippi and then,
when the price dropped, to turn around and bet Navy to catch
it both ways. Jimmy would be laying 11-to-10, or $33,000 on both
sides, with a spread of five points. So he was actually putting up
$3,000 and would win $60,000 if the result came inside the
spread.

The night before the game, it was Ole Miss by one and a
half. "Take me off," Jimmy told Gil. "I want to bet thirty-three on
the Navy."

"All right," he said. "I'll take you off tomorrow. Don't worry
about it. We'll move it back to Ole Miss by one, but you won't
have to pay the juice." That meant Jimmy would not have to lay
11-to-10 on his Navy bet, saving him $3,000.

The next morning, New Year's Day, the phone rang in his room at the Mount Royal Hotel. Jimmy never mingled at night with the guys at the joint. He liked them, but he preferred to be a loner.

It was Gil on the phone. "Greek," he said softly.

"What's the matter?" Jimmy asked.

"The boys raided the place last night."

"What boys?"

"The Canadian Mounted Police. The fucking Royal Mounted Police. They got everything."

"They can't do that," Jimmy yelled, meaning they could not just leave him with $33,000 on Ole Miss.

"The hell they can't. They did."

The police had impounded the books and some of the money, but not all of it. Some was stashed in other places. That did not help Jimmy. He did not have a dime on Navy as far as the book was concerned.

Navy beat them, 21–0, and Jimmy was in Montreal with $7 in his pocket. He called Joannie. "Anything in the bank?" he asked.

"About $260," she said, "but I haven't paid the rent yet."

"I just want to write a check."

"What happened? What's the matter?"

"Nothing. Everything's great." That was always one of his rules: never to tell Joannie when things were bad. He believed there was no reason for both of them to worry about it.

Being broke was not all that bad, comparatively. At last he was off the hook for that $40,000 loan.

Chapter 6

Unfriendly Timing

TOUGH GUYS WITH guns are not the only ones who can rob you blind. Jimmy once got ripped off by his friends with the help of his own pocket watch. It happened in 1946, after he went to Philadelphia to pick up $70,000 he had won on a series of baseball bets. He went to Atlantic City and took a suite in the Ambassador Hotel to kill a few days before the College All-Star game in Chicago.

Jimmy's suite became a gathering place for all the top gamblers in town, and there happened to be a bunch: Harry Rosen, one of the country's top bookmakers; Kingie Schwartz, the Canadian who could read the pool numbers on a tote board and give the odds for place and show instantly (he was also one of the highest players in horse-racing history); New York Nate Linnett; and Cheesecake Ike Berger, somebody's guest since the day he put on long pants; plus a few others. They sat around all afternoon betting horses with each other.

Jimmy kept a pocket watch in those days, one his father gave him, and he had it propped on the desk. Around 3:00 P.M., Jimmy received a phone call he took in his bedroom. He returned in time for the next race, which was a one-and-a-half-mile race for jumpers. He was ahead for the day, and everybody wanted to bet him on one horse, a long shot aptly named Long John II. Jimmy took $500 here and $1,000 there. Long John II came in at 11-to-1. Jimmy finished up a loser for the afternoon by more than $137,000.

That night he was walking on the boardwalk, feeling snake-bitten, when he ran into Slim Silverheart, the Pittsburgh book-maker who was his friend — his "Uncle Joe"— for so many years. Slim walked along with Jimmy, and after a while, he said, "Greek, what time you got?"

Jimmy took out his watch and said, "Ten-fifteen."

"That's funny," he said, "I got twenty-five after. Your watch must be wrong, Greek."

Then it hit Jimmy. The boys had past-posted him on the race. They knew the result before they put their money up. He had a hunch it was more of an accident than a plot. One of them might have called for a baseball score and found out the result of the race too. Maybe Jimmy's watch was already slow, or maybe one of them set it back while he was in the next room. Either way, once they knew, they could not resist betting Jimmy. Slim let him know what happened without telling him.

Jimmy did not say anything to him, either. He did not say anything to anyone. He just pretended he did not know what happened. He started scheming how he could get revenge.

He had not made a bet on the College All-Star game yet. The Los Angeles Rams were sent out as an eight-point favorite, and in Jimmy's mind, that was a wrong number. The All Stars had guys like Pat Harder and Elroy Hirsch and they were loaded. Jimmy believed the game was a toss-up.

The next afternoon, everyone was back in Jimmy's suite again, and Jimmy picked up the phone right there and called Mel Clark's in Chicago. "I'll take the Rams," he said, "and give the eight for $50,000." He had not raised his voice, but he spoke clearly so all the boys could hear him.

"You like the Rams minus eight?" Cheesecake Ike asked.

"I'm just monkeying around with it," Jimmy said. He saw the others were all ears too. These guys were mainly horseplayers, and none of them had the time or the interest to keep up with sports the way he did. They respected his opinion on a football game because they were aware that he knew what he was doing.

Jimmy left the next day, a Thursday, and went to Chicago. He immediately went up to Clark's place.

"What's the game?" Jimmy asked.

"It's up to twelve," Mel said.

"Yeah? Where is all the money from?"

"We got a lot of money from the East on it. Most of it came in yesterday."

The day of the game Jimmy went back to Clark's, and by then, the Rams were favored by thirteen. "How about a straight price?" Jimmy said.

"You're entitled to 3½-to-1," Mel said.

"I'll take it for $20,000, and from now on whatever you take at thirteen, I'll pay you two percent of it." This was a strong offer. Clark customarily gave bets away in return for one percent of the winning side.

"You got it," he said.

Now Jimmy was off his original bet on the Rams and played the game in the middle. They did not think anything of it. If a bookmaker gave eight and it came thirteen, it was a natural move. He also had the All Stars with the odds, in addition to the points.

On the way to the game, Jimmy was in the elevator at the Blackstone Hotel when Nate Linnett got on at another floor. "Say, Nate," Jimmy said, "who'd you bet on?"

"Because you bet on the Rams," he said, "I made a big bet on them too."

"I didn't tell you to bet on the Rams."

"I heard you on the phone. You bet $50,000."

"I'm playing the game even," Jimmy said.

"But I heard you bet the Rams," Nate said.

"I'm not kidding. I played the game out."

Nate shrugged. "I gave nine. I'll stick with it."

Hirsch and his boys beat Bob Waterfield and the Rams, 16–0. Jimmy got $70,000 for his straight bet and came out $60,000 ahead on the points. It made him about even for the week, including Long John II, and it gave him the personal satisfaction of squaring with those guys who past-posted him.

The next winter in Florida, when Nate and the rest passed the story around, Jimmy had an answer for them. "That's right," he said, "but how much did you bet on the Rams?"

The College All-Star game in the 1940s was like the Super Bowl. Gamblers came into Chicago from all over the country.

They came to the Blackstone and the Sherman and the bets flew. Tommy McDonald's was another popular gambling joint. Both McDonald's and Clark's were right off Clark Street in the Loop. They had cigar stores in front, but the layout was wide open and so was the whole town.

Every summer Jimmy stayed after the game and spent two or three weeks in the room at Clark's, matching wits with one of the greatest handicappers of all time, Professor Charles McNeil. McNeil had been a college professor at the University of Illinois in Champagne–Urbana, not far south of Chicago. He never wore a tie, but he always wore a white shirt and somehow looked like a professor. He started coming up to Clark's and making little bets, fifty cents and a dollar. After a while, he began betting $2. Then he was putting down $5 and $20. Before long he was betting $100 and $200, and finally Mel and Jakie Summerfield saw what he was and they said, "Hey, come in with us." McNeil was reluctant.

Jakie said, "You can make more here than you can teaching arithmetic."

"Calculus," McNeil corrected.

"Whatever it is, this has got to be more fun," Jakie said. McNeil agreed.

The professor was the first to put up the teasers, where the bettor could move the line seven points up or down, but he had to make a two-team parlay and lay 11-to-1. It works out that a 6½-point teaser is even money. Today, bookies shade it so you have to lay 11-to-10 with six points, and with 6½ they want 6-to-5 or 13-to-10 and 5-to-4. One day Jimmy said, "Mac, let's make a 12-point teaser, with three teams." He did and got a lot of play, though the bettors were actually getting a one-team bet at 6-to-5.

During the winter, Mac and Jimmy would match wits on basketball especially. One year he said, "I'm always giving you the numbers. Why don't you give them to me, the night before, and I promise to bet you three or four games." He meant he would take either side of Jimmy's line and lay him 11-to-10. He would bet $1,100 a game. He told Jimmy to call him every night around 7:00.

After a couple of weeks, Jimmy was not doing well at all. He would win fifteen and lose ten, and seldom would it come his way, even with the 11-to-10 in his favor. One afternoon, Jimmy phoned Clark's and was talking to Jakie about it.

Jakie said, "I'll give you a tip. Instead of giving him the line at 7:00, give it to him at 9:00."

"Why?" Jimmy asked.

"Do what I tell you."

That night Jimmy called at 7:00 and told Mac that something came up at the office and he could not get back to him for a couple of hours. He said, okay, and Jimmy called back at 9:15. Jimmy said, "Are you ready?"

He said, "Yep, yep. Any time, ole Greek." This did not sound like the professor, who was usually eloquent and formal. Jimmy read off the numbers and he started at the top and bet every game.

What Jimmy did not know was that McNeil had a nightly custom. He stopped working at 7:00 and spent the next two hours downing a quart of Scotch. When sober, he only bet the three-point games. But when he was drinking, he would even bet the one-pointers. Those were practically toss-ups, and that was the difference in the whole advantage. Now Jimmy was winning twenty and losing seventeen, and the 11-to-10 edge starting mounting up. Jimmy took a lot of McNeil's money that season by calling at 9:00.

He did not always have something extra going for him when he made a bet, but those were the bets that stuck best to his memory. He had a subsidy working through one entire basketball season because he knew the trainer at a college in West Virginia. He was on Jimmy's payroll in a small way. This was a high-scoring team and played a major schedule. Its star player had a bad knee, and the trainer had to work on it just before every game. The kid was one of the nation's highest scorers, but when the knee was stiff his scoring slacked off. An hour before game time, the trainer would call Jimmy. If the knee was okay, the trainer would bet on his team. If it was not, he said he would not bet the game that night.

Of course, Jimmy bet every game, one way or the other. He won eighteen out of nineteen bets on the trainer's team that season.

There was nothing "wrong" there, but the key to the team's

performance was the physical condition of its best player. It was only one step from that, however, to the mental condition of a key player. Professional gamblers always knew basketball was the most susceptible to outside manipulation than all the other team sports. There are five players, instead of nine or eleven. On the average team there are only two players, at the most three, who are vital to the team's success.

Since Paddy Ryan was knocked out by John L. Sullivan in 1882, the lore of betting in the United States had been rife with tales of tigers who went into the tank. That was easy enough, one on one, man against man. When Jimmy was a kid in Kios, Primo Carnera was knocking out guys named Farmer Lodge and Sam Baker and Bearcat Wright, and a couple of years later, he knocked out Jack Sharkey for the heavyweight championship—after Sharkey, who did not have the heavyweight title at that time, beat him in fifteen rounds. Larceny was a convenient arrangement inside the squared circle.

It was only a quantum leap from one to five, when basketball took the court. One day in Steubenville, Jimmy got a call from a bookie he knew in New York. He asked for a price on NYU against Buffalo in the Garden. Jimmy told him to call back in twenty-five minutes. He had files on all the basketball teams in the country in the late-forties. He put a pencil to it, and it looked as though NYU would be playing reserves in the fourth quarter. When he called back, he told him the game was fifteen. He said, "I got a guy here who wants to take thirteen for $5,000. You want any part of it?"

Jimmy said, "Hell, yes."

"You got it, for $2,000."

A little while later he called back and said, "This guy wants to go another $5,000 to twelve. You want some?" Jimmy told him if he would take money at thirteen, he sure would take more at twelve.

It was Jimmy's habit in basketball season to call around the country and see who was betting what. He called Minneapolis and got Lou Walker, who later came to work for him. He asked him, among other things, what he had on NYU and Buffalo. He said seventeen. Then Jimmy asked him who was betting the game. He said, "Jimmy, you know I can't tell you that."

Jimmy asked him if Billy Hecht, the boss, was there. Billy said the betting was out of New York. Jimmy did not like it. Nobody was going to bet him and take twelve and thirteen and give fifteen and sixteen in Minnesota. He asked Billy who in New York was betting. Billy did not want to say. Jimmy said, "Billy, this is basketball season, but football is coming too." Billy leaned on Jimmy for his opinions on football.

Finally, Billy said, "Well, between you and me . . ." He named the guy who called Jimmy for thirteen and twelve.

Jimmy said, "Uh-oh, this is wrong. Why would the guy do this?" A half hour later, Jimmy called Minneapolis back and it was sixteen; a little later it was fifteen, dropping to fourteen. Jimmy told the kids in his office in Steubenville, "Okay, let's go. We got to get off and get well. Call every small book in our neck of the woods." Jimmy came out ahead on the night, when NYU won by nine, but he was determined it would never happen to him again.

Jimmy had gained a certain reputation by that time, and International News Service — which later merged with United Press to become UPI — called him from New York to get the point spread on the games in Madison Square Garden. After this Buffalo game, when INS called, Jimmy told them he did not have a line. "I can't give you the numbers," he said, "because I don't know how to handicap games in the Garden."

A few years later, in 1952, New York District Attorney Frank Hogan broke open the basketball scandals — but in the meantime there was a lot of paranoia. During this time, Jimmy got a call from a New York friend, Butch Tauris, a former song-and-dance man who fell to predictably hard times. He wanted to know something to bet. Jimmy gave him Denison plus six over Ohio U., because Jimmy had just made a small bet on the game.

Later when Jimmy called Billy Hecht, he learned that the price had dropped to two. "And in New York," Billy said, "it is off the board," meaning no New York books would take action on the game.

Jimmy's song-and-dance man had called every friend in town and told them Jimmy the Greek was betting Denison; therefore, Jimmy must have the game in the bag. Denison won, and the next day, the whole Ohio Conference was barred by every bookmaker in the country.

Big betting scandals followed both world wars because there was so much black-market money around that could not be placed anywhere except in gambling. These were profits from dealing in whiskey and cigarettes. After World War I came the Black Sox sellout of 1919. The basketball fixes of 1950-1951 stemmed from a lot of guys trying to be bookmakers who did not know enough about it, and they were losing. A lot of people like Charley McNeil, Jimmy the Greek, Jakie Summerfield, Jerry Zarowitz, Bobby Berendt, and Eddie Kurd were beating them with superior handicapping.

In 1946, Jimmy won the biggest basketball bet of his life. He was in Florida, as usual, for the winter. He rarely came back from Florida with any money, because whatever he won at basketball he dutifully contributed to the racetrack the following day. This time he won so much money on basketball, near the end of his stay, he had no chance to lose it back on the horses. He had nothing but winners through the first rounds of the National Invitational Tournament at the Garden.

He was betting at a little cigar store in Miami Beach across from the Roney Plaza. Slim Silverheart introduced Jimmy with the magic words, "Whatever this guy wants . . ." There was a high-stakes poker game going on right upstairs. It was a fine place to bet because it was run by a guy from Chicago, and any bets made were sure to be paid. If somebody reneged, he was in serious trouble.

For the final game, between DePaul and Rhode Island, Jimmy came up with a gimmick that got all the other guys to bet him. Rhode Island was a high-scoring team, but it had a loose defense. Jimmy had DePaul the winner, but that was not enough. Finally, he came up with an idea that would make them think he was wrong. "Fellas," he announced, "I have a proposition. I'll take six-to-five that DePaul sets the NIT scoring record tonight." This was the team that had George Mikan, the greatest pivot man in basketball up until that time. They lined up single file to bet him, covering $52,000—until there was only one man left, a little fellow who seemed shy. Jimmy said, "What are you going to do, Pops?"

He said, "Would you give me $100 of your side?"

DePaul and Mikan broke the scoring record by eight points.

That spring in Florida Jimmy came up with another gimmick bet that attracted even more play, this time on baseball. All
the gamblers were talking about the coming season and Joe
DiMaggio's return to the Yankees after three years in the army.
One night on Twenty-third Street in Miami Beach, where all the
gamblers hung out, a guy said, "He'll have a great year. He'll hit
.350 because he's the one guy who can pick up right where he
left off."

Jimmy did not think so. He had been reading about DiMaggio's domestic troubles. He was breaking up with his wife and
there was a little son involved. Jimmy knew that made it worse
for him, because Jimmy himself was going through torture with
his daughter for the same reason. DiMaggio being Italian had
something to do with it too. There is definitely some similarity
between Greeks and Italians when it comes to children. Other
people love their children, but it seems they live for their children.

In order for Jimmy to bet against DiMaggio, he had to come
up with someone he thought would hit higher, who was not an
obvious choice. He knew nobody would give him Ted Williams
— it had to be someone out in left field, so to speak. Because Jimmy was living in Ohio, the Cleveland Indians were important to
him, and one player in particular, shortstop Lou Boudreau,
especially had his attention. Jimmy lived vicariously with every
play he made, every hit he got. If he could have changed places
with anyone in those years, it would have been with Boudreau.
He had hit .306 the previous season and .327 the year before
that. He figured to hit a solid .310.

So on Twenty-third Street, Jimmy started announcing that
he liked Boudreau to outhit DiMaggio. "You're crazy, Greek,"
someone said. "Boudreau isn't even in DiMaggio's class."

Jimmy said, "I'll take six-to-five that Boudreau hits for a
higher average than DiMaggio does." He gave it to Jimmy, and
then they all started jumping aboard. Jimmy made them lay him
7-to-5, 8-to-5, and then 9-to-5 because they were so anxious to
back DiMaggio. Adding it up, Jimmy had over $100,000 riding
on it.

Going into the last day of the 1946 season, Boudreau was at
.293 and DiMaggio was just a couple of base hits behind him at

.292. Boudreau had pulled himself from the lineup most of the last month because he had a bad ankle. DiMaggio was in Philadelphia for a doubleheader. Jimmy had a spotter in Shibe Park telephone him every time Joe came to bat. DiMaggio went 1-for-7 and finished at .290 — the lowest average of his career until the season he retired.

Chapter 7

Marriage:
The Biggest Bet of All

JIMMY STROLLED THROUGH New York's Central Park Zoo one spring when he made an important biological discovery. Turning to a friend, he pointed at the cages and said, "You know, there must be something to it. There's a he and she in every one."

Companionship was not a bad game plan, but it had a way of leading to the biggest bet most of us ever make — getting married. When Jimmy made his first bet on marriage, he lost.

Looking back, he believed he lost because he violated one of his own rules. He did not research the situation properly. This was one time when he should have kept his mind and his field glasses on the tote board.

He was in a box at Tropical Park, on a mild March afternoon in 1942, when he noticed a lovely, blue-eyed blonde in the next box.

"Who," he asked one of the people with him, "is that?"

"Sunny Miles," he said. "Her father is J. H. Miles."

Jimmy knew about her father. He was a big truck farmer in Indiana, a millionaire. He owned some racehorses. For once, Jimmy was not interested in getting information on horses. He wanted to know more about Pauline (Sunny) Miles. He arranged to be introduced.

She was engaged, but they went out that night. They went out the next night too. The night after that, they were married in Fort Lauderdale. How, or why, it happened so fast he could never explain. He was not drunk and did not have any other acceptable excuse. He was twenty-two, and she was twenty-six. They just drove up the coast to Fort Lauderdale with Sunny's mother and two of Jimmy's Steubenville pals, Cans Jones and Cecil Gallagher. They found a justice of the peace, and thirty minutes later, they headed back to Miami Beach.

It was the sort of impulsive, romantic thing people were doing that year, in the early months of a spreading war. Jonesy turned to Jimmy, in the back seat of the car, and grinned. "Well, Greek," he said, "you'll remember March 28 for a long time."

It was like drawing a curtain over a window. "I'll never forget March 28," Jimmy said. "I'll never forget that date." For a moment, Jimmy started to get angry. March 28 meant only one thing to him. It was the day his mother was killed, the anniversary of his mother's death.

Jimmy felt a knot in his stomach as big as a fist. *My God,* Jimmy thought. He had not even realized what day it was. Out of respect for his mother, he never would have chosen that date to wed. One more day, two more, a week would have made no difference.

Jimmy was not usually superstitious about anything, but the month of March always upset him. He once counted eight family members who died under the sign of Aries, including his mother, aunt and uncle by the gun, and another uncle in a plane crash. Even in old age, he refused to fly on March 28 and was uncomfortable flying during the month of March — period. He laid odds 2-to-1 that when he died, it would be in March. (He would die in April.) Jimmy never felt the ill-chosen date to marry was an omen. He simply believed they did not know each other well enough to stake a marriage on it. Two days: some people take that long to select a magazine off the newsstand.

There might have been couples who won the bet, but they were not among them. Their first year was not too bad. Then their daughter, Victoria, arrived. Sunny had to stay home with the baby, and that cramped her style. She liked to go out, and even in Steubenville there were bright lights and music. Sunny had to take care of Vicki, and she was not the type who enjoyed changing diapers and heating bottles. Not that Jimmy was the perfect husband, but on the side, she was seeing another guy. One day a friend of Jimmy's phoned.

"She's with him right now."

"I don't believe it," Jimmy said.

"Then go see for yourself."

He gave Jimmy the address. Jimmy saw red — a flaming, matador red. He kept a .38 in those days. With the money he carried, he had it for protection. That day, at that moment, he had a different reason for carrying it. He did not care what she was doing because she did not mean that much to him anymore, but she was the mother of his child. He was going to kill her and her lover.

He jumped into his black Chrysler and tore down Market Street hill when the car started wobbling. It was a flat tire. And it happened to be the luckiest flat he ever had. In the time it took him to change the tire, he cooled off. He was too tired to commit homicide anyway, after loosening lugs with a wrench, sweat rolling down his face. Jimmy realized that the best thing to do was to divorce her. That was what he did.

As lucky as he was with the flat tire, he was just as unlucky in the divorce settlement. She got everything, including the thousand shares of Reynolds Metal he had bought with the idea of holding it for ten years. He bought it at $14\frac{7}{8}$. It climbed to 35, but he sold it to pay off Sunny. Ten years later the stock, after splits, was worth nearly $2 million. He never would have had to work again.

There was one thing Sunny did not get. Jimmy kept Vicki, who meant a lot more to him than Reynolds Metal. But he always had the fear that Sunny would come back to take Vicki away from him. He had heard too many stories about wives who signed over their kids, changed their minds after six months, and then went to court to get them back.

One of the turning points in his life came the week after Christmas in 1947, when Vicki beat him to the telephone and answered, "Hello? My daddy likes Texas." That sent a chill through him. He decided that was it. He closed his Steubenville office and moved to Florida. Jimmy knew that no one had control over how a judge would rule especially if he thought a gambler was somebody who lived under a rock. For the next few years, he kept a low profile as a bettor, getting money down through a partner if at all.

The next time Jimmy married, his instincts were just as swift, but he better researched matters this time around. He checked into the Kenilworth Hotel in Bal Harbour for the first North-South college football game in 1948, Christmas night. Jimmy's man, Herman Hickman, the Yale coach, had the North squad, and a few days before the game they were heading to Joe's Stone Crab Restaurant for dinner. His room at the Kenilworth was on the ninth floor. Herman's was on the second. Jimmy was coming down in the elevator when it stopped at eight. When the doors opened, a beautiful brunette, in a classy, white evening gown, looked at Jimmy.

"Are you the elevator boy?" she asked.

"Yes, ma'am," Jimmy said, alertly. "What floor are you going to?"

"Are you sure the elevator is working?"

"Yes, ma'am," Jimmy said. "I'm sure it is."

"It has come back three times, up and down," she said, suspiciously. "But there hasn't been an elevator boy on it and I won't get on."

"Where are you going, ma'am?"

"To the lobby."

"I'll take you there, ma'am."

Jimmy knew what happened. When the elevator boy had his dinner hour, the elevator was put on automatic. Jimmy pressed the "L" button and down they went.

"Thank you," she said.

"You're welcome, ma'am."

In the lobby, she was met by her date, a college boy Jimmy recognized as one of Herman Hickman's players, Jack Geary. Jimmy rode the elevator back to the second floor and walked into Herman's room with an announcement.

"I just met the girl I'm going to marry."

Herman and his wife, Helen, laughed. He could not blame them. Jimmy had been divorced for several years and was dating maybe a dozen different girls. He weighed about 175 pounds then, with decent looks, plenty of money, and a Cadillac convertible. He had the world by the chain.

"Who are you kidding?" Herman said.

"I mean it," Jimmy insisted. "I really mean it."

"What's her name?"

"I don't know."

That broke it for Herman. "You're going to marry her," he said, his eyes almost watering, "but you don't know her name."

"I'll find out."

The next day, Jimmy checked her out. Her name was Joan Specht. She and her sister, Marge, were on Christmas vacation from St. Mary's of the Woods College in Terre Haute, Indiana. Their father owned the Hercules Manufacturing Company in Evansville, Indiana. George Specht was one fine human, and Jimmy's strategy was to get to know him first. Jimmy always got along well with older people.

One night when George was with her in the lobby, Jimmy sidled over and whispered, "Who is that young lady next to you?"

"I'm sorry, Jim," he said. "I didn't introduce you. This is my daughter, Joan."

Jimmy took it from there. She spent most of her time with the Yale football player, but Jimmy had an edge. The Yale student manager was in charge of travel arrangements. Jimmy knew him from having visited Hickman's practices, and had once done him a huge favor.

"When are the players leaving?" Jimmy asked him.

"Some leave on the twenty-eighth, some leave the twenty-sixth."

"When is the tackle leaving?"

"He leaves on the twenty-eighth."

"You mean the twenty-sixth," Jimmy said, slipping him $20.

"Yes, sir, the twenty-sixth," the manager said.

The day after the game, several players were in the lobby with their bags. Outside, a bus waited to take them to the airport. The kid from Yale was there, talking to Joannie, while Jimmy positioned himself in a corner. He watched as the manager made sure everyone who was on the list got onto the bus. When the bus pulled out, Joannie walked by Jimmy on her way to the elevator.

"Miss Specht," Jimmy said, "now it's my turn."

She glared at Jimmy and kept on walking. Jimmy's plan did

not call for him to make a big play for her right away. He had become quite friendly with her father and earlier in the day had invited him to dinner.

"That's fine, Jim," he said. "I'll have the family."

Jimmy hoped he would say that. They went to one of the finest gourmet restaurants on Miami Beach, with the captains hurrying around, pouring wine, lighting cigarettes — the whole number. Jimmy laid it on pretty strong. He could tell Joan enjoyed herself, and that impressed her father. It went on that way for the rest of the week, without him making any kind of move on Joannie.

Jimmy wanted to take her to the Orange Bowl game on New Year's Day. He had tickets on the 50-yard line, up high, where you're supposed to sit to watch a game. When Jimmy mentioned it to her on New Year's Eve, she asked if her father could go too.

"Well, yes," Jimmy said. "I do have another ticket."

"He has to sit down low," she said. "He has a heart flutter. He's not allowed to walk up steps."

Jimmy swallowed hard. "I don't know if I can change my seats," he said.

"I'm sorry, but if he can't go, I can't."

Jimmy looked at his watch. It was 2:00 A.M., twelve hours until game time. He drove Joannie back to the Kenilworth, then he hurried down to Twenty-third Street where he had his contacts. Painfully, he parted with his 50-yard-line seats, up high, for three that were field level. It was the worst possible place to watch a game, with the exception of the bench, but he could not complain. He was with Joan, and he had Texas and seven points against Georgia. Texas won big, 41–28.

"Well, you won your bet," Mr. Specht congratulated him.

"Yes, sir," Jimmy said. "I won $10,000 on Texas."

"Ten thousand!" he repeated, shocked by the amount.

"I try to win my vacation expenses," Jimmy said.

Actually, Jimmy won $50,000, but he cut down the amount so Mr. Specht's heart would not flutter. He did not want a heart attack on his conscience. It was funny, in a way. Here was a prosperous businessman who often threw around $50,000 in his business, but he could not imagine anyone betting that kind of money on a football game. As it turned out, he could not imagine anyone betting $10,000 on one.

Joan returned to school and Jimmy began commuting to Indiana. St. Mary's of the Woods was a strict Catholic college, whose rules did not allow students to leave the campus during the week. When Jimmy drove up in his Cadillac convertible, he brought a bag of sandwiches with him. They drove around and parked to talk and eat the sandwiches and drink Coke and then he returned her to the dormitory. It was the purest, most innocent time of his adult life, a change of pace after dating some top models in New York. They toasted each other with Coke, because if those nuns caught her drinking anything else, she would have been expelled. If that happened, Mr. Specht would have expelled Jimmy Snyder.

In the years that he courted Joannie while she was in college, Jimmy lived in Florida. He made trips to see her at school, and meanwhile spent a lot of time with Ray Ryan at his home office in Evansville, Indiana, just a few miles south of Terre Haute. Though Jimmy's first oil deal had nothing to do with Ryan, he met a pair of drillers, Bob Tulley and Truman Carter, through him. They gave Jimmy five-eighths of a well they were sinking on the Otto Chase farm across the river from Evansville, outside Henderson, Kentucky. It hit, too, for a thousand barrels a day, and Jimmy thought, *This business is a cinch.* Then he learned that it was a "lime" well and the flow died down quickly. Ryan got all excited when they hit and offered Jimmy a flat $750,000 for his share. Jimmy laughed at him. That was his first mistake in the oil business, but certainly not his last.

Another one of his mistakes in the oil business occurred when he, again, mixed his women with his money. As with Sunny and the Reynolds Metal ordeal, Joannie, on one occasion, indirectly cost him a fortune.

At an engagement party for her sister, Marge, and Dr. Owen Slaughter, later a prominent Evansville surgeon, Joan and Jimmy had a riot of an argument. Jimmy could not even recall what it was about, except that it ended with one of them telling the other, or maybe simultaneously, "Go to hell!" Jimmy stalked out.

He chartered a private plane and carried his temper that night to New York, where he was supposed to sign the papers to start drilling an oil well on some Indiana property. The next day, one of his drilling partners, Bob Tulley of Tulley and Carter, called.

"Jim," he said, "you're due to start drilling in two days. Did you forget?"

"To hell with it," Jimmy snapped.

"What are you talking about?" he said.

"I'm not interested in the well," Jimmy said, not thinking clearly, still brooding over his split with Joannie.

"Take the property if you want it. You can have it all."

"Are you serious?"

"Send me the papers. You can do anything you want with it."

"If you say so," he said.

That lease produced eleven oil wells. He would have been a wealthy man. He kept the property around it, but the five wells they drilled there were dry. That was what happened to him whenever he mixed his women with his money.

But even though Joan cost him a fortune on one occasion, she indirectly saved his life on another. It was in 1949 or 1950 and it was one of the many times he resolved to marry her before making it official. He was in New York with Harold Salvey and divulged his plans.

"You're crazy," Harold said. "She's still a schoolgirl. Her father is a respected businessman. You're a gambler. Believe me, Greek, it's not a good mix. It'll never work."

"I'll make it work," Jimmy said. "I'm gonna buy her a ring."

"In that case," said Harold, "I can get it for you wholesale."

They went to Tiffany's first, found the ring he wanted, a four-carat marquise diamond, and priced it. It was $13,000. Then he followed Harold into a cab and they headed for the diamond market. It was a beehive with shops, stores, and vendors. People were practically selling from pushcarts. The sight was so vivid to him. There were little Jewish men, with their full beards and yarmulkes, who had placed their money in gold and diamonds and escaped from Germany before the war — the ones who were lucky.

Jimmy and Harold found a friend of Harold's named Sam, and in a few minutes he produced the stone Jimmy wanted, wrapped in tissue paper. The price was $4,500. Jimmy described the setting he wanted, platinum, with a baguette on each side, and he needed it in time to catch a flight to Miami the next morning.

Sam threw up his hands. "Impossible," he said. "You come back late in the afternoon. Ve haf it then."

"So you stay another day," said Harold. "What's the difference?"

The next afternoon they went back to pick up the ring. At the corner Harold bought a newspaper and as they drove away from the diamond market he said, "Greek, what was the number of that Eastern flight you were supposed to catch?"

Jimmy told him.

"Well," he said, "you're a dead man." He handed Jimmy the paper. The Eastern flight had collided outside of Washington with a small plane, where a Bolivian Air Force pilot was *practicing*. He bailed out. Everyone aboard the Eastern jet was killed.

Now, gambler's luck does not usually lend itself to sparing gamblers' lives, but something or someone did not think it was his time to go when he missed that flight. Even more ironically, the same force intervened again in a similar fashion in January 1969, two weeks after the Super Bowl and after his surgery. The night he left the hospital in Santa Barbara, he caught a flight for Los Angeles, figuring to change planes there for Denver, where he was involved in a mining deal. They landed in Los Angeles on a foggy, dreary, miserable night and Jimmy suddenly realized how weak he was from the surgery. He decided to cancel his connecting flight, take a cab to the Beverly Wilshire, get a good night's rest, and fly to Denver in the morning.

The United Airlines plane he would have taken went down a few miles outside of Los Angeles, crashing into the Pacific. Only a few passengers survived.

Jimmy never dwelled on the whims of fate or the deeper meanings of life, or asked, *Why me?* These were just cases where he beat the odds, his good bets cashed.

Chapter 8

H. L. Hunt:
High-Rolling Gambler

JIMMY CONTINUED TO KEEP a low profile in the gambling world and placed many of his bets through Ray Ryan, who played the role of partner. Jimmy had known many guys who bet money in his time; that was his life. But he never knew of a higher roller than Ryan. Ryan was an unforgettable character in his experience.

Jimmy first met Ryan at Marty Gilfoyle's gambling joint in Miami. Ryan was a tall, handsome guy with an upbeat personality. Everything was always happy with Ryan, whether he was flush or busted. He looked like a movie star, with straight brown hair brushed back flat on his head — something like a latter-day Richard Arlen. He liked Jimmy's style and Jimmy liked his.

Ryan had bounced around as a teen on his own, much the way Jimmy had, though Jimmy remained within the confines of Steubenville.

In a sense, Ryan's betting losses on the horses or sports made Jimmy feel like a piker — because for him, oil and gambling mixed like oil and water. Where Jimmy plunged $150,000 on one game, Ryan did that on five or six games.

Ryan once told Jimmy that he bought two 80-acre fields outside of Centralia, Illinois, on a tip. If you're well liked in the oil business, you get information. A truck driver, a worker you lent $10 to six months ago — anybody can tip you to promising leases. He had these two fields and owed a man in Chicago $19,000 from betting horses. Ryan went to a representative of the Texas Company offices in Centralia and told him he would sell one of the fields for $19,000. Ryan knew the man well.

The guy said, "Ryan, I know the field is worth it, and probably more, but why $19,000?"

Ryan said, "I want the money by 10:00 A.M."

"That's impossible. The company will want the title proven, and other technicalities."

"Tomorrow, or the deal will be off," Ryan said.

"How about both sides for $38,000?"

"No," Ryan said, "one is all I'll sell."

Ryan went back to his hotel. On his way upstairs, he noticed the gambling layout on the second floor: race results, dice, and roulette too. An hour later, the Texaco man called his room and said, "Come over and get the check."

The check was made out for $38,000. The company said both fields or none, because it would not run as much of a title risk that way.

Finally, Ryan said okay. He went down to Western Union and wired the $19,000 to Chicago.

Ryan said he knew he had just pissed away a fortune. Disgusted with himself, he went back to the hotel. That evening at 6:00 he got into his car and took off for a vacation to Florida. He spent the afternoon losing the other $19,000 playing the horses.

Both fields came in and produced over 5 million barrels of oil apiece. At $3 a barrel, the rates at the time, in one afternoon Ryan had squandered away $15 million betting horses that ran second.

Ryan was known as a high roller about the same time as Jimmy. Damon Runyon put the label on him. Runyon wrote in a column: "Every generation seems to produce its own fabulous figure in lofty gambling. As Nick the Greek has been used to connote high rolling for years and before him Pittsburgh Phil Smith, now it is Ray Ryan. He plays the highest gin rummy of any man since the game was invented."

This publicity attracted another high-rolling gambler, oilman H. L. Hunt, who filled a significant chapter in Jimmy's life because he knew Ryan well. Hunt fancied himself the greatest card player in the world, second only to his talent at checkers, where he claimed absolute superiority throughout all history.

Hunt started calling Ryan trying to get him to set up a gin game. Both were busy men. Finally, Hunt learned that Ryan had booked passage to Europe on a luxury liner, and he bought a ticket on the same ship. Their ocean crossing was one high-stakes gin game — at $10 a point, where $30,000 changed hands within twenty minutes — and Ryan stepped ashore on England with $243,000 of Hunt's money.

Ryan liked to hobnob with actors, possibly because he had the looks and personality to be in show business himself. In later years, William Holden and he went into partnership to create the Mount Kenya Safari Club in Africa.

Ryan was a regular in Las Vegas before Jimmy ever went there. One day Ryan was going into the hotel dining room out there when he was stopped by Johnny Myers, the Howard Hughes publicity man. "Ray, let me have $5,000," Myers said. "I've got a real pigeon for a gin game." Ryan gave him the money.

Later, Ryan's meal was interrupted when actor Bruce Cabot rushed to the table. Cabot needed some cash. "I've got a sucker tied up for gin," he said. "It's like finding money." Ryan backed him.

The baked Alaska and a faint suspicion arrived at Ryan's table in a dead heat. Ryan hurried to the card room, and there were Myers and Cabot, playing head to head. The joke was on him.

Ryan was a restless guy. Any time he had a deal on, he totally concentrated. Then when it was settled, he wanted something else. He loved to bet on anything, and he loved to bet big. Once, Jimmy and Ryan were in the Warwick Hotel in New York with some friends, and Ryan decided he wanted to bet on gin rummy but he did not want to play. A waiter had just arrived with some drinks and sandwiches.

"Young man," Ryan said to the waiter, "do you know how to play gin?"

"Yes, sir," the kid said. "I play all the time."

"Good. I'll tell you what we're going to do. You play my hand, and if you win, you keep half the money. If you lose, I'll cover you. Fair enough?"

The kid thought he was either nuts or drunk, but New York waiters are inured to anything. "Yes, sir!" he said.

In the next two hours the phone rang a few times. It was room service wanting to know if the food had arrived, because the waiter never came back. Jimmy was not in the game, so he answered and told them the kid delivered the order and left.

The kid was winning, but he did not have any idea how much because he did not know how high the stakes were.

"We're going to dinner now, young man," Ryan finally said. "Here's your money." Ray took out his money clip and peeled off $5,000. Jimmy thought the kid was going to faint.

"Take it," Ryan said. "You play gin very well, young man."

The next day, Ryan thought it was so much fun, he wanted to do it again. He called room service and asked for the waiter, Eddie.

"I'm sorry, sir," the voice at room service told him. "Eddie quit working here last night."

During the two years Jimmy had known Ryan, he was after him to come in with him on betting football games. He thought Jimmy was the best handicapper on college football, and he was.

"I'll put up all the money, Greek," he said, "and you've got a third of it. You just give me the teams to bet."

Until then, Jimmy had decided to keep a low profile in betting for Vicki's sake. He had never taken Ryan up on it. Finally, he told him he would accept the deal on one condition. He would cover his third, but he wanted to stay in the background. "I don't want anyone to know where the bets come from," Jimmy said. "I don't want to talk to anybody or make bets with anybody on anything."

The first week of the football season that year they happened to be in New York, this time at the Savoy Plaza. Jimmy had him bet the Arkansas–Oklahoma A&M game. They had some other bets going, but this was the big one, a triple bet. It turned out to be a triple loser — $100,000 worth. Jimmy was sick. This was their top bet, and they blew it.

That night, when Ryan came back to the hotel room, he knew the result. "Now, look," he said, "I know how you feel about it, but don't worry. I got plenty of money. I can carry you if you need it. But most of all, I believe in you." Knute Rockne

or Vince Lombardi never gave a better pep talk as far as Jimmy
was concerned.

The next week Jimmy had a big winner, and the rest of the
season it continued with Jimmy collecting all the way.

Then Ryan introduced Jimmy over the telephone to H. L.
Hunt in Dallas. The old fellow was already a legend. When *Life*
magazine finally got a photograph of him, by using a telephoto
lens as he crossed a downtown street, they were so proud of it
that they ran it full page. When J. Paul Getty was asked if he or
Howard Hughes was the richest individual in the world, Getty
said, "In terms of personal wealth, there is only one — H. L.
Hunt in Texas."

The stories about Hunt soon became clichés — how he always brought his lunch to the office in a brown paper bag, and
how he drove an old Ford and parked it blocks away to save the
parking fee. All were true, but were clichés, nevertheless.

Jimmy called H. L. once a week, on Saturday mornings, and
after a few weeks they talked of other things besides football. He
told Jimmy that he won his first big stake in the oil business playing poker, taking a man's lease with three queens over two pair.
He said he quit smoking when he figured that just taking the
wrappers off cigars had cost him $380,000 over the years — that
was how valuable his time was.

H. L. loved to bet on games in the Southwest Conference,
and Jimmy's expertise concentrated on the Southeastern Conference. They bet $50,000 a game, head to head, with no 11-to-
10 either way. His accountants settled up, sending a check to
Ryan's office as if it were another expense of the oil business.
Ryan occasionally sent a check to him when they lost. H. L.
would call Bookie Shaeffer's joint in Chicago and get the line on
the games. He would pick three games against the line, giving or
taking points, and Jimmy would take three the same way.

One Saturday well into the first season, H. L. said, "Young
man, I think we should delete the Southeastern Conference."

"Well, sir," Jimmy said, "that's your prerogative, but if we
delete the Southeastern Conference, I think we should delete
another conference of my choice."

"That would be fair," he said.

"All right, then we'll delete the Southwest Conference."

There was a big pause, as H. L. realized he would never be able to bet on SMU again, and he said, "No, we'll leave it as it is."

As usual, Ryan and Jimmy tried to use any edge they could get. Ryan gave Jimmy the name of a secretary in Hunt's office to call in the latter part of the week. The old man had a habit of jotting down his favorite team on a notepad at his desk, and he placed a star or two beside the top choice. The secretary told Jimmy who he liked as a best bet. Jimmy would have Ryan bet $20,000 on the team with Bookie Shaeffer, so when Hunt got the line on Saturday, his top choices would be a half point less (or more). At other times, when H. L. picked a team Jimmy thought was right, he would get Ryan to lay off the whole $50,000.

After two seasons they had hit him for $600,000, $200,000 of which belonged to Jimmy as per his agreement with Ryan. By then, Jimmy had other interests, and H. L. did not seem reluctant to call off their arrangement.

For one thing, it was not a good year, 1951, to be using the telephone, as the Kefauver hearings soon established. But Jimmy did not forget his old friend, H. L. Hunt, or his unlisted number. Their next contact was in 1957, after Jimmy had tapped out in oil and gone to the holy land, Las Vegas, to repent.

Jimmy became close friends with Bernie Einstosh, who owned the Horseshoe Club in Reno, and together they reactivated Jimmy and Ryan's former arrangement with the old man. That was the last year Hunt gambled, and he quit, owing Einstosh and Jimmy $140,000, half of it which belonged to Jimmy. There was a good reason, much in character for this hard-bargaining old mule-skinner. Hunt told anyone he owed to go to Johnny Drew and collect it. Drew was a colorful guy, a bookmaker who moved between Vegas and Chicago, said to be chummy with some of the Capone mob. He was fined once for running a crooked dice game at an Elks convention.

H. L. had lost a lot of money to Drew and paid him. Then Hunt went on a hot streak and won, Jimmy heard, close to a million, and Drew cheated him. So when he told Bernie and Jimmy and others to see Johnny, it was his way of putting the pressure on, in hopes of collecting what was due him.

Jimmy wanted no part of that. He only called back once, in 1962, when the Justice Department cleaned him out and Tina, his daughter, was deathly ill. Jimmy asked H. L. to pay the $70,000 he owed him.

"I hear Johnny Drew is still alive," he said, "why don't you get it from him?"

Jimmy said, "H. L., you know Johnny isn't going to pay me."

"Well, Jimmy, you know I've always fulfilled my obligations. But I got screwed by Drew and I'm just not going to pay."

"In a way," Jimmy said, "I can't blame you. But it really isn't fair to put your problems on me. If someone didn't pay me, and I laid off some of your bets, I'd still be responsible to you."

"I'll think about it."

"I wouldn't call you," Jimmy said, "if I didn't need it."

"Yes, I realize that."

The conversation ended pleasantly, but Jimmy never collected and he never brought it up again. Hunt quit cold. When Drew welshed on him, he never gambled again, with anyone, on anything. And Hunt loved to bet. That was his weakness — sports and politics. Sometimes he and Jimmy talked a half hour on the phone, five minutes about the teams they were betting and the rest of the time on politics.

He was a man of unshaken convictions, but they were not always consistent. He tried to persuade Gen. Douglas MacArthur to accept the Republican nomination in 1952, though he considered himself a Democrat. He did not like Ike, contributed a ton of money to the cause of Senator Joseph McCarthy, loved Barry Goldwater, but voted for John Kennedy against Nixon in 1960. "Nobody," he said, "can convince me that old Joe Kennedy's boy is a liberal."

The last time Jimmy saw H. L. was years after he stopped gambling. In 1970, a nutty outfit called the Bonehead Club in Dallas gave his son, Lamar, an award for his role in the pro football merger. The terms of the merger included an $18-million indemnity by the AFL, a payoff that seemed even more ironic after Lamar's Kansas City Chiefs won the Super Bowl that year, the last one between the disunited leagues. As the previous winner of the Bonehead award — for making the Colts a seventeen-point favorite over the Jets the year before — Jimmy had the honor of introducing his successor.

Lamar and his father were both seated at the head table.

H. L. was over eighty, a tall, disheveled figure in a suit two sizes too big for him, a wisp of white hair circling his head like a halo. Lamar said, "Dad, you remember Jimmy the Greek, don't you?"

The old man studied Jimmy. "Jimmy the Greek," he repeated. "Yes, I know you. You were strong on the Southeastern Conference."

Johnny Drew and H. L. Hunt both died in 1974, about six months apart. Drew died first, of a heart attack. Hunt was eighty-five. Jimmy sure could have used the money due him, but he understood how H. L. felt, and his memories of him were always friendly.

Chapter 9

Kefauver Hearings:
No One Listened

JIMMY HAD TO SUFFER a national embarrassment, along with a lot of other people, because a senator from Tennessee, a fellow who later became famous for his coonskin cap, was determined to rid the United States of the evils of gambling.

One afternoon in March 1951, Jimmy came home from the racetrack to his big house in Miami at 995 Venetian Way. He was doing well and could afford to have a couple, Walters and Katie, live in and run the house for Vicki and him. On this particular day when Jimmy got out of the car, Walters was outside waiting for him.

"Mr. Snyder," he said, "I heard your name on the radio."

"What about?"

"That thing up in Washington, the hearings."

Jimmy realized what he meant. The Kefauver Committee was conducting hearings in an investigation of organized crime in interstate commerce. "They even mentioned the house number," Walters said. He was wide-eyed.

"Don't worry about it," Jimmy said. But Jimmy worried enough for both of them. He had been "having a ball," with plenty of money and a steady income from his coal-stripping company, and did not want anything to spoil it. There was always his basic worry about Vicki, that notoriety would endanger his custody of her. Sure enough, the next morning in the *Miami Herald* there was a front-page story labeled, "Kefauver Hearings — Jimmy the Greek Consulted Coaches Before Making Bets."

Several years earlier, before Jimmy closed his Steubenville office, he bet with a guy in Milwaukee named Sydney Brodson. It was not until the Kefauver hearings that he knew his first name was Sydney. Everyone knew him as "Shoebox" Brodson— because he once showed up at a bookmaker's carrying his figures in a shoebox. Jimmy had not talked to him since then, until the previous football season, when "Shoebox" called him at home one night.

"How'd you get my number?" That was the first thing Jimmy wanted to know. It turned out a guy from Miami ran into "Shoebox" at the Chicago Airport and they had nothing better to do than exchange Jimmy's home phone number. At that time, Jimmy had no contact with gamblers. Even before, when he was doing business with them, his social life was kept separate. When he entertained, one night he had gamblers, another night all the young crowd. The third night he had politicians and older people. He was part of all three groups, but never mixed them socially.

"Shoebox" called to inquire about the weather. Miami was opening its schedule against Georgetown. "It's sprinkling," Jimmy said.

"I thought you might be doing something on the game," he said.

"There's a lot of talk up here that it's pouring down rain there. Miami's the big favorite and everyone's taking the points."

"I don't like anybody," Jimmy said. He was not interested in the game at all. His interest now was in the oil business.

They must have checked "Shoebox's" telephone calls, because here he was before the Kefauver Committee telling the world about Jimmy Snyder. As follows:

MR. DOWNEY RICE, ASSOCIATE COUNSEL FOR THE COMMITTEE: Directing your attention to a man by the name of Snyder down in Miami, will you tell us how you met him and who he is; James Snyder?
BRODSON: Yes. I first knew Mr. Snyder, in the form of an okay.
RICE: You got an okay on him?

BRODSON: Yes, and I assume he must've gotten an okay on me or he would not have done business with me.

RICE: You did not meet him formally?

BRODSON: I did not. In fact, I never met him for a period of four or five years, and never had occasion to meet him until last year.

RICE: And you met him down in Miami when you were there?

BRODSON: Yes, when I was there for a vacation.

RICE: Now, sir; is Snyder from Steubenville, Ohio?

BRODSON: I believe so.

RICE: What type of business do you do with him; the same thing?

BRODSON: No. Snyder is no longer in business.

RICE: He is no longer in business?

BRODSON: No.

RICE: Well, when you were doing business with him, was it the same type of business?

BRODSON: Yes.

RICE: Football?

BRODSON: Basketball.

RICE: Football and basketball?

BRODSON: Primarily.

RICE: And you bet back and forth with Snyder?

BRODSON: Yes.

RICE: Did you do anything else with him? Was he an information getter or anything like that?

BRODSON: Yes.

RICE: Tell us about that.

BRODSON: Well, Jimmy had an opinion which was very, very well respected.

RICE: On what?

BRODSON: On basketball and football games.

RICE: Yes.

BRODSON: And when you say you respect a man, the man comes up with many more winners than he does losers, and that is what makes him good. In this business if you come up with losers you are a bum; and that is the sole distinction. Jimmy was known to have — to come up with more winners than losers, and consequently —

RICE: Did it come to your attention that possibly the reason he came up with more winners was because he knew a few coaches?

BRODSON: No, it didn't come to my attention.

RICE: Do you know that?

BRODSON: I don't know why Jimmy came up with more winners than losers. He had his sources of information which I never inquired into.

RICE: Did you call him from time to time and discuss the situation with respect to certain teams before making a bet for purposes of research, shall we say?

BRODSON: Yes.

RICE: And you considered him an expert along those lines, and had a good source of information to tell you the condition of the teams, the players and the chances?

BRODSON: Jimmy might — I don't know what his sources of information might be. He might have known coaches whom he spoke with.

RICE: As a matter of fact, he told you sometimes he was in touch with some coaches, did he not?

BRODSON: Yes, but lots of people tell you they are in touch with coaches, who are not actually in touch with them.

RICE: I did not hear your answer.

BRODSON: I say a lot of people tell you, and they are not.

RICE: Did he tell you that?

BRODSON: I believe he may have mentioned that; yes, sir.

RICE: All right, sir.

BRODSON: I don't believe — Jimmy may have conceivably known coaches on a social basis; I don't think there was ever any question that coaches or anybody else were making the results go in conformity with Jimmy's desires.

RICE: We understand that.

BRODSON: He might have conceivably known a coach who might have told him that his team was not in good shape; that it looked bad in practice all week.

RICE: More or less through inadvertence, not knowing that Jimmy —

BRODSON: Not knowing that Jimmy was using it for gambling. He might have told him strictly on a friendly basis.

RICE: Yes.

ESTES KEFAUVER: Mr. Rice, in that connection, I think I feel that some improper inference might go out — what you are talking about is not with respect to any coaches.

BRODSON: I am not talking about the veracity of any coaches.

KEFAUVER: Just a minute. That any coaches would be selling out to him, but he would worm his way in and try to find out information about how the coaches felt, how the players felt, whether they had any casualties, or that some players were laid up.

BRODSON: Yes.

KEFAUVER: And whether they thought they had a good chance of winning.

BRODSON: Which, so far as I know, is a perfectly bonafide and legitimate inquiry.

KEFAUVER: And in the case of this fellow, Snyder, he was posing as being an oilman of some sort.

BRODSON: That I don't know.

RICE: You say he got out of the business. What happened to him?

BRODSON: Pardon me?

RICE: You say he got out of business. What happened to him?

BRODSON: What happened to him? Well, Jimmy, I believe, had been very successful and had accumulated a relatively large sum of money as a result of his endeavors, and that I know only by hearsay.

RICE: Yes.

BRODSON: I believe he had some marital trouble, and there was a question arose as to the custody of the child, and I believe when the question about the custody of the child arose, it —

RICE: Let us not go into that. He is out of business?

BRODSON: Yes.

RICE: How long would you say he has been out of business?

BRODSON: About three years, I would estimate.

SENATOR ALEXANDER WILEY (WISCONSIN): Mr. Chairman, I do not want to divert from that, but I do think that the particular idea that you brought out in your question might be well amplified in view of this man's large experience. Do you want to give it, as your judgment that, by and large, the basketball coaches and the players of this country are not selling out; that [there is] only the occasional sellout?

BRODSON: I would say to the best of my knowledge no coach has ever sold out. I have never ever heard of it in the grapevine that a coach has sold out. I heard in the grapevine that a coach might occasionally be conceivably betting on his own team to win. I have never heard of a coach betting against his own team.

SENATOR WILEY: That is the grapevine. But let us get it straight so that everyone else doesn't get the idea that all colleges and all players of this country have gone to hell.

BRODSON: They haven't; believe me, they haven't.

SENATOR WILEY: No.

BRODSON: They are in the very small minority.

RICE: Getting back to Miami, with respect to telephone numbers 82-5543 and 82-5544, listed to James Snyder, 995 North Venetian Way Drive, Miami, Florida, did you ever discuss with him conversations that he might have had with professional football players?

BRODSON: You go back to James Snyder? I missed the beginning of your question.

RICE: Incidentally, do you bet professional football games?

BRODSON: Occasionally; yes.

RICE: Did you ever discuss with him conversations with professional football players he might have had?

BRODSON: No; he did not discuss any conversations he had. He had convictions on certain professional football games, but I can't say he got them on the basis —

RICE: Did he indicate to you that he was in touch with certain professional football players?

BRODSON: I don't think he did.

RICE: Would you say that he did not?

BRODSON: What I mean by that is I can't remember any particular players that he may or may not have been in touch with. He might have intimated that he got his information from somebody, but as for mentioning any specific player or any specific team, I can't say that he did.

RICE: It would not surprise you then if he was in touch with certain professional football players; is that not right?

BRODSON: I can't say it would surprise me; no.

RICE: Did he ever tell you —

BRODSON: But, on the other hand, numbers of people are.

RICE: Did he ever tell you he was from Steubenville?

BRODSON: Yes; that is right.

RICE: Who put an okay on Snyder down there in Miami?

BRODSON: Who put an okay on Snyder in Miami?

RICE: Yes.

BRODSON: Well, my first contact with Mr. Snyder was in Steubenville.

RICE: You started doing business with him when he was in Steubenville?

BRODSON: Yes.

RICE: He was okayed by whom in Steubenville?

BRODSON: Nobody actually okayed him. What happened was when I first got started in this business, I didn't have an office, and I used to go down to Chicago, and I knew he did business with a couple of reputable houses in Chicago, and was found to be of good reputation, and they were satisfied I would be satisfied.

RICE: Who were these reputable houses in Chicago?

BRODSON: Well, there are several recognized houses in Chicago.

RICE: For instance?

BRODSON: I would have to say — you mentioned the name Clark.

All this transpired only a few weeks after the disclosure by the New York district attorney's office of fixed games on college basketball. Brodson's testimony that Jimmy was friendly with many college football coaches made it appear that he might be a master fixer. He learned later that the Kefauver Committee had a list of Jimmy's phone calls a few months earlier when he was talking to more than a dozen coaches and a few players around the time of the Clemson–Miami Orange Bowl game and the North–South game.

Senator Charles Tobey of New Hampshire wanted to subpoena Jimmy, but Estes Kefauver talked him out of it. Kefauver had Jimmy checked out and found no arrests. The way Jimmy understood it, Kefauver told Wiley, "If Snyder had talked to one coach, well . . . but he talked to a dozen, all of them famous men. Nobody would believe all these men were involved in anything wrong."

The coaches Jimmy had talked to during that period were Bud Wilkinson, Paul "Bear" Bryant, Ray Graves, Wally Butts, Andy Gustafson, Jim Tatum, General Bob Neyland, and Red Sanders. Jimmy invited them to the party he gave every year during the week of the game, which fell on Christmas night. Casually, out of the usual cocktail conversation that develops at such socials, came a bet for $150,000 on Kentucky against Oklahoma in the Sugar Bowl. Kentucky was the underdog, but Bob Gain was on that team and Jimmy liked them for $50,000. Some comment by Wilkinson — something beyond the usual expression of coaching gloom — prompted Jimmy to press his bet for another

$100,000. Kentucky won the game, 13–7. Jimmy figured Bear Bryant owed him that one — he had lost $250,000 betting on his team against Santa Clara in the Orange Bowl the year before.

The point was, none of these coaches knew Jimmy gambled. The end or even the middle of a season was never the best time to talk with them. The time to get what he considered hard information was before the coach opened the season. He liked to gauge his mental attitude — what coach he was mad at, what team he wanted to beat most — because he instilled this into his players.

Several months after the long Kefauver hearings ended, Jimmy was staying in a penthouse apartment in New York, two doors from the Gotham Hotel, where he bought newspapers. One evening he strolled over there in his slippers to get the early editions when this statuesque man approached him. "How do you do?" He said. "I'm Estes Kefauver. I'm running for the vice-presidency."

"I'm Jimmy the Greek Snyder," Jimmy said. "You mentioned me in your hearings last year."

"I remember the name," he said. "You were the gambler. What are you doing now?"

"Same as I was doing then. I'm in the oil business."

"You were the fellow who knew all the coaches. Did you really know them?"

"Yes, sir. I knew them as casual acquaintances."

"That really impressed me," Kefauver said, "that anybody could know so many coaches and great players."

"That was my business," Jimmy said. "And when I quit gambling, we remained friends."

Chapter 10

Jack Chrysler Blew It

IT WAS TRUE WHAT Brodson said in the Kefauver hearings about Jimmy having accumulated a happy sum of money. He had nearly $800,000 and wanted to get away from betting altogether — at Joannie's request and because he knew her family would not approve of their marrying unless he was involved in a legitimate business.

Jimmy took a piece of Ray Ryan's oil action here and there, never anything more than a fraction, but he did much more on his own — like drilling twenty-one straight dry wells. The twenty-second try was a lulu, though. He hit oil!

This was in the Denver–Julesberg basin in Colorado near Fort Collins, where Jimmy had 160 acres. Earlier he had almost gotten into a deal with Bud Robineau of Frontier Oil on a refinery in Florida. It fell through. Now Robineau called Jimmy about the Colorado strike.

"Jimmy," he said, "let's make a deal."

"What kind of deal?"

"You can't lose. We'll give you everything you've invested in the well so far, plus a $25,000 profit. Then we'll take it over, drill it, and you'll get twenty-five percent of it."

"No, siree," Jimmy said, "this baby is all mine. This time Jimmy the Greek is getting on a pipeline."

Jimmy smelled the oil that saturated the coring. He rubbed his fingers in it. The gas pressure was high. This had to be a winner or why would Robineau offer him anything? Now he had to raise the drilling money.

Joannie was out in Colorado with him. One morning he got up early and took her big diamond engagement ring and a diamond bracelet from her jewelry box. He borrowed short on them. He called Steubenville and got George to mortgage his house for him — that good old house he had broken Slim Neal to get. That meant $10,000 more. He got the rest from his Uncle Anthony in Baltimore.

It reminded him of the time Ryan told him about a deal of his: "We went to Louisiana, got some money, and bought some leases —"

Jimmy interrupted, "Wait a minute. Where did you get the money to buy the leases?"

Ryan gave him a puzzled look. "Where?"

"Yeah, where did you get the money? Did you win it, have it, or borrow it?"

"Listen," Ryan said, "for an oil deal you get the money wherever you can: your mother, your brother, your maiden aunt, your friends, your enemies. You just get the money."

Now Jimmy could relate.

In a few days, Jimmy raised $37,000, enough to drill the well. They found oil, all right, but they drilled into what is known as "a low." There was oil there, but there was also enough water to make it worthless. It kept coming up that way, oil diluted with water, at $1,000 a day for equipment and manpower.

"What can we do about it?" Jimmy asked his foreman.

"There's nothing we can do," he said. "We can't shut the water out of it."

"Then plug the goddamn thing!" Jimmy said.

That was it. His $800,000 was gone. He decided he had spent the past two years gambling at another man's game. Now he had to go back to his own. It is impossible to make odds on Mother Nature.

Joan put up with more than the average suffering housewife. In the years when Jimmy was gambling, he was not the most consistent husband in captivity. Three months after they were married, she left him. She could not understand how he did well one day and poorly the next. She had not heard about the IRS filing a lien against people. The separation did not last long, but while they were apart, he flew to Paris, after settling with the government. If one wished to be distracted, this was not a bad place to begin.

One night in Maxim's, Jimmy noticed he was being observed by two gentlemen at the next table. He judged them to be from the Middle East. Finally, one of them moved his chair around and spoke to him.

"Pardon me, sir," he said, "but His Highness is very impressed with the suit you are wearing. May we ask where you purchased it?"

"Thank you," Jimmy said, "It was made in Los Angeles. My tailor there is Tony DiGrandis. It's a midnight-blue mohair."

Jimmy did not believe this was the standard Paris nightclub dialogue, but they invited him to join their table. He was curious to see if His Highness was on the level. He turned out to be Prince Fahid Ibn Abdul Aziz, the sixth son of King Saud, who ruled a chunk of real estate known as Saudi Arabia. This young man had a nice pension, but there was nothing pompous about him.

"Call me Freddie," he said.

After dinner Jimmy invited them back to his hotel. He had just picked up six new suits in New York, and the prince and he happened to wear the same size, "perfect 38's." Jimmy opened the closet and handed him a couple. You would have thought he gave him the offshore oil rights to Texas. For the next two weeks, they were inseparable.

Every night at 5:00, his secretary ushered into Freddie's suite six of the most exquisite girls imaginable. The ratio was always the same — four to two, blondes to brunettes. They selected their dates for the evening.

It was out of the Arabian nights. All they needed were the big satin pillows and the belly dancers.

Freddie was the perfect host. He always let Jimmy choose first, but the secretary tipped him off that His Highness preferred blondes. As the perfect guest, Jimmy always picked a brunette. Even though there were four blondes, he did not want to risk selecting the one who most caught Freddie's fancy.

It went that way every night. They drove off to the fleshpots of Paris, and later, with their blonde and brunette of the moment, drifted gently into that great boudoir in the sky.

One night they went to a gambling house in the Paris suburbs, where the big attraction was a no-limit *chemin de fer* game. Jimmy knew nothing about the game, but he took a shot at it. He bought $100 worth of francs and sat at one of the smaller tables to study the rules. After a few hands, he left and bought another $3,000 worth of francs. He figured he might blow it, but he was going to get a run for his money.

In *chemin de fer*, you play with six or eight decks of cards in a box known as a shoe. That night, a burly, wealthy plunger from Switzerland was dominating the game. He kept saying, "Banco," meaning that no matter what anyone put down, he booked it all.

That was not for long. Jimmy's first turn, he laid out the whole $3,000 worth of francs and got lucky. He won six times in a row. He swept up nearly five million francs and, with Freddie cheering him on, bought champagne for everybody. One of the people in the club that night was a man named Jack Chrysler. Yes, *that* Jack Chrysler. Jimmy once owned one of his cars.

They met again not long after that, on the *Queen Elizabeth*, when Jimmy was returning to New York with Prince Fahid and his secretary/talent scout. The second night out, they bid on how many knots the boat had done in the last twenty-four hours. Chrysler, at the next table from them in the dining room, bid two or three times and lost, Jimmy noticed.

The next night out the bidding was about to begin. "Jack," Jimmy said, "how high you going?"

"I can't, Jimmy," he said. "I'm out of money."

"Beg your pardon?" Jimmy said. Was this *Jack Chrysler* talking?

"They won't cash a check on the boat," he said.

"What do you need?" Jimmy asked.

"No, thanks," he said. "I'll survive."

"I'm serious," Jimmy said. "I happen to have some cash on me. Tell me what you need."

"Well, if you have $2,000, I'll give you a check."

Jimmy reached into his pocket, peeled off a $5,000 package, and handed it to him. "I don't want a check," Jimmy said. "I'll stop by your office in New York."

Jimmy did not do this entirely for humanitarian reasons. He had in mind getting to know Jack Chrysler better. You never know when you might need someone with his assets. When they docked, Jimmy moved into the Madison Hotel, where he got an apartment. A day or two later, Jack phoned.

"When are you coming by?" he asked.

"I'm going away for the weekend," Jimmy told him, "with the Prince. I'll see you Monday."

After hearing Jimmy recite one of his tales of the oil frontier on the boat one evening, Freddie mentioned an Arabian oil deal he thought Jimmy might help put together. That weekend he explained it in more detail. Jimmy's mouth watered. It sounded like a sure thing, but it was going to take a tidy sum, $100 million, to get it going. You do not produce that kind of money fishing for dimes through manhole covers. This was where Jack Chrysler would come in. When Jimmy dropped by his office, to get his loan back, he slid it into the conversation.

"Tell me more," Jack said.

He had an office the size of a ballroom in the Chrysler Building — carpeted, paneled, tasteful paintings, his own stock ticker flashing against the wall. The more Jimmy talked of the oil deal, the further Chrysler leaned across his desk.

"See if you can get me in on it," he said.

That was all Jimmy wanted to hear. He flew to Saudi Arabia with the Prince and sat in on six meetings. He taped them all, carrying a translator wherever he went. Back in New York, he played the tapes for Jack in his office. His interest grew even warmer.

"Look," Jimmy said, "as far as I'm concerned, this is out of my league. If it goes through, I'll get a finder's fee and a little stock, but that's all."

That was all right with Jack. It was all right with Jimmy too. The finder's fee would come to $5 million, plus two and a half points of the stock. The final detail was for Jack Chrysler to put it together —raise the money, organize the board of directors. That looked like a cakewalk. Jimmy was a big favorite now.

Then, all of a sudden, he was informed that the whole thing collapsed. He phoned Freddie; except it was not Freddie anymore. He was the Prince.

"What happened?" Jimmy asked.

"Your man made a mistake," he said.

Among the board of directors, Jack had selected a wealthy New York real estate man, whose recent $2 million donation to Israel was well publicized. It killed the deal on the spot. There were no second chances. When the Arabs saw that name, it was kaput.

Jimmy himself was nearly kaput. He had spent every cent he had trying to tie up the deal. The day it collapsed, he did not even have cab fare from the Madison Hotel on 53rd and Madison to the Chrysler Building, a dollar ride in those days. He walked the mile; at least it seemed like a mile. For a fellow who was a big favorite to collect $5 million, that was some letdown.

Even though Jimmy had made Chrysler a loan on the voyage to New York, he was not about to borrow money from him. It was against his code to show weakness. He had an apartment at the Madison and wore a $200 suit. He did not look like a guy who was busted, and there was no way he would admit he was.

As an old gambler, he knew he could get money somewhere else. He went to a friend who owned the Hickory House Restaurants in New York and Miami, both hangouts for gamblers. He found his man, Pops Popkin, a horse lover and a work of art. He lent Jimmy $3,000 to fly to Paris to plead his case with the Prince. It did not work. If he had been in it alone, Jimmy might have had a chance, but there was no way he could persuade the others to change their minds, short of tanks and jet fighters.

All of his luck was not bad. Joannie met him when he returned to New York and they patched it up again. She took him back when he was busted.

This prompted him in 1956, at age thirty-seven, to take a close look at his finances. There was no savings account, and the checking account had only a little money for existence. He decided the only real bankable commodity he had was his lifelong knowledge of sports and the manipulation of odds and point spreads. Federal laws and the intense publicity pressure resulting from the Kefauver hearings made gambling a bad risk throughout the country — except in the only place where it was legal, the state of Nevada. Jimmy took what few assets he had and went there.

"I have to go back to gambling," he told Joannie.

"Why do you *have* to?" she asked.

"Well, you want to eat, don't you?"

She said she did not know if she could live with the uncertainty of that kind of life. He asked her to give him "a couple of years," and he would send for her. That is what they finally agreed; although, when Jimmy asked for "a couple of years," he really had in mind four or five.

Las Vegas in the fifties was a small town, with maybe 40,000 people. The Desert Inn Hotel was the glamour spot. The Stardust, Caesar's Palace, and the Frontier had not been built, but the place already bore all the glitter and excitement of a fantasy land. That is the key word for Las Vegas: excitement. It was then, and it is now. Flashing neon in the middle of a sand pile; a flame in the desert that drew moths. You have to drive a long way through a lot of nothing to get there, or drop in out of the sky, out of an Arabian night. When a gambler gets to Las Vegas he says to himself, "No one can touch me now, I'm going to bet my money legal."

Jimmy understood the appeal of the place, but it never touched him quite that way. The longest he had ever stayed in Las Vegas was three weeks, with Ray Ryan in 1948. What grabbed him then was the concentration of guys who matched wits and money. He had seen that green felt jungle all of his life, the tables and the wheels and the blackjack layouts. They say there is no cure for the dice bite, but any type of gambling where he could take a piece of paper and figure the percentage against him turned Jimmy cold.

A casino was just something he walked through to find the action he wanted. They always built them so you had to pass the tables to reach the coffee shop or the bar, and that is where Jimmy's people would be sitting, hanging around. For seven years this was almost a nightly ritual for him, a tour of the big casinos on the Strip. In those days, before the corporate setups took over, every hotel was owned by ten, fifteen, or twenty stockholders, and all of them were players. They gambled.

There is a feeling one gets once inside a Las Vegas casino going full blast that is guaranteed to make the adrenalin pump. Jimmy could stand at the top of the stairs and hear the jungle sounds rising, the chirp of the croupiers, the clicking of chips in nervous hands, the jingle, cough and clatter of coins spilling from the one-armed bandits, even as he checked out the room. The tables were laid out like a mine field, and Jimmy walked right around them.

He had seen people transformed by that music, as though they had walked through a veil. It was contagious. In everyone's hearts, we all are high rollers. The bellmen bet on which way the elevator would go. A housewife, who was once pacified with a book of trading stamps, would break your arm if you approached the nickel slot machine she planned to play. Las Vegas Judge Myron Leavitt once performed a wedding ceremony in front of the keno booth at the Horseshoe, because the happy couple was on a lucky streak and did not want to leave. The players on the floor barely noticed.

Las Vegas always glorified in its reputation as a city of sin, gin and din. (Now, however, they seem anxious to reestablish themselves as a family-oriented town. Only time will tell if that is possible.) The late-fifties were a kind of heyday, at least as Jimmy saw it. From Monday to Thursday, the town belonged to the professionals. The public riding free junkets came in on the weekends. Almost any big bettor who flew in from anywhere in the country was known by name by the floor men and pit bosses. Until about 1961, it was a world of its own.

Then the computers and the business people began taking over, and it got bigger and bigger. The casino hotels became attuned to the masses, instead of the elite, and to Jimmy, the place lost some of its romance, intimacy, and excitement. The high roller stopped coming, and the slot machines were lined up row after row. In the times he liked best, the bigger casino hotels would not deign to have slots because they felt it detracted from the atmosphere. Jimmy agreed.

Today most of the major hotels are owned by public companies. You can buy their stock in the market. But those gamblers who built Las Vegas are gone. Some died, some got rich and semi-respectable, others grew old and complacent and sold out.

Hookers are part of the mystique of Las Vegas, but it is not the industry some people seem to think. The sexiest girls in the world go there, and in many cases, they do enjoy the kind of temporary visa. Any schoolteacher, secretary, airline hostess or model who wants to supplement her income can go to Las Vegas for a weekend and score. They come from all over the United States — straight girls and housewives who turn professional from Friday to Sunday.

These girls from Utah, Texas, Nebraska and thereabouts cannot miss. They may earn $500, $1,000, or $1,500, depending on how pretty or cute they are, who they run into, and how well his luck runs at the tables. A few have scored big, from $10,000 to $15,000, because the guy they were escorting got hot at the craps table and shared his winnings with her. Any pit boss in town can give you a story like it.

In Las Vegas even the hookers tend to look like ingenues. They are in demand because gambling is a sensual sport, and a fellow can grow attached to his lady of the evening. A friend of Jimmy's from Salt Lake City used to come down every year. He loved to play, and the price was $25 the first time he lined up with Yvette. The next trip to town, the price was $50, and a year later it was $75. Two years passed before he happened to call again. This time she told him her rate had gone up to $150. "Goddamn," he bellowed, "you just priced me out. Inflation got to you, too, huh?"

All of this was later, but Las Vegas in the fifties was Jimmy's kind of town. He would walk through the Riviera to the restaurant and find one of the owners, Gus Greenbaum, a guy who could not resist a challenge. He would like Johnny Saxton over Basilio in a title fight, and Jimmy would like Basilio. He might like the Dodgers over the Giants. Whatever it was, Gus wanted to get something going.

When Jimmy first settled in Las Vegas he was offered a piece of the action by certain casinos to go with them. He already had enough of a "name" within the business. He would not go with anyone immediately because he did not want them to know he needed a job. Whenever he was broke, he made it a point not to let it show. A friend from his Ohio days owned a big restaurant in town, Luigi's, and he borrowed $7,500 from him. For the first few weeks, he did all his betting downtown, along the Gulch, because Niggy Devine had a place down there where he could get credit. Niggy had owned a spot in Cincinnati when

Jimmy was operating out of Steubenville. From the start, Jimmy moved into a place right on the Strip, the El Rancho, and lived there for the next two years.

One of the first fellows he ran into in Las Vegas was the owner of a small gambling club who knew his reputation for setting up betting propositions that attracted business. He was a big, heavyset guy with a dynamic personality, and was quite a lady's man. One of the Gabor sisters said, "I never knew what it was to be a woman until I spent a night in his arms." Even considering the talents for exaggeration in the Gabor family, this was a high rating. We will call him Frank Crandall. His name has been changed because he turned out to be, what Jimmy termed, "a crummy, lying, crooked, dangerous shit-heel, the grand champion of all the bad numbers I'd ever known." That is, he stole his money and then tried to get him maimed when he complained about it.

In his first days in Las Vegas, Jimmy needed a place to drop anchor, and Crandall kept begging him to "come in" with him. "Make book out of my club, Greek," he said. "I'll back your play and whatever you win, we'll split even."

This happened to be the week of the Tournament of Champions at the Desert Inn, and all anybody could talk about was golf. Jimmy did not know anything about the pro golf tour, but wondered if there was some new way to bet on it. He spent a day or two looking at it from every angle; then he came up with a fresh one. He grouped the players according to their Vardon Trophy scores, their strokes per round through the season, and he made it 6-to-5 so you could back one guy against any other guy in that group. He put Billy Casper, Gary Player, and Arnold Palmer in one group, for instance. They were all shooting 70.8, so it was even money whoever you took.

Jimmy agreed to book these bets out of Crandall's club. It was a big success, and it went like he figured. He made $26,000, which is just what he should have made, because he handled about $220,000 altogether.

Jimmy went over to Crandall and said, "You got thirteen and I got thirteen."

Crandall said, "Keep it. Stick around, move in. We can keep it going."

Jimmy did, and keeping his propositions carefully over the next six months, he built $480,000, which he left in the cashier's cage at Crandall's club. Any time he needed money for a bet, he went to the cage and got what he wanted.

That summer in 1957, Sugar Ray Robinson was coming up for a rematch with Gene Fullmer in Chicago for the middleweight title. Fullmer had won a fifteen-round decision in January and now he was a 5-to-2 favorite, but Jimmy really liked Robinson to win and bet $10,000 that way. He was out of town for a few days before and after the fight, which Robinson won with a perfect left hook in the fifth round.

When he returned to Las Vegas, Jimmy picked up the $25,000 from his bet and took it to the cage. He noted that his "draw" was down to $400,000. When he asked about it, the guy at the cage said, "Crandall drew $80,000."

Jimmy went over and asked Crandall what that was all about. He just waved a hand at Jimmy. "Aw, Jimmy," he said, "after you left I got a call from Gil Beckley in Chicago. He was there for the fight and he said he had good information on Fullmer. So I bet the $80,000 for us."

"But you knew I liked Robinson," Jimmy said.

"Yeah," he said, "I know, but Gil was so sure he had the straight information. I figured I would cover for you."

"Where'd you place the bet?"

"Oh, Gil placed it."

"Oh."

In the next few months the money in the cage went down to $126,000, which meant Jimmy's half was $63,000. When Jimmy wanted to make a good bet on TCU, the cashier told him there was no draw left.

Crandall was sitting at his usual table near the bar. Jimmy said, "Frank, there is a misunderstanding in the cage. I want to draw $60,000 to make a bet."

"Don't bother me with the penny-ante crap," he said. "I've got troubles. I've got to pay a guy $200,000."

"What's that got to do with me?" Jimmy said. "There's $63,000 of my money in that cage." The Greek's temper started to erupt, and he said a few other things too.

Crandall said, "Greek, you got sixty seconds to get out of

here, or I'll have you thrown out." Then he looked over his shoulder and for the first time noticed an empty wall. "Ralph," he shouted. "Where the hell is Ralph?"

Ralph Lamb and the rest of his "security" people had conveniently disappeared. Lamb knew Jimmy was getting screwed and wanted no part of it.

Jimmy said, "You know something, Frank? You could gag a maggot." He left.

The rhubarb with Crandall was all over town in a few hours, which is the way stories flew in Las Vegas. Then it got back to Jimmy that Crandall was saying that he was the one who had blown the money. That figured, too, along the line that the best defense is a good offense. But even Crandall's credit manager, Johnny Dunn, knew better.

A year after all this went on, Jimmy was in the Horseshoe Club downtown and ran into an old hustler he knew named Natie. He was an old second-story man gone straight. Jimmy trusted him, on the theory that there was no one more reliable than a reformed thief. He used him as a courier for out-of-town bets. From time to time, friends of his would be in jail, and Jimmy lent him the money to bail them out. This night he was at the bar with two other people.

"Greek," he said, "I want you to meet a couple of friends of mine from L. A."

Jimmy shook hands all around. Natie had the dignified look of a banker. The two strangers looked like longshoremen.

"They made this trip especially to meet you," he said.

"What for?"

"They came to town," Natie said, "to break your legs." The two guys laughed, but Natie did not laugh. "Your old partner sent for them, but when they got in they called me, wanting to know who was Jimmy the Greek? I told them who Jimmy the Greek is, and what I want them to do is go break the legs of the guy who sent for them."

"What?"

"That is, if it's okay with you."

The two guys looked at Jimmy, expectantly. Jimmy felt like he had them on a leash and all he had to do was let go. "No, no," Jimmy said, "forget it. I couldn't live with that. But thanks anyway. It's only money."

Nobody ever did anything to Crandall, and in his heyday he cheated guys with whom you would be afraid to be in the same room. Las Vegas was his sanctuary. Nobody wanted to make any violent trouble there.

In fact, it is everyone's sanctuary. It remains a matter of record that people connected with gambling do not meet violent deaths in Las Vegas. They might meet them down the road a ways, such as in Phoenix, where poor Gus Greenbaum and his wife were found with their throats cut, ear to ear, or in Los Angeles, where Bugsy Siegel was gunned down.

That does not happen in Las Vegas. No gambler, no mobster, no so-called bad guy has ever gotten himself killed or dismembered there. It is a kind of unwritten law. This is the last place, the last haven, a modern equivalent of Butch Cassidy's Hole-in-the-Wall, and no one wants to risk ruining it. If they blew Las Vegas, what is left? Gamblers have been chased out of England and Puerto Rico. Where can they go? Mexico?

Besides, there were more subtle ways of putting someone out of circulation. Jimmy had his own experience with that.

His place at El Rancho Vegas was a private cottage on the grounds. One night, in the small hours, the screen door on his porch went bang, followed by a knock, and he heard a girl's voice call, "Jimmy?" He opened the door only a crack, and a girl he had never seen before was standing there.

Before he could ask what she wanted — he thought he knew — she started screaming, then she ran off the porch, tearing at her clothes. Jimmy just stood there for a minute or two, stunned. Then he sat on the bed and puffed a cigarette. Thirty minutes later, the telephone rang. It was the police. It seemed they had a girl at the station who claimed Jimmy raped her, and she was prepared to sign a warrant for his arrest.

Jimmy got dressed and went downtown, crowding the speed limit. He knew both of the cops handling the complaint. The girl was in the next room.

"This is a lot of bullshit," he roared.

"Yeah, Jimmy, we know," one of them said, "but what can we do? We have to take the warrant."

This was one of the times in his life that he let his pure Mediterranean temper all hang out. He started yelling that he was going to sue everybody in sight for false arrest. Then he said they had damned well make her submit to a medical exam. He demanded it. It was the only way he knew he could be cleared.

He was in luck. In what was surely one of the rare occasions in this woman's adult life, she came up clean. There were no traces of recent sexual intercourse. She was irate and insulted; she thought they were testing her for gonorrhea.

The case was dropped, and he went back to the El Rancho to get what sleep he could. The whole thing, the question of who tried to set him up, was no mystery. Jimmy believed at the time he did not have an enemy in the world, but he sure had one hell of an ex-partner.

Chapter 11

The Sixties:
A Decade of Destruction

JIMMY THE GREEK WAS born with gambler's luck: on top of the world one minute and lower than a snake's belly the next. Life had been this way for as long as he could remember, high points and low points with nothing in between. One of the lowest points came during the decade of the sixties. Looking back, that decade represented little more than death, suffering, financial devastation, and injustice. Death and suffering began in 1954, when Joan gave birth to Florence, who died at only three weeks of age. At the time they did not know why she died. All they were told was that something was wrong with her.

Two years later, Jamie was born. Though the doctors gave him a clean bill of health at birth, about a year and a half later he was diagnosed with cystic fibrosis. Joan and Vicki constantly took care of him, not knowing from one day to the next if he would make it.

Then Stephanie was born and escaped the deadly gene. For years, Joan was unable to leave the house. Jamie required constant care. Jimmy was out trying to earn money to pay for cumulating medical costs.

Eventually, he was able to get into business for himself, with the Vegas Turf and Sports Club. Joannie's brother, George Specht, came in as fifteen percent partner and licensee. The club was downtown, a couple of miles from the hotels on the Strip, and before long they were doing eighty-five percent of the book-making business on sports and horses.

They sold Jimmy's odds nationally to people at $25 a week and made a $1 service charge for every follow-up telephone call they made. In the first few weeks, they had 161 people buying the odds and phoning the offices.

Then the federal law was enacted forbidding interstate transmission of gambling information for purposes of betting. It did not stop them. For one thing, they did not know if it was being enforced anywhere. For another, they thought because they were home-based in a state where gambling was legal, it might not apply. That was naive — even dumb. But when you have been doing something routinely for almost thirty years, it is hard to get it in your head overnight that it is illegal.

At the time, Jimmy was getting calls from a Salt Lake City mortgage banker named Jimmy Dunn, who liked to play. "Utah goes against Utah State tomorrow," he said one night. "What price do you think it will be?"

"Utah is the home team," Jimmy said. "It should be about four, Utah. That's how it looks to me."

A month later, there was a grand jury investigation in Salt Lake City regarding gambling. They subpoenaed some of the businessmen there to find out what was going on. Somehow the question came up about how they got their odds, and Dunn answered innocently that everybody got the odds from Jimmy the Greek in Las Vegas. Who else would they get them from?

Suddenly, the whole jury investigation was forgotten. The target now was Jimmy the Greek, as he discovered that Friday night when the phone rang at his home.

"Jimmy," one of his men at the Vegas Turf and Sports Club said, "you better get down here. The FBI is here."

Jimmy did not bother to finish dinner. Two agents were waiting for him. "We want to see your books," one of them said.

"Be my guest," Jimmy said. "I've got nothing to hide. I'm paying $10,000 a month in taxes to you people."

They were looking for the black book, the one with the names of the big bettors. They never found it.

In four months, Jimmy was out of business. He soon discovered that he needed all the money he put aside and then some for attorney fees. That was when he found out who his real friends were; guys like Eddie Levinson and Paul Wyerman, two of the owners of the Fremont Hotel who came up with $75,000 cash in the middle of the night so he could post bond. There were others, like Irving Devine, who owned the New York Meat Company, Sid Wyman, and Milt Jaffe. Jaffe became one of the executives of the Stardust Hotel, but Jimmy knew him many years earlier from around Pittsburgh when he had part of the Bachelors Club and was managing Billy Conn, the boxer. Wyman was one of the owners of the Dunes. They lent Jimmy thousands of dollars without even asking for it — no collateral, no interest, and no time limit. "You must need it," Jaffe said. "Pay it back when you get it."

Jimmy's attorneys were never convinced that the charges against him could have held up in court. But, since he lost his source of income, he could not afford the cost of a trial. He also could not risk having a trial in a city where he had little chance of winning. His defense had to be based on the fact that he operated out of a legal gambling house; he paid taxes and he owned a license issued by the state of Nevada. To the good Mormons of Salt Lake City, Las Vegas was awaiting the punishment of God. He was under federal indictment in Salt Lake City, and his attorney hoped for a change in venue. Salt Lake City was rampant with Mormons who frowned on gambling, among many other things. Jimmy requested the trial be moved, preferably to Nevada, or at least to any state that had a racetrack or some understanding of gambling. The federal judge in Utah denied the motion. This was at a time when Joe Valachi told the FBI about hidden mob interests in Las Vegas, and Jimmy was in the headlines elsewhere on the same front page. It made him look like he was one of the characters too. He heard later that the Justice Department moved in on him because they thought that since he was handling some $2 million a week, he had to have some Mafia connections.

Of course, he had about the same Mafia connections as the Reverend Billy Graham. That, however, was impossible to prove in Utah. He also had another powerful adversary in the case, U.S. Attorney General Robert Kennedy. Kennedy sent some of his task-force people to Salt Lake City to make sure Jimmy faced trial there.

"I don't have a chance," Jimmy told his attorney.

"We can always appeal it," he said.

"Isn't there anything else we could do?"

"With the judge's permission," the attorney said, "you can plead *nolo contendere* in Las Vegas." That is a legal phrase, Jimmy discovered, which admits your case is too weak to contest in court. In effect, it is a plea for mercy.

They gave up and decided to plead *nolo contendere*, shortly after they checked out the presiding judge. Judge Christopher was a man who drank no stimulants. When he went hunting, on those cold miserable mornings Utah is famous for, he carried cold water in his thermos instead of coffee. He did not drink Cokes, preferring Dr. Pepper, a soda with a prune extraction content. He was an extremely fair man, but they did not see how he could be sympathetic. The judge was reluctant to agree. He delayed his ruling of the request, and Jimmy suspected Kennedy's influence. Alfred Wright of *Sports Illustrated* wrote in the magazine:

> It's not that Jimmy Snyder could seriously be undermining the moral fibre of the nation, but the Attorney General of the U.S. has had agents by the hundreds sifting through every piece of paper in Las Vegas in his efforts to pin the donkey's tail on Jimmy Hoffa, who has been pouring teamster funds into the area. Snyder was just a minnow that happened to be boated during the Department of Justice's angling expedition.

In early September of 1962, President John F. Kennedy met with the U.S. attorneys at the White House to report on the drive against organized crime. In a speech later reported in the papers, he told them: "One Las Vegas gambler is supposed to have said he hoped we'd be as tough on Berlin as we've been on Las Vegas. Well, we intend to be."

The gambler was Jimmy the Greek, as the Justice Department by then already knew, and what Jimmy actually said was: "They lost in Laos; they lost in Cuba; they lost in East Berlin; but they sure are giving the gamblers a beating."

That was one of the costliest sentences he ever spoke. Most of his government troubles, Jimmy believed, could be traced to that statement. It appeared in a *Sports Illustrated* story, "The Bookies Close up Shop," by Bob Boyle, in the issue of September 3, 1962.

The guys at *Sports Illustrated* just about killed Jimmy with kindness. They had long been favorites of his; they gave him his first national exposure and quoted his odds on many major events. Few had heard of Jimmy the Greek until December 1961, when Gil Rogin wrote a test piece on his career as the last of the oddsmakers, under the title, "The Greek Who Makes the Odds."

Almost from the day the magazine began as Henry Luce's legacy to sports, Bob Boyle had been after Jimmy to tell his story. He resisted, not out of modesty, but on the theory that his life was going to get a lot more interesting in the next few years. It sure did, but not in the way he planned. His ambitions never anticipated being arrested.

That foreign policy quote, Jimmy was told, led to some angry phone calls from the Justice Department to the executive offices at Time-Life. Bobby Kennedy did not have an enemies' list; he had a shit list, and it did not do to get on it. Jimmy later learned from his friends in the FBI office in Las Vegas that Bobby was calling every few weeks, asking, "What's happening with Jimmy the Greek? Have we got anything?"

It was not exactly a vendetta. Bobby had a special distaste for Jimmy, based on his department's belief that he was a bigger fish, a shadowy guy who got his money from the mob or Hoffa. Supposedly, Bobby felt that Jimmy wrongly knocked the Kennedy administration in the worst possible place — the pages of a sports magazine. If it had been the editorial page of *The New York Times*, no one would have remembered it.

Finally, the judge agreed to accept Jimmy's plea and toss the minnow back. This was the first and only time in his life he was ever arrested, much less charged or sentenced. Once again Jimmy was busted. He owed $10,000 on his fine. What was even more important, he felt a compulsion to change his image — and as quickly as possible. He needed some respectability.

He dropped in to see Hank Greenspun, the editor of the *Las Vegas Sun*. "I want to be a columnist for you," Jimmy said.

Greenspun acted puzzled. "What are you going to write about?"

"Odds." Jimmy said. "Let me present the odds in my column — on football, baseball, the political elections. You name it and you'll have the odds in the *Sun*, in my column."

"You've got a job, then," Greenspun said. "One column a week for $25."

The money was a joke, but the money was not the important thing.

There were more important variables, like the destruction that still hovered over the Snyder family. After Stephanie was born, Joan had two miscarriages. Then she gave birth to Anthony. Anthony was born healthy and somehow escaped the deadly gene like Stephanie had. Finally, Joan gave birth to another child, whom they named Christina. "Tina" was born with the gene. Her first day of life was spent in surgery. She had a blockage in her intestines and had to have a colostomy. Within a few weeks, the doctors explained, "We're going to turn her over to you now. There is nothing more we can do for her." Now Joan had to go through everything again with Tina that she had done with Jamie. Somewhere she found the strength to do what had to be done.

Tina survived for only two and a half years. Though her life was short, it had been long enough to devastate the family. Jimmy grieved deeply. He became angry at God. He refused to go to church or to pray. It was agonizing to watch his children die. He knew God had his own reason for doing things, but he could not help questioning His motive. Jimmy became so deeply saddened by Tina's death that he even wrote about her in his column. It was an emotional release for him. Joan, however, was angered that he could expose something so painful and private.

The column read:

> You all have seen many All-Americans perform in the field of sports. You have seen Oscar winners in the field of movies. You have seen Emmy award winners in the field of television. And many of you have had top performers right in your own home that no one else has seen — except YOU. Such was the case of Tina, who was our Little All-American, in the game of fighting to live.
>
> Tina's game started on December 26, 1965. On the kickoff she was almost tackled in the end zone, but somehow man-

aged to bring the ball out to the one-inch line. The game was only six hours old when her coach decided that for Tina to break through the eight-man line, the defense she was using, she had to have the help of special coaches. For seven hours, these added helpers labored, cutting out and digging new passages in her little body. The odds were 1,000-to-1 that she would never make the three-inch line.

After 90 days of playing touch-and-go at the hospital (Sunrise), her coach decided that she should go home and let her mother teach her to play the game, as the game was only beginning.

There were mist tents, shots, vitamins from A to K and five different medicines three times a day. Her rooting section consisting of her mother, father, sisters Vicki and Stephanie and brothers James and Anthony, celebrated with lemonade and birthday cake with one candle. On four different occasions of that first year, the referee had counted nine over our champion, but somehow she always managed to make it up before the bell rang.

Up to now, Tina had never tried anything but feints through the middle of the line — then faded back for the doctor to give her shots or for her mother to give her medicine. But on this day, she tried her first running play, all on her own, and gained. A smile for the first time in a year passed over her mother's face. Her trainer (Mrs. Myers) clapped with joy.

Anthony ran to the closet and brought out the games and toys he was saving to play with his Tina and no one else. The defense was getting mad and called their first time out — they would change their game plan. They threw up the "virus defenses," sent in the mumps and chicken pox, but Tina avoided them all with the "isolation play" that her mother had taught her.

It took her another year to make the two-yard line. But what a performance she put on to make it. It was a year that will never be forgotten. She sang and danced, threw passes and kisses and by now could call a few plays on her own. She had three favorites: the "auto play" (a ride up and down the Strip to see the lights), the "Coke play" (a ride to the 7-11 store for a Coke icee) and the "cookie play" (she would blindfold herself with her blanket and pick a cookie out of the cookie box). She called these plays daily and sometimes twice a day — if she thought she could get away with it. And most of the time she did.

She gained another five inches in the game of life — and the defense called their second time out. This had gone far enough they decided. From now on they would triple team her. First they sent in dysentery to weaken her, then followed with a virus and then crushed her with a congestion in her lungs which were already crippled with a cystic condition.

Her mother rushed her to the hospital and called all her coaches. For nine days she battled the three ailments and on the fifth day she almost pulled the "end around" to lick the first two, but the cystic condition was too much. The offense called time.

Now the Commissioner from up above was watching all this time and decided to draft this gallant little player. With the experience she had, He thought, she would make a great coach for his "Little Angels." The draft went through Saturday afternoon and with the help of Father Baldus, she was sent on her journey up to the "Little Angel League" Monday noon. The game was over — who was the winner?

Only those who had the opportunity to watch this Little All-American perform. True, she had her bad days on the field, but the happiness and joys that she gave on her good days far overcame the bad ones. These, we, her rooting section, will never forget — and for these days that will never be forgotten, we are very thankful and grateful to the Commissioner above.

This column received overwhelming support from the readers. The Snyder family received hundreds of letters of sympathy. Joan withdrew her anger.

In addition to all these problems that plagued the Snyder family during the sixties, there was another. In 1967, Jimmy was again brought before the court because he was slow in paying the $10,000 fine assessed when he had pled *nolo contendere* to concealing interstate wagering activities. Jimmy had accumulated extensive medical costs from his son Jamie's cystic fibrosis treatments. In fact, in one year, his costs ran $35,000. He had already filed bankruptcy. The judge ordered him to pay $600 a month until the fine was completely paid.

Little was known about cystic fibrosis at the time the Snyder family was cruelly introduced to the disease. They were told that Jamie would never live past the age of two. He lived to be twenty-six. This was six years beyond the average life expectancy of cystic fibrosis patients. Jamie was a fighter. He never gave in to the condition. He researched the disease and tried everything he believed would help him overcome — from strenuous exercise to experimenting with vitamins and minerals and proper nutrition. Despite his optimistic belief that he would be researching cystic fibrosis until he was "old and gray," he died while attending college at the University of Las Vegas in Nevada.

With Jamie, James, Jr., Jimmy felt a lot of guilt. He loved him but never spent a lot of time with him. It was difficult for him to get close to him. Jamie felt that his father feared intimacy because he was afraid of losing him. That was true.

Jimmy had buried his mother and aunt, his uncle, his three-week-old daughter, Florence, two unborn children, his two-and-a-half-year-old daughter, Tina, and now at any moment it would be his oldest son, who was named after him.

Jimmy continued for many years to write his newspaper column, and was ultimately able to earn more than $25 per column. It was extremely helpful to him at a pivotal point in his life. He remembered Bryan Armstrong, the paper's managing editor, saying to him, "I don't know you, Jimmy, but this is without a doubt one of the smartest moves I've ever seen a man make."

It was not a bad move for the *Sun* either, but it helped Jimmy more than it helped the paper. It made him an instant celebrity in Las Vegas again, a respected member of the community.

The lingering cloud was lifted on December 18, 1974. It may have existed mostly in his own imagination, but it existed, nonetheless. On that date he received a full and unconditional pardon, signed by the president of the United States, from his conviction eleven years earlier.

He paid the fine and served his probation. Few people thought of him as a felon, but he was. He lost his right to vote, not to mention his business and $500,000 in accounts receivable on the books that were written off.

That conviction was like a scar that always seems more visible, more unsightly, to the one who has it than to others. He lived in a quiet fear that it would come up at troublesome times, embarrassing his wife and children. Naturally, he did not go around wondering if people were whispering, "Psst, he's a felon." But it was there, never too far from his thoughts.

Twice it came up in instances where companies were considering him for their public relations accounts. Fortunately, they investigated deeply enough to determine the circumstances, and it was overlooked. Everyone seemed willing to overlook it but him. He never overlooked it, stamping his feet and beating the floor with his fists, screaming "miscarriage of justice."

Jimmy had the distinction of being the first nationally known figure to be tried under the new gambling law, passed by the Kennedy administration in their sweep against organized crime. A member of the Nevada Gaming Commission told Jimmy, with some regret, that Jimmy was to be made an example. His timing was horrendous. The Justice Department had just lost a big gambling case in New Orleans, involving Gil Beckley and others. Joe Valachi was singing about the *Cosa Nostra* and titillating the country with expressions like "the kiss of death." In Las Vegas, the story had broken of an attempted shakedown of a wealthy gambler, who happened to be Jimmy's friend, Ray Ryan.

The headlines everywhere were about crime and gambling, and few people could separate the two. Jimmy was lucky, in a way, that he did not get the electric chair for that lousy phone call.

He made light of it at times over the years, even boasted that he must have been a bigger man than he thought, if it was so important for the government to get Jimmy the Greek. He wanted the pardon, wanted it with a passion, and his attorneys filed the application the first moment he was eligible in late 1971.

For the next two years he was investigated — it was standard procedure — by the federal and state law agencies. He did not mind. They talked with more than a hundred people, friends, some not so friendly, business contacts and neighbors. The local FBI office, the sheriff, and the U.S. attorney in Las Vegas gave him the most glowing recommendations of all. They nearly eulogized him. He later saw copies of the letters. You would have thought they confused him with Father Flanagan.

Now all he could do was wait. The request for a pardon went through the office of Senator Howard Cannon, to the Justice Department, and, hopefully, on to the president. Jimmy was on the telephone to Washington so much, one of Cannon's aides had to calm him down. "Hey, Jimmy, take it easy," Chet Sobsey said one day. "We can't push these people too hard. There's a limit. It has to go through certain levels."

Jimmy heard the wheels of justice turning, ever so slowly, inches at a time. He constantly feared something would go wrong at the last moment and wreck it for him. Something almost did. In the summer of 1974, he was told the pardon was getting close. By August it would be on the desk of President Richard Nixon.

About that time, Jimmy had dinner with Jack Anderson at Duke Zeibert's, his favorite Washington pit stop. They were having a warm discussion, as they often did, on the honesty of politicians. Jimmy expressed his opinion that those in Nevada, his state, were more honest than most. He told Jack that he knew of cases where big money had been refused for special favors. Why, he had once heard a fellow boast he would pay $500,000 if the governor issued him a gambling license in Las Vegas.

That conversation was filed away in Jack Anderson's agile mind, and a few days later he mentioned it to one of his staff people and told him to look into it.

Jimmy quickly forgot about it. That summer he checked into the Duke University Clinic at Durham, North Carolina, hoping to shed a few pounds on their famous rice diet. There, a call reached him from the U.S. attorney's office in Nevada. An Anderson column appeared in which his remarks demonstrated the honesty of Governor Paul Laxalt of Nevada, but in a way sounded like Jimmy himself was the one who offered the bribe.

At first Jimmy treated the whole thing as a joke. Then the seriousness of it hit him. He could just see his pardon being tabled while this matter was resolved, and then never surfacing again. Jimmy caught the first plane back to Las Vegas and went before the Gaming Board. He even took a lie detector test.

He did not blame Jack. He probably made it sound less casual than it was, and his staff did the rest. This is what actually happened. At a party one night Jimmy warned the governor about a rumor he heard, that a fellow was in town boasting he would pay $500,000 to anyone "who could get me a gambling license." Laxalt knew him by reputation and so did Jimmy. Paul laughed it off. "That fellow," he said, "could offer 50 million dollars and it wouldn't make any difference. He couldn't get a license to sell apples on a corner."

The matter quieted down, and Jimmy went back to his nervous vigil. Then the first of August, with Watergate coming apart like a grenade, he received word that his request for a pardon was on Nixon's desk. It was still there on August 8 when Nixon resigned.

His only hope now was President Gerald Ford. Jimmy had met him years before, in the home of Bob Maheu. He was a congressman then, and Jimmy's impression of him never changed. When he took office, Jimmy told anyone who asked that the Ford presidency would be neither fancy nor tricky. "He played center on his college football teams," Jimmy pointed out. "Centers only know to do one thing: go straight ahead. They don't have room to maneuver." That was Ford. That will always be Ford. Right or wrong, he met the moment head on. He never changed.

Jimmy believed that was the case when Ford pardoned the former president. Maybe he thought: *I've got to do it sometime; we can't put an ex-president in jail. Why not now?*

But the reaction that erupted around the country did not bode well, Jimmy thought, for getting his own slate cleaned. He would not make a price on his chances after that. For the next few weeks, he moped around. Then in December, he was in his hotel room in Indianapolis, where he was doing a promotional film for a client, the Delta Faucets Company, when the phone rang. It always rang when he was in hotel rooms, but this was the most welcomed call of his life.

"Jimmy," the voice said, "this is Paul Laxalt, and as my first official act as the newly elected junior senator from Nevada, I have the pleasure of informing you that the president has just signed your pardon."

Paul was elected in the seat vacated by the retiring Alan Bible. The senator stepped down a few days early to give his successor a slight jump in seniority.

Jimmy could not recall what he said or what he did, but he remembered his heart leaped like a fawn. He called home and told Joannie, and after that, he had room service send up some good German wine, Bernkaestler Doktor, at $35 a magnum.

The stigma was gone, no more a threat to Joan or his children, and he could vote again, a right we all take for granted in this country. Imagine the irony he felt. Here Jimmy the Greek studied the candidates like few others, did massive research, had a ton of information, and for eleven years could not vote for the candidates he thought were most qualified. Now, once again, he could. The decade of destruction had come to an end.

Chapter 12

Public Relations: Nothing to Hide

AFTER THE JUSTICE DEPARTMENT arrested Jimmy in 1963, making the country safe for decent folk, he sat down and did some heavy thinking. He began a planned and measured campaign to bury the image of Jimmy the Greek as a gambler.

It was a conscious act, one that disputed the habits of a lifetime. For several years he moved in quiet corners, keeping a low profile. A gambler has little use for exposure outside his circle.

He started by making himself available to the news media — his odds, information, and hospitality. He was looking for acceptance, not publicity. No call or request went unattended. In return, he asked nothing. He just wanted them to know who, and what, Jimmy the Greek was. Under his circumstances, broke again and on probation, he saw only one route to become respectable, and he took it. Making the odds gave him contacts all over the country. Now he turned that into a new career in public relations.

He figured it would not hurt to have writers and television people on his side. They had made Jimmy the Greek.

In 1965, he formed his own public relations firm, called Sports Unlimited. A few months before he picked up his first big account, Caesar's Palace, he developed one of his less-inspired ideas: the Las Vegas Air Races. At the time it seemed a lively way to promote the city and attract new convention business.

Such races suggested a more romantic time, of scarves and goggles and Chester Morris going down in flames. Actually, most of the contestants were test pilots who flew their own propeller planes, World War II vintage. The show itself was tremendous, but it was a financial disaster.

Wilbur Clark, Jimmy's friend and political betting nemesis, the owner of the Desert Inn, agreed to back Jimmy and posted $50,000 in prize money. The pylons were erected and the course was laid out over a private field at Boulder City. In late July, with the races less than a month away, Wilbur left for a business trip to Disneyland, where he planned to build a hotel. Jimmy reminded him that he had just enough cash on hand to cover expenses and to meet their payroll through the third of August. "Don't worry," he said. "I'll be back by then."

He was, but in a coffin. The day before the money ran out, Wilbur Clark died of a heart attack in a San Diego hospital. The death of a close and devoted friend made the prospect of a business setback seem trifling; but the combination of the two was unspeakable. Jimmy wavered between grief and guilt.

Still, obligations had to be met. Jimmy borrowed all the money he could get his hands on. The races were held with all the appropriate pageantry, before grandstands so empty the planes could have landed in them. Great numbers of people came to town to see the races, but Jimmy overlooked one minor detail: He forgot to hire a detachment of armed guards to pry them out of the casinos.

Private buses were arranged to pick up the passengers at each hotel, where hundreds had signed up. But when it came time for the buses to depart, maybe six people got on from the Dunes and ten from Caesar's Palace, and it went that way all over town.

Jimmy ended up losing $130,000. He was busted and back in debt again. He *did* make an important discovery with that experience. He learned that you cannot compete with that green cloth and the big marquees with all the lights.

In September of 1965, Jimmy landed the public relations account for Caesar's Palace, one of those Las Vegas luxury hotels that seemed to be built with King Farouk in mind. It was only a month after it opened and the place was a mausoleum.

Half of the rooms were empty. Jimmy began by bringing in entertainment writers from around the country, relays of them, just letting them get a whiff of the scene.

At the same time, when anyone called for a reservation, the operators were instructed to tell them the hotel was full, but if they had a cancellation they would give them a call. They always did. In sixty days, Caesar's caught on, not because of the gimmicks, although they did not hurt, but because of the greatness of it.

In many ways, the hotel business is a self-contained world, with all the human complications. Caesar's had three partners: Jerry Zarowitz ran the casino; Nate Jacobson watched the money; and Jay Sarno was the promoter. When the hotel began to prosper, each one thought he had done it all by himself. If a story or a layout appeared on one, Jimmy unfailingly expected complaints from the other two. All three were never happy at the same time. *West* magazine once did a feature spread on Caesar's Palace, with Sarno on the cover, sprawled on a couch in a white toga with slave girls feeding him grapes, the whole bit. The other two sulked and grumbled, but it would have been nice to collect commission on every customer that cover brought in.

Even with the petty jealousies that existed in this and all partnerships, Jimmy was always given carte blanche treatment. They never questioned his expenses. He was valuable to them because he had a job they did not understand.

One day Fletcher Knebe, a *Look* magazine writer, flew into Las Vegas and phoned Jimmy. "Come over tonight for dinner," Jimmy told him. "Whatever you want here, you have an open door."

Knebe was a brilliant reporter, later the author of a best-selling political novel, *Seven Days in May*. He was no ham-and-egger. At Caesar's that night, Jacobson was visibly disturbed. He came over to Jimmy's table and called him aside.

"You know about this guy?" he whispered.

"I know he's a helluva writer," Jimmy said.

"He's here to do a butcher job on Vegas," he said. "I don't want him around here."

"If he's going to butcher us," Jimmy argued, "he's going to butcher us. We won't stop him with rudeness."

"Get him out of here," Jacobson said, his voice rising.

Before Jimmy could say anything, he noticed Fletcher getting up from the table. He had overheard Jacobson and was walking out on his own. Jimmy gave him points for that and walked out right behind him. The next morning Jacobson called and asked Jimmy to stop by his office. He lectured him for ten minutes. When he finished, Jimmy said, "What have you got to hide? You have a great hotel. Let him see it. Take him everywhere. Show him the books. Gambling is not illegal in Nevada. You're running a legitimate business, licensed by the state. Hell, Fletcher might even praise us a little. What have you got to lose?"

Jacobson straightened in his chair. "You're right. Absolutely right. Tell him I'd like to apologize."

Jimmy called Fletcher at the Tropicana, where he moved after the incident in the dining room.

"You want to interview Jacobson?" Jimmy asked.

"You're kidding, of course. You've got to be kidding."

"No," Jimmy said. "Mr. Jacobson wants you to be his guest tonight at dinner."

That night at dinner in Jacobson's suite, Jimmy could not stop him from talking. He was, Jimmy thought, overcompensating for his discourtesy from the night before. Two months later, the story appeared. Only two hotels received any praise: Caesar's Palace and the Tropicana. All the pictures in the layout were taken at Caesar's.

"Turned out well," Jacobson told Jimmy.

That was all he said, but that was enough. It was part of his job, except it would not be his job for much longer.

Actor Telly Savalas, another Greek, was the innocent cause of Jimmy leaving. Caesar's decided to offer Broadway musicals instead of using an entertainer in the nightclub. The management was negotiating to get *Fiddler on the Roof.*

One day Jimmy was in the health club, taking a steam with Savalas.

"Jimmy," the actor said, "put in a good word for me. I'd love to play Tevye." That was the lead part in *Fiddler.*

"You can't," Jimmy said, winking at him. "You're Greek. That's a Jewish part in a Jewish play."

"Listen," he said, with a laugh, "I can play a Jew better than any Jew can."

Jerry Zarowitz told Jimmy that the negotiations to bring in the play were complete. The next day Jimmy wrote a publicity release, which went to every major paper in the country. It began: "Telly Savalas is a 2-to-1 favorite to play Tevye, the dairyman, in *Fiddler on the Roof* at Caesar's Palace. . . ."

The next voice Jimmy heard was Nate Jacobson's. "Greek," he screamed at Jimmy in his office the next morning, "do you realize what you've cost us with this release?" He had it in his hand, shaking it at Jimmy.

"What are you talking about?"

"I'm talking about a half a million dollars," he roared. "That's what you cost me. We don't even have *Fiddler* signed yet. They'll want another half million for it now. Why didn't you let me see this before it was sent out?"

"I've been sending out releases for nine months," Jimmy said, "and you never asked to see them."

"From now on, I want to see every single one."

"Cool off, Nate, I'll be back in half an hour."

Jimmy walked through the lobby and out to the grounds to let the sun hit him in the face. The more he walked the more he realized the account was not for him. He was paid a fat salary but worked seven days a week. He was in the office in the morning, afternoon, and back at night. He seldom had time for his family. Tina, his daughter, was suffering from cystic fibrosis and her condition was worsening. He decided to resign.

Jimmy turned around and went back into Nate's office. "You and I have become pretty good friends," Jimmy said. "I'd like to keep it that way."

Jacobson understood. Jimmy left with Nate's friendship and a check for $7,500 in severance pay. There had been talk of Jimmy eventually getting $7/10$ of a point in the Caesar's ownership, but now that was out. It would have soon been worth $400,000 (a clue to the value of a going Las Vegas health spa).

When Jimmy walked into his home that night and announced he had quit, his wife and children gave him a standing ovation. Jimmy welcomed the chance to become reacquainted with his family. However, it would not be long before he had a new client named Howard Hughes, and once again his time would not be his own.

For the most part, Jimmy was fortunate in one aspect: He was able to earn a living doing something that came naturally. His worlds overlapped. Often accounts came through his interest in sports and politics. One example was John J. Hooker, the chairman of the board for STP Motor Oil (a client) whose path he first crossed in Tennessee, where he was a candidate for governor in 1968.

While other polls showed him in the lead, Jimmy's projected him as the loser in a close race. John J. lost, a defeat that cut deep. He was one of those people born to be a politician, the son and grandson of Tennessee governors. His great-grandfather, a Union general, won an even more enduring fame by lending his name, unintentionally, to a certain category of professional ladies. It was General Hooker's custom to celebrate military victories with a party, to which he invited those girls, camp followers, who for patriotic and economic reasons attached themselves to army field units. They became known as Hooker's girls, a phrase shortened even more, in time, by popular usage.

You had to like a fellow with that kind of heritage. Jimmy was even more sold on John J. Hooker when he saw how he handled adversity, a quality with which Jimmy was familiar. Hooker was one of the founders of a company called Minnie Pearl Fried Chicken. He once told a meeting of financial people about the rise and fall of his fortunes.

"The stock took off," he began. "My holdings were suddenly worth 10 million dollars . . . 20 . . . 30 . . . 40 . . . my God, 50! But then the day came that it started going the other way . . . 40 . . . 30 . . . 20 . . . 10 . . . and finally, minus two." He paused. "Gentlemen, I want you to know one thing. When my holdings were plus 50, that was great, but it was all on paper. The minus two was real. That was mine, and it was cash."

It took John J. a year or two to pay off his debts, but to his credit, he paid off every dime.

His story illustrated the vagaries of high finance, a world similar to the one Jimmy knew. The major difference was that on a bet you put up your money immediately.

The two did not meet until 1972, at a party Jimmy gave in New Orleans on the eve of the Miami–Dallas Super Bowl. John Y. Brown, who made a fortune in chicken (Kentucky Fried),

brought Hooker, who had lost a fortune. Before Brown introduced him, Hooker breezed into the room and said, "Greek, if
you hadn't made me an underdog, I believe I still could have
won that race."

Jimmy laughed and said, "I'm sorry, John, but that's how it
showed."

He patted Jimmy on the back. "That's all right, Greek. You
called it like it was. I'm not mad at you."

Jimmy discovered in the course of the years that sports, politics, and business marry well. They did in the case of John Y.
Brown, a power in the Democratic Party who produced the tele-
thons that paid off the party's huge debts left by the losses to
Nixon. Brown was also a devout sports fan, whose wife, Ellie,
became the first woman to own and operate a major-league franchise (the ABA Kentucky Colonels). He later divorced Ellie and
married Phyllis George, who would be Jimmy's colleague at *The
NFL Today*. That is another story altogether.

An exciting sports event is to business what a Sinatra ballad
once was to the back seat of a car. It was after the Ali–Frazier
fight in New York, in March of 1971, that John Y. offered Jimmy
the national account for H. Salt Fish and Chips, a subsidiary of
Kentucky Fried Chicken. Jimmy had been pitching it for a year,
and in the process, they became friends. The Browns were his
guests at the fight.

That night they toasted their future success as the kingpins
of the fish-and-chip industry. The next day, John Y. visited Wall
Street, where talks began that led to his selling out of Kentucky
Fried Chicken, including H. Salt. It was not really a loss for the
Greek. Brown soon acquired the Lum's fast-food chain, and
Jimmy landed that one.

It was through Brown that Jimmy enjoyed one of his great
moments of theater. Colonel Sanders was at the Democratic
Convention in 1972, and one night they were sitting together in
John's box. NBC put a camera on them, and John Chancellor
commented that there was a piece of Americana — Colonel
Sanders, sitting with Jimmy the Greek.

The Colonel gave Jimmy some fatherly advice. "Greek," he
said, "you do a helluva job. But it's only in the newspapers.
People talk about you, but they don't recognize you. Let me tell

you what you should do. Start wearing a white suit. Do it. You'd be a famous man."

Jimmy loved him for that, but never took the Colonel's advice. A white suit would not have looked right with Jimmy's blue, low-top tennis shoes.

If one wants to survive in the public relations business, he needs more than a gimmick; he needs a philosophy. Jimmy's approach was a little different from that of the orthodox public relations types. He believed in promoting the head of the company. To sell a product, to really expose it, has always been difficult. It became harder after the payola scandals. Today, magazines will rarely, if ever, lend space to stories about products. They will, however, give space to people: interesting, dynamic, authentic people. So he worked hard on the head of the company, and identified him with the product. If the public recognized him, they would know what he was selling.

One of Jimmy's rules was to never lie on behalf of a client. When the client hired Jimmy the Greek, he bought his credibility. Once, when Jimmy agreed to do a television commercial for Edge shaving cream, a New York ad agency sent him the story boards, which called for him to say, " . . . for a smoother shave, it's Edge, three-to-one." They included the results of the poll from which the figures were taken. Jimmy checked them out, and it figured five-to-two.

Jimmy told the account man that the commercial had to be changed. The guy was upset, as ad men so often are. "What the hell's the difference?" he demanded.

"The difference," Jimmy said, "is that it's not three-to-one, it's five-to-two." And that is how they filmed it, "Edge . . . five-to-two."

Jimmy found it as practical to apply odds to a marketing effort as to a game or an election. Another of his clients was Aurora Products. He could walk through their toy fair with the president of the company, Chuck Diker, and look at the lines and give him odds on which would sell and which would not.

Jimmy's public relations business took him around the world. In 1973, the government of Greece (at that time the military junta of Col. Georgios Papadapoulos) invited him back to his father's land to discuss representing them. Jimmy researched that too. The idea of a dictatorship was unacceptable to the American spirit, though, as a practical matter, we tolerated several over the years, including Spain and Yugoslavia. Jimmy found that a sizable majority of the Greek people approved of the government. The economy was getting stronger. Greece was building schools and hospitals. Jimmy went there with an open mind, and took his family along to visit Kios. He wanted them to enjoy the sun and the sea, the fig trees and fruit produced by the rich earth, to see it all as he saw it as a young boy.

He met with the premier and his cabinet. Papadapoulos said to him, "Jimmy, we have been so pro-American. We love America. The bases are here, the sailors are here, we want your country's friendship. Her enemies are our enemies. Why do the American people dislike our government?"

Jimmy answered him in Greek. "Mr. President," Jimmy said, "you have to understand what Greece means to us. It was the cradle of democracy. Americans think of that, the culture, the traditions. That was the Greece they knew. All you need to do, somewhere down the line, is hold the elections. Put it to a vote."

He looked at Jimmy sharply. "We will have an election," he said, "in time. But when Greeks vote, brothers start killing each other. In the last 169 years, Greeks have had 200 elections. What good has it done?"

Jimmy did not get the account. In late 1974, the Papadapoulos government was thrown out and elections were held. His question waits to be answered. The idea of an election, Jimmy wished he had told him, was to give the people the right to make their own mistakes. It is a hard lesson for men of power to learn.

In a sense, Jimmy had been in public relations all his life and did not know it — doing favors, making contacts, putting people in touch who could use each other, pressing the flesh in a hundred ways. He was slow to discover he could get paid for it.

In fact, he was the one who put Dean Martin and Jerry Lewis together. They were playing at a little joint in Atlantic City. Dean Martin had the first act and Jerry Lewis was the second act. One day they started monkeying around and Jimmy said to them, "You need to get together, for Christ's sake. You'd make a good team." The rest is history.

Dean Martin was from Steubenville, too, and Jimmy and he grew up together. Dean was the neighborhood bully. When Jimmy was about eleven and Dean was almost thirteen, Dean used to beat him up every day. But by the time Jimmy was thirteen, he had spurted into a big guy. One day when Dean picked on Jimmy, he gave him a tough beating. The whole town was screaming, "Hit him again, Jimmy." They did not like Dean at all. They all knew how he used to beat up Jimmy and got pleasure out of seeing him fight back. He hit Jimmy, and Jimmy did not feel a thing. Jimmy said, "Oh shit, let me get this guy once and for all." That was the last time anyone would ever bully him around.

The wildest public relations experience of his career, and in a way the biggest coup, involved the celebrated tennis match between Bobby Riggs and Billie Jean King in August of 1973 on the floor of Houston's Astrodome. When the publicity for the show began to take off and it became apparent that this was not going to be a sports event but a "happening," Charley Diker, president of a Nabisco subsidiary, wanted Jimmy to get involved.

Nabisco's candy division sold an all-day sucker called the Sugar Daddy, which seemed to fit right in with the male chauvinist angle Riggs had pushed for months. All Jimmy wanted was for Bobby to present Billie Jean with a giant Sugar Daddy, which they would bill as the "world's largest," at midcourt, before the match, on national television. The company was prepared to pay them $15,000 apiece.

Jimmy made the proposal first to Riggs and Jerry Perenchio, the promoter of that cosmic event. Jimmy Welch, the president of Nabisco candies, was with Jimmy. They almost laughed them out of the room. "Think it over," Jimmy said, looking at Perenchio but talking to Riggs. "After the match this may be all he has. He ought to get it while he can."

The idea began to grow on Bobby, as did the $15,000 Jimmy offered him, and a contract as the tennis host at the Tropicana for $100,000 a year. In a few days Perenchio called and said it was set. Billie Jean had agreed to go along. Jimmy's only concern now was that Riggs would carry it too far and get them all thrown out of the arena. But the night of the match turned out to be a press agent's dream. The ABC cameras covered the whole ceremony. (Billie Jean, who had refused during the weeks of the buildup before the match to lower herself to Riggs' level, maintained her dignity by entering the Astrodome on a litter borne by male galley slaves. Under one arm, she carried a piglet, which she gave to Riggs after accepting the Sugar Daddy.)

Fifty million viewers looked on, with commentary by Howard Cosell. It was one of the last great moments of pure comedy the country ever knew. Bobby gave his all, even wearing a yellow warm-up jacket with "Sugar Daddy" emblazoned in blue across the back. He did not discard it until after the fourth set, trailing early and headed for an inglorious, upset defeat.

What all this had to do with tennis was never made clear, but it turned on the whole country. For months afterward people still asked Jimmy if Riggs (Jimmy made him a 5-to-2 favorite) had thrown the match.

The answer was "no." He lost because he wore himself out promoting it. He wore himself out in another way too. It may have been billed as "The Battle of the Sexes," but Jimmy could tell you that Bobby collaborated like hell with the enemy. He needed those 400-odd vitamins he was washing down daily. Over the ten-day period preceding the match, Bobby entertained a total of twenty-six ladies in his room, around the clock. That number was an educated guess. Jimmy may have missed one or two, but Bobby did not.

The night before he was to meet Billie Jean, Jimmy told Riggs he was going to lose. "You've done a great job," he said, "but you forgot one thing, the tennis match." It was just a tired old man who lost to Ms. King the next evening, before an international crowd of 30,000, who dressed like they were at the opera.

Sugar Daddy was one of the night's biggest winners. They got a million dollars' worth of television time for $30,000. Sales for the first quarter after the match went up nearly thirty percent (although Jimmy Welch said sugar costs did too).

For Jimmy's money, Bobby Riggs established himself as one of the great public relations men of all time, better than some of the acknowledged giants of the field: Joe Namath, Evel Knievel, even Muhammad Ali. Jimmy based this on what he had to work with, a fifty-five-year-old body and a face like Bugs Bunny.

Within months, Riggs virtually disappeared from the national scene, turning up at an occasional event to lend a little fringe of color. That was the weakness of public relations: When it is all over and you have lost, the image you created is what you have left.

Few people remembered Bobby Riggs once played at Wimbledon. They only remembered that he lost to a girl who wore glasses. The circus was over.

Chapter 13

Howard Hughes
Had a Pattern

IN FEBRUARY OF 1970, at a time when famine was upon the boxing game, Jimmy received a call from a promoter named Harold Conrad. "I'm here in Vegas," he said, "with Bob Arum. We'd like to see you."

Arum was an attorney for Muhammad Ali, who was unlicensed to box and still appealing his conviction as a draft resister. A fight between Ali and Joe Frazier, Ali's successor as the world heavyweight champion, was worth millions, but no state would take it.

It was a bad time for boxing. Promoters went right on, gamely selling second-rate fights at high prices, as if their hearts were not breaking.

Conrad and Arum were shopping for a state that would license Ali to meet Frazier, in a dream match between unbeaten heavyweights in the prime of their years. Jimmy had known Conrad since 1963, when he promoted the second Liston–Patterson fight in Las Vegas. He had been back with Ali and Patterson in 1965. Not long after the phone call that day, they were in his office.

Conrad got right to the point. "Can you help us here?"

"I don't know," Jimmy said. "I'm sure the governor is opposed to it, but I know him well enough to sit and talk to him."

"If you get it on," Conrad said, "you're in for three percent."

Such a deal is not unusual in boxing (or in Las Vegas), but this one represented a substantial amount — $30,000 out of every million. Jimmy wanted it clarified.

"Of the gross," Jimmy said, "not the net."

"The gross. Three percent of everything."

"The live gate, the TV, everything," Jimmy said. "The gross of the whole shebang. I don't want to hear about expenses."

"The whole shebang," Conrad said.

"I'll see what I can do," Jimmy said.

Jimmy arranged a meeting at which Conrad and Arum would make their pitch to the governor of Nevada, Paul Laxalt, and the members of the state boxing commission. The night before the meeting, Jimmy had dinner at the Sands with the governor and Charles Barron, a retired air force general who had no sympathy for Ali. Laxalt had knocked out an Ali–Patterson bout in 1967, shortly before Ali refused induction into the army, so Jimmy knew he was an underdog. But if he was honest with him, told him the whole story, he figured he would at least listen.

"Governor, this is a big score for me," Jimmy told him, emphasizing his three percent. "Please consider it."

He said he would, but did not commit himself either way. The next morning, Jimmy was in the lobby of the El Morocco Hotel, five minutes before the meeting was scheduled. From behind the registration desk, the switchboard operator paged Jimmy for a phone call.

"Jimmy," said the voice on the phone, "Mr. Hughes doesn't want this fight." He later learned that it was Bob Maheu's son, Peter, who made the call.

"Mr. Hughes" was Howard Robards Hughes, Jr. Jimmy did not say a word. He replaced the phone, gently, and walked over to Conrad and Arum. "I just found out," he told them, "that you don't have a chance. Don't even propose the fight. Before the meeting starts, thank the governor and tell him that maybe you'll be back when the climate for a fight is better."

They understood. That was the end of whatever chance Las Vegas had for the fight and whatever shot Jimmy had at his three percent. Jimmy never knew what Governor Laxalt would have recommended in that meeting. He did know, however, that if an Ali–Frazier fight in Las Vegas had grossed the $20 million it grossed in New York a year later, Howard Hughes cost him about $600,000. Jimmy did not have much of a choice. At the time he worked as a public relations consultant for the Hughes Nevada Operations.

No, he never met Howard Hughes and, no, he never talked to him. He saw him once, from a distance, in a dining room, years before he settled in Las Vegas. Except for the mustache, he had the kind of face people can never describe to the cops.

One thing was sure, for someone that no one could see: His presence was everywhere. To be involved with Hughes in any way was to feel like a character in the second act of a play.

Jimmy's orders came from Bob Maheu, a bulky, balding ex-FBI agent who headed Hughes' Nevada holdings. He was the second most powerful man in the state, until the night of the long knives, Thanksgiving week of 1970.

Bob Maheu never met Hughes either, though he started working for him in 1953, handling security jobs, which included keeping an eye on some of Howard's lady friends. Maheu moved to Las Vegas four years earlier to act as a surrogate for the boss. Bob spoke often to Hughes in his penthouse hideaway on the top floor of the Desert Inn, but he was even reticent about that.

"Those who talk to him, don't say," Maheu told Jimmy, "and those who don't talk to him, may say."

The power of Howard Hughes radiated from that top floor, which had a mystique all its own. Except for his six personal aides — the "Mormon Mafia," chosen because they did not smoke, drink, chase women, or have liberal ideas — no one really knew what the inside of the penthouse looked like after Hughes had it remodeled. The story became a Las Vegas legend, how Hughes checked into a suite at the Desert Inn in 1966 (again, on Thanksgiving Eve) and five months later was asked to move because other guests had reserved the rooms for the Tournament of Champions. Rather than move, he bought the hotel lease for $13.6 million.

Once he owned it, he took over the entire top floor. Indulging his passion for secrecy and confusion, Hughes let the story spread that he imported a group of carpenters from Los Angeles to remodel one part of the space. After them, a new shift of carpenters arrived from Houston and completed another section.

Then a third group, from Dallas, finished the job. That way, there was not even a carpenter who could describe the entire suite. It was a clever story, except that it never happened. The suite was never touched.

From the privacy of the top floor — "up there," Jimmy always called it, with reverence — Hughes ruled a business empire reputed to be worth $4 billion. His Tool Company, aircraft company, Nevada Operations and airlines employed some 65,000 people. His holdings were rivaled only by those of J. Paul Getty and H. L. Hunt, Jimmy's old gambling buddy.

Hughes invested nearly half a billion dollars in Nevada real estate, though for reasons of his own, the figure he allowed them to quote was never higher than $200 million. His holdings included five hotels — the Desert Inn, Sands, Frontier, Landmark and Castaways — and two casinos, the Silver Slipper in Las Vegas and Harold's Club in Reno. It was out of the Silver Slipper, which was privately owned, not a corporation, that Hughes made his political donations, including the now famous $100,000 to Nixon (and $50,000 to Humphrey). The donations were made in cash.

The wealth of Howard Hughes, so freely used, gave Las Vegas a new image and a new vitality. A few years before, Las Vegas was regarded as a haven for mobsters and outlaws. Bugsy Seigel opened the Flamingo Hotel, the first of the fabulous hotels on the Strip, before he died one night of hyperventilation, caused by several large bullet holes in his chest. The town was corrupt.

Later on, Las Vegas meant lavish entertainment and show biz superstars, such as the Sinatras and the Martins and the Hackets who earned in a week for their acts what most people do not make in a lifetime. Then almost overnight, in 1966, Howard Hughes became the town's biggest industry. Once he began to buy up the state, this invisible billionaire emerged as a Las Vegas folk hero.

Gambling and tourist income increased more than twenty-five percent a year, twice the rate before he came. Suddenly, more people *trusted* Las Vegas. The place was nearly respectable. As a public relations man, privy to the conversations of his inner circle of executives, Jimmy learned quickly about Hughes' likes and dislikes. For one thing, he did not like prostitutes.

"Chase those girls," were Bob Maheu's orders to his hotel people. "Mr. Hughes wants them out."

Soon each of the Hughes hotels became a "mom-and-pop" joint. The only problem was, it was difficult to make money in Las Vegas with a "mom-and-pop" joint. The prospect of meeting a lady of the night at the bar, or in the cocktail lounge, is what made some of the Las Vegas hotels so successful. Clean was nice, but Jimmy always believed that anyone in business in Las Vegas should not stray too far from the "sin city" image.

One had to respect Hughes for ordering the prostitutes off his premises. In Las Vegas, that took nerve. It also confirmed a theory of Jimmy's: There is no one more pious than a reformed hell-raiser, after age has quieted the glands. In his heyday, Hughes boasted of deflowering 200 virgins in Hollywood. According to Jimmy's calculations, by 1974, Hughes had not had sex in eleven years including the six years he did not sleep with his wife, Jean Peters.

Still, Jimmy admired Hughes for the reclamation job he saw being done. For nine years, the Landmark Hotel tower was a Las Vegas joke. Incomplete and unopened, it represented failure. To the people who financed it and those who worked on it, the hotel represented a big loss of money.

"Mr. Hughes is buying the Landmark," Bob Maheu told Jimmy. "He thinks it's an eyesore."

Hughes could have bought it in bankruptcy for $13 million. He did not do it, knowing, Jimmy suspected, that a lot of small contractors would be ruined. He paid 100 cents on the dollar, a total of $17.5 million. He did the same thing when he bought the Frontier, which was shaky.

It was not easy to analyze a phantom, but the evidence suggested to Jimmy that Howard Hughes had a conscience. He pledged $6 million for a Nevada medical school, a gesture not unrelated, Jimmy thought, to his own near brush with death in 1947. He was obsessed, of course, with aircraft. Long before he was rediscovered by the public as the world's richest hermit, he had established speed records in planes he designed. He had flown around the world in 1938 and had received a ticker-tape parade on Broadway that rivaled Lindbergh's.

In 1947, Hughes was nearly killed test-piloting one of his

own planes. He crashed it in the street in Beverly Hills, avoiding any homes. His face was burned and cut and he broke more bones than the doctors could count. He grew a mustache to cover some of the scars and began to retreat from people.

Jimmy knew this story from a pretty good source — Cans Jones, his old Steubenville pal whose younger brother, John, was the doctor who put him back together. The money Jonesy won from gambling helped put John and another brother through medical school.

The day Hughes was released, after months of surgery and treatment, he handed Dr. Jones an envelope with a check in it. The doctor put it in his desk without looking at it. The next day he handed the envelope to his secretary and said, "Here, you'd better deposit this." He still had not looked at it.

A moment later the secretary walked back into his office. She looked puzzled. "Dr. Jones," she said, "there's no amount written in. It's just a blank check, signed by a Mr. Hughes."

Dr. Jones filled in an amount of $100,000 and donated it to charity.

Anyone exposed to the Hughes organization soon developed a thing about doctors and medical care. Once, around New Year's 1969, Jimmy left the office feeling puny and went home to rest. Minutes after Jimmy got there, Dee Coakley, his secretary, phoned.

"Do you feel better?" she asked.

"Not really," Jimmy said. "Worse, if anything."

"Let me talk to Joannie."

"She's not here. She must be out with the kids somewhere."

"I'll be right over," Dee said, slamming the receiver in his ear.

By the time she arrived, Jimmy was stretched out on the couch in the living room. She phoned Bob Maheu for advice. "Just stay there with Jimmy," he said.

In a few minutes, one of the two Hughes company physicians, Dr. Robert Buckley, arrived in an ambulance. "We're going to Santa Barbara — now," he said.

With its sirens screaming, the ambulance roared down the Strip to the private hangar at McCarran Field, where a Hughes plane, a Cessna 402, was waiting with its twin engines running. Jimmy was loaded into the plane. When they touched down in

Santa Barbara, California, another ambulance was waiting to take them to College Hospital. There, more doctors were waiting for him. In his room, the bed sheets were even turned down.

Jimmy's problem was diagnosed as an abdominal obstruction. He needed immediate surgery. Later, in the recovery room, he had just come out from under the anesthesia when one of the doctors leaned over him. "We got that thing out," he said, "but we have to send it to be analyzed, just in case. You understand."

"I know," Jimmy said. "In case it's cancer."

"Don't worry," the doctor said. "I doubt it is. I doubt it so much, I'll give you 100-to-1 odds that it isn't."

"I'll take it," Jimmy said, smiling.

Luckily for Jimmy, he lost that bet. Either way he owed his comfort to Bob Maheu, a fellow he grew to like. He could relate to him. He *saw* him. He got into the habit of calling him "Uncle Bob," and it was the kind of thing he enjoyed. What Maheu's inner feelings were about Hughes, Jimmy could not tell, but he seemed to be as loyal as an old bird dog.

Every now and then, Jimmy received orders to set up the Hughes private jet to transport a critically ill child to a hospital that was hundreds, maybe thousands, of miles away. Once Jimmy asked Bob about one of them.

"Does he know the child?"

"Not that I know of," Maheu answered.

"That's a good story," Jimmy said.

"But you can't put it out. Mr. Hughes doesn't want any publicity. You know that."

Jimmy did know that. It was one of the ground rules the day he was hired. In fact, the key part of his job was to keep his name *out* of the news.

How Jimmy was hired in the first place had to do with his talent for running into people at the moment they had a problem. In 1968, Hughes, through Maheu, was negotiating to purchase Air West, an airline with sixty jets that fanned out from Nevada to seventy-three cities in eight western states, Canada, and Mexico. Jimmy had known Bob Maheu slightly but crossed paths more frequently with his son, Peter, a sociable fellow in his late twenties. They were near Jimmy's table one night at the

Sands, and Peter invited Jimmy. Bob began to talk about the problems that had developed in the Air West negotiations.

"Do you have any ideas?" he asked Jimmy.

"Give me twenty-four hours to put a pencil to it," Jimmy said, "and I'll give you a prospectus. If you like my suggestions, you take the credit for them. If you don't, throw them away."

"Send me your ideas, Jimmy."

Jimmy went immediately to the office, leaving behind a pouting wife and some puzzled dinner guests. He knew nothing about airlines. That night he telephoned an airline executive in Los Angeles, a friend, who flew in the next day and helped him prepare a prospectus for Air West. It included a list of political and business leaders who might support a Hughes takeover. It must have been a decent prospectus, because a few minutes after Bob Maheu received it he was on the telephone with Jimmy.

"Can you produce on this?" he asked.

"If I didn't think so," Jimmy said, "I wouldn't have suggested it."

"All right. You've got four months, through January, because by then our offer for Air West will have expired. How much do you want?"

Jimmy said he wanted $50,000.

Maheu hesitated. Instantly, Jimmy moved in. "If you're worried," Jimmy said, "I'll play you double-out."

"Beg your pardon?"

"Look," Jimmy said, "we're talking about $50,000 over four months. I'll play you double or nothing. If we win Air West by that time, I get double — $100,000. If we lose it, you don't owe me a penny."

"You mean you'd do that?"

"Try me," Jimmy offered.

There was a long pause. "No, let's do it at the $50,000 figure," he said, "win or lose. I'm sure that won't affect your dedication to the project."

"You'll get a full and total effort," Jimmy said.

He soon got Air West, or Hughes Air West as it was known; whereupon, Jimmy went on the payroll, full-time. Not long after that, he was in Bob's office when Peter Maheu showed him a report on the underground atomic testing in Nevada with megaton-plus explosives.

"Can you do anything about this?" he asked Jimmy.

"I can do anything about anything," Jimmy said. "What do you want done?"

"All we can tell you is, Mr. Hughes doesn't want megaton-plus testing in Nevada."

"What else?"

"That's all."

"What do you mean, 'That's all'?"

"That's all we can tell you, Jim."

"Nothing else?"

"Except that Mr. Hughes' name is not to be used in any way."

"You always make it easy," Jimmy said.

It was a touchy assignment. Hughes' companies enjoyed a lot of government contracts, so it was not just modesty that prevented him from taking on the Atomic Energy Commission. On the other hand, Hughes was ecology-conscious before it was fashionable. He preached the conservation of air, land, and water as far back as the forties, and that was at the heart of his fight with the AEC.

Still, it *was* the United States government, and if you are going to battle them, it helps to have your own army. Jimmy had a small revolt in his own office. "I won't do it," said Dee Coakley, Jimmy's secretary. "It's unpatriotic. I refuse to work on this."

"Maybe it is," Jimmy said. "Or maybe Mr. Hughes is right. Why don't we research it before we judge it?"

They did not have to dig deep. Radiation had affected some cows, ruined their milk, poisoned some babies. Measurable amounts were found in the water. There was concern about an earthquake. The more they researched it, the more they came to believe in their own opposition to the testing. Since they could not connect Howard Hughes with it, they made their point indirectly. They flooded science writers with copies of newspaper and magazine stories that supported their viewpoint. In no time they sent out packages as thick as a phone book. Within six months, the Atomic Energy Commission announced that it was halting the megaton-plus testing in Nevada. Bob Maheu was pleased.

Jimmy never heard from Hughes. Only once did he get

what he might describe as a personal reaction from him. It was the result of what he considered one of his more brilliant ideas. His office was preparing a feature story, a roundup of Hughes' first four years in Nevada, to offer to the wire services. It was the usual public relations mix: the growth of Vegas, new residents, higher employment, the increase in tourist traffic.

The last photograph anyone had used of Hughes was taken in 1946, when he was forty. Jimmy knew it was impossible to produce a new photo of him, but he had a brainstorm. He gave a print of the last Hughes picture to artist LeRoy Neiman, and he said, "I want you to age this face. Show me what he should look like fifteen years later."

Neiman did a masterful job. He added gray to the temples, a little salt and pepper in the mustache, and a few lines for character. It was a handsome portrait and Jimmy was delighted. They delivered it to Peter Maheu for the approval of Mr. Hughes. Pete said, "I'll let you know."

Days passed. Jimmy held up the feature, in hopes of being able to offer it with photographs of a Neiman painting of the elusive Howard Hughes. Jimmy kept asking about the portrait. Finally, Pete said, "Come on over. I have your answer." Jimmy went to his office and there, on his desk, was the painting, with an original comment by Howard Hughes: an X slashed across his face.

Of course, Jimmy's standing in the company was secure enough to sustain small setbacks. The last time his advice was ignored had been in the matter of an *Esquire* magazine piece promoted by Dick Hannah, of the Carl Byoir office, who handled public relations for Hughes for years. (He later arranged the famous telephone conference call, during which Hughes slandered Maheu.) Hughes was strong for the *Esquire* story, which dealt with the Hughes Nevada Operation.

They were having a meeting on it, and Maheu tapped a pencil and said, "What do you think about it, Jimmy?"

"Ben Gazzara," he said.

They all looked at him blankly.

"*Run for your life,*" Jimmy said, which was the title of a television series popular then, starring Gazzara. "Stay away from the story. They'll cut you to pieces."

The story ran in an issue that featured a fake photo sequence on the cover. The photo was purported to be of Hughes, chasing a photographer into the trees around his pool. You can imagine what a hit that was. From then on, nothing that had to do with public relations moved in or out of the Hughes office without being bounced off the Greek.

With Hughes, there was a new cause every week. They lobbied against dog racing in Nevada and won. They kept a rock festival out of Las Vegas. When a mechanic at the Hughes private airport pumped the wrong gas into a small plane that crashed, killing three, Jimmy kept it out of the newspapers while the lawyers settled with the families.

One of the more curious assignments began on a January morning in 1970, when the telephone roused Jimmy from a sound sleep. "Jimmy," said Peter Maheu, "stay close today. We're going to have something special for you to do."

In Jimmy's daily routine, he stopped by the Hughes Nevada offices about 9:00 A.M. and stayed there for maybe an hour, on the way to his office. That day he was there by 8:30.

"What's up?" he asked Peter.

"We're waiting for something."

"For what?"

"Something."

Jimmy should have known better than to ask. It was hours before "something" materialized. Finally, he was handed a typewritten statement:

> This is not a decision reached in haste; and it is done only with the greatest regret. Our marriage has endured for 13 years which is long by present standards. Any property settlement will be resolved privately between us.

As Jimmy read those brief sad lines, Peter sensed what he was thinking: This is a front-page story in every newspaper in the land. "The order," he said, "is not to change one word of this statement, and deliver it to the two wire services. Just the two wire services."

Looking back, Hughes' problems seemed to grow — his investments suffering, his distrust of everyone deepening — from the day of his divorce statement. Some of his Nevada interests were losing big money. Air West, it was reported, had dropped $32 million in 1970. There were rumors that he had developed pneumonia.

Other rumors began to circulate, as early as August, that Bob Maheu was about to be fired and that Hughes was bound for the Bahamas. Maheu asked Jimmy to deny them, and that was enough for Jimmy. The fact that Hughes did not deny them meant nothing. He never confirmed or denied anything.

At that time, Jimmy believed he knew as much about Howard Hughes, his history and his habits as anyone alive. Or, at least, he knew where the information was. One of Jimmy's first acts had been to direct his staff to find, copy, and compile clippings of every story written about him from his years in Houston and Los Angeles. It made for a dossier 500 pages thick, and Jimmy had it distributed on a limited basis to the higher Hughes executives.

Passages from that file turned up years later, as source material for Clifford Irving's non-book about Hughes. He claimed it was from a computer printout. Jimmy did not know whether to be furious or flattered.

Jimmy assembled the file for the usual good reason: to let his bosses know he was on the job, and because there was something he needed to know about Howard Hughes: his pattern. Everyone has one. Jimmy discovered his.

Hughes picked up and left every four years. You could set your calendar by him. This was of no small interest to Jimmy. He was in the public relations business and had only one account. He went to Bob Maheu and told him that his research indicated Hughes got itchy feet after four years, and where did that leave him?

Bob was amused. "Jimmy," he said, reassuringly, "Mr. Hughes is going to spend the rest of his life right here in Las Vegas. Your job is secure."

It was as secure, it developed, as Maheu's. For Maheu, the difference between winning and losing was the fact that the purchase of the Stardust fell through. Hughes, who was prepared to pay $42 million for it, backed off when the Justice Department threatened to bring a monopoly charge. There was no objection to his buying the Landmark, which was bankrupt, and he did.

Instead of owning the Stardust, which showed a profit of over $12 million a year, Hughes now had a hotel that was losing seven. That was a difference of around $20 million per annum. When an investment goes bad, wealthy men get unhappy. It is a short step from there to calling someone a thief. Jimmy was a kind of firefighter for the company, and if Bob Maheu had been a thief, sooner or later, he would have known it.

There was another small but enlightening fact Jimmy discovered about Howard Hughes. He sat behind a desk that was custom-designed, one with special wiring so that any phone could be placed on it and the sound magnified. Hughes was hard of hearing. Wherever he went, the desk went. Jimmy seriously thought he might have been kidnapped, until he heard his desk was gone. It was part of his pattern, just like the four-year cycle.

On the eve of Thanksgiving 1970, exactly four years to the night that Hughes had arrived in Las Vegas, Jimmy had dinner at the Frontier with Governor Laxalt. As they left the hotel, Jimmy looked across the Strip, up to the top floor of the Desert Inn, and nudged the governor.

"Excuse me," Jimmy said, his hands clasped as if in prayer, "I've got to say hello to God up there."

"It won't do you any good, Jimmy," the governor said. "There's nobody up there tonight."

His remark went right over Jimmy's head. It hit him a few hours later, and Jimmy intended to call him the next morning, but it was Thanksgiving Day and he did not bother.

When he walked into the Hughes Nevada offices on Friday morning it looked like a Marx Brothers' comedy. Everyone was running in and out of doors.

"Hughes is gone," someone told Jimmy.

"Where did he go?"

Nobody answered. Jimmy figured, at that moment, no one really knew.

"How did he leave?"

There was no answer to that one, either. The power struggle between the old-timers in the Hughes empire and the Maheu faction was in the open now. From where Jimmy stood, Maheu had represented Hughes well. He was like a successful football coach who snubbed the board of regents. Aligned against him were Raymond Holliday and Frank Gay, executives of the Tool Company in Houston, and Chester Davis, the Hughes attorney. They had been with Hughes forever. Gay started out as one of his original Mormon helpers.

Jimmy had Maheu release a statement expressing his concern for the safety of Mr. Hughes, hinting that his sudden departure may have involved duress. Maheu had the sheriff's office break into the Hughes penthouse. It was empty.

With nothing else to do, Jimmy left a day or so later to keep a business trip to Chicago. He was having dinner with friends when he was paged. (When you worked for Hughes, you left a number where you could be reached at all times.)

It was Bob Maheu. "They're trying to move us out, Jimmy," he said. "They came in like the Gestapo. But we're not going to give up. We're going to do the best we can to protect our people."

Jimmy said, "Bob, you mean Mr. Hughes: protect Mr. Hughes, don't you?"

"Yes, yes, that's right," he said. "Mr. Hughes."

Jimmy felt Maheu had to take the position that he was the one looking out for Howard. As far as Jimmy knew, he still worked for Howard Hughes and to him, Bob Maheu *was* Hughes. When Jimmy boarded a plane back to Las Vegas that night, he thought to himself, *Greek, you sure got yourself into a sweet one this time.*

The battle lines could not have been clearer. The old guard had been around Hughes for twenty-five years. Jimmy never saw so many people on a payroll with jobs no one knew anything about. Whatever else people might say, Hughes was loyal to anyone who had been loyal to him in his younger days.

Jimmy suspected that, to a point, Hughes enjoyed a little intrigue among his executives. He liked to pit them against each other. A little infighting kept them honest, kept them on their toes. He often challenged his people by giving them an assignment right on a deadline, to see how they executed under pressure.

There was no doubt, the old soldiers viewed with suspicion the growth of Maheu's power. In a sense, Maheu was in business on his own. He had unlimited use of the company Cadillacs, helicopters, and an airplane. He bought into a housing development in Los Angeles, and was a partner in several consulting firms with the Hughes security chief, Jack Hooper. He had a yacht, and all the trappings of power.

Davis and Gay led a task force of auditors and security cops swarming into the hotels and casinos and Hughes Nevada offices. They publicly announced the firing of Maheu.

A meeting was held at Maheu's home, on the grounds of the Desert Inn, beside one of the golf fairways. There was no small irony to that. It was a home Hughes paid for, and when it became apparent that construction costs were running $50,000 over estimates, Maheu sent Hughes a memo, offering to pay the extra costs.

Hughes sent him a memo back: "You're going to live in it the rest of your life. For another $50,000, don't worry about it."

There Maheu was, more or less evicted from his own office. Outside, they could see plainclothesmen from Intertel, the security agency hired by the Tool Company executives. Among those at the meeting were the Maheus; Dick Danner, who managed the Frontier Hotel; Al Benedict, the liaison with all the hotels, who later ran the MGM; their attorney, Tom Bell; and Jack Hooper.

Jimmy asked Hooper the key question again: "How did he leave?"

Hooper still did not know; no one else knew either. To this day, no one can say for certain. One theory is that he took the interior fire exit down nine floors to the parking lot. Another was that the Mormons carried him down. Who knows? Maybe he just walked out through the lobby. Who knew what he looked like anyway?

The point of their meeting was to devise a game plan to counter the takeover of the old guard. Each side filed an injunction, Maheu claiming that their power of attorney was forged and only Hughes could fire him. They hired so many detectives that they spent most of their time trailing each other.

It was all over for Maheu when Paul Laxalt reported that he received a call from Hughes, from Paradise Island in the Bahamas. He said Hughes confirmed that the Tool Company executives acted under his orders. Maheu was fired. As one of the few who directly spoke with him, Laxalt was convinced that the voice he heard was that of Howard Hughes. Among the first to be fired with Maheu were Jimmy the Greek, Hooper, and Danner, who had delivered to his friend, Bebe Rebozo, the Nixon campaign money.

There was no way Jimmy could not believe the governor. He was a friend and tennis partner of Maheu's. Maheu was out, and so was Jimmy the Greek. There was still a matter of money owed for past services, specifically, a bill Jimmy submitted for $121,000. When it got to Chester Davis, the portly, crusty old lawyer roared when he saw it. "What the hell did you do," he demanded, "to earn all this money?"

Jimmy said, "In twenty-four hours, I'll have a memo on your desk, listing some of the things I did, with copies to all the other attorneys and Hughes himself."

Two days later Jimmy had a call from Hughes' man in New York. "We're going to agree to X amount of dollars," he said, "but we're going to deduct twenty-eight percent from that. You would win if you took it to court, but it would take two years and attorney fees."

Why the twenty-eight percent? Jimmy never figured that one out. He settled for $74,000 and closed the account. Jimmy never knocked Hughes, which surprised a few people. Can you see it? Jimmy the Greek shaking his fist and threatening, "I *made* you, Howard, and I can *break* you."

Jimmy's philosophy was simple: He who pays me has a right to fire me. And Jimmy was well paid (six figures a year).

On paper, Maheu won big. In December of 1974, a jury awarded him punitive damages of $2.8 million in his slander suit against Hughes, who, in that ill-timed telephone conference with newsmen, referred to Bob in language not recommended for general audiences. Liar, thief, and son-of-a-bitch were among the gentler descriptions.

How long the settlement could be delayed by Hughes' attorneys remained to be seen.

Jimmy's own final brush with the Hughes experience came some three years after he left his employ. Questions were still being raised about the purchase of Air West, and on three separate occasions, Jimmy was called to testify before the Securities Exchange Commission. Jimmy was suspected, not found, of having driven down the price of Air West stock — before the sale was closed — by spreading unfavorable statements. It was not so. Poor management drove down the company's stock. In California it was know as "Air Worst."

A joke about the airlines quoted one of the Air West hostesses praying on takeoff: "Our Father, who art in heaven, Howard be thy name . . ."

On final reflection, Jimmy had to say it was one of the more interesting periods of his life. Working for Hughes, in some ways, was like putting a message into a bottle and casting it out to sea.

Hughes could not be described as consistent. He did not hire Jews or blacks, but he donated generously to charities (the list was seven pages long) that provided for Jews and blacks.

He did prove one thing. Few things capture the imagination of the American public faster, or assure a larger fame, than someone who craves privacy and goes to great lengths to obtain it. For more than a year, a person could not pick up a paper or a magazine without reading about him. There was the Clifford Irving hoax. There were fantastic rumors and all the gags, you know the kind:

"I just got a call from Howard Hughes."

"How do you know it was him?"

"Had to be. When I picked up the phone, no one was there."

Chapter 14

Oddsmaking: Wrong Again

FOR THE LAST SIX weeks of the 1968 season, Jimmy created a mild panic in pro football because of something he did not do. He did not establish a line — a point spread — on the Kansas City Chiefs. In betting parlance, they were "taken off the board."

Now it is true that people in sports panic more easily than those in other fields, with the possible exception of high fashion. This story explains why the odds are made and sometimes not made, what moves them, and to what purposes they are used.

It gets close to the core of the sports experience in this country. That is, the games can be enjoyed; one can fall in love with a team, just as long as he believes they are honest and above suspicion. Always, the alien presence is *gambling*. People bet. When they bet they tend to do two things: (1) look for an edge and (2) justify their losses by screaming "fix." Both ways can spread alarm, and sometimes, in rare and dramatic instances, there is reason.

Jimmy did not bar Kansas City in 1968 because of any suspicious behavior by the players. He barred them because what gamblers call "unnatural money" began to show up on their games. Actually, it was more like unnaturally *big* money. It was winding up in Las Vegas gambling shops, but not directly. The bets were being laundered, sent in from cities other than the source of the original money.

Jimmy began to check around, and learned that the names of three Kansas City players were being misused by some unsavory characters. The full story took a year to break. Ironically, it broke the week of the 1970 Super Bowl, before the Chiefs met Minnesota. At the time, all Jimmy knew was the following.

Lenny Dawson, the quarterback, one of the straightest arrows in the league, was getting phone calls from a Detroit gambler named Donald (Dicey) Dawson (no relation of his). Jimmy seriously doubted that Lenny had any idea what the other Dawson did for a living.

Johnny Robinson, the halfback from LSU, was thinking about opening a restaurant and sports club in a building thought to be owned by the Mafia.

A third player (whose name cannot be used) was mixed up with a crowd in Kansas City suspected of stealing cars and dealing drugs.

Jimmy knew what was happening to the line. Say that the Chiefs were favored by seventeen over Denver, and Dicey Dawson took the points. His friends, the people around him, would say, "Dicey talks to the quarterback. He *knows* something . . ." The line would drop to sixteen and *their* friends would start betting, and soon it was down to thirteen.

The suckers would come in and the line would fall to eleven. The fellow in Detroit would bet that — take Kansas City and lay the points — and now he had the game middled. He was on both sides with maybe a six-point spread. That was beautiful — for him. He was *using* the public, and that was why Jimmy barred the Chiefs. The point spread is there to protect the public. It is a barometer. You can read it, measure the teams, test the winds of sentiment, see where the money is flowing and how fast. Some weeks it was like a novel.

Pete Rozelle, whom Jimmy admired, and others in high places in professional sports, took the position that betting was not an essential part of team games. Fan interest did not depend on it.

That was absolutely true. If all gambling somehow disappeared tomorrow, pro football and the rest would still exist. Unfortunately, Jimmy lived in the real world. In the real world, people were betting $10 billion each year on pro sports. It was not a question of something funny going on with the Chiefs. They only lost twice all season. But the *suspicion* of guilt can be as deadly as the real thing.

Jimmy would have to bet his life that Len Dawson and Johnny Robinson were clean (and lie detector tests later vindicated both). As for the third fellow, he only knew he got involved with bad company and became an unsettling influence on the team.

The first week the Kansas City game failed to appear on the line, the calls began flooding in from all over the country. Pete Axthelm of *Newsweek*, Dave Anderson of *The New York Times*, and Mort Sharnik of *Sports Illustrated* wondered if Jimmy had heard any rumors. Jimmy said that it was impossible to handicap them at the time because of their injuries — they had some — and left it at that.

The Chiefs won their last five games that 1968 season, then were blown out by Oakland in the playoffs.

Each week there were more calls, more questions. When Jimmy barred them, everyone did. The National Football League office, which does not like to acknowledge that people bet on games, was having convulsions. It became a suspense story: Would this be the week a point spread appeared on Kansas City?

Later that winter, Jimmy learned that the NFL had investigated the rumors and asked several of the Chiefs to submit to lie detector tests. Len Dawson was the first to volunteer. The case was quietly closed, or so it seemed.

When the 1969 season was about to open, Jimmy got a call from one of his favorite sports columnists, Bud Furillo of the *Los Angeles Herald-Examiner*. "An old friend of mine," he said, "is wondering if you're going to put the Chiefs on the board this season. He'd appreciate it if you did."

Bud did not identify his old friend, but Jimmy knew it was the commissioner. Rozelle had been the general manager of the Rams in the early fifties, when Bud was covering the team. Pete understood that when a team was kept off the board, it was performing under suspicion. He wanted the suspicion removed.

The Chiefs were back, and the matter rested until Super Bowl week 1970. Suddenly, with tens of thousands of football fans congregated in New Orleans and the press hovering like fruit flies, an FBI gambling investigation broke wide open. It centered in Detroit, and there the name of Dicey Dawson was publicly linked to the Kansas City quarterback.

Rozelle's office moved quickly to reveal the results of its own tests to clear Lenny. The timing was hellish for a team preparing for the biggest game of the year. The strain, the pressure, the distraction was intense. That was all anyone could hear that week. The average fan figured it would blow Kansas City right out of the game.

Immediately, Jimmy moved Minnesota from a three-point favorite to nine, for two reasons, neither of which had to do with Len Dawson's frame of mind. He moved it because fans *thought* he would be affected, and because the Chiefs had an injured cornerback (and that is where those big sixes are scored). The gamblers closed the game at thirteen, which showed that the money was still coming in on Minnesota.

There was, thankfully, a lighter side to Super Bowl IV. The Chiefs proved all the amateur psychologists dead wrong when Len Dawson gave an inspired performance. They led at the half, 16–0, as Jimmy sat in the company of Phil Iselin, owner of the Jets; his coach, Weeb Ewbank; and Governor Paul Laxalt of Nevada, who did Jimmy's arithmetic. The Vikings had to score five touchdowns to beat Jimmy's handicap.

He was barely paying attention as the half-time show unfolded below them, a noisy, extravagant reenactment of the Battle of New Orleans. Cannons exploded. Horses bolted. Costumed soldiers fired rifles and crumpled to the ground. ". . . And when the smoke cleared," the voice on the stadium loudspeaker said, "the British had lost 1,975 men, while the American casualties were six."

Out of the Kansas City section in front of them, a heavy voice boomed out, "*And one Greek.*"

Jimmy laughed along with everyone around him. After the Chiefs finished polishing off the Vikings, 23–7, Jimmy caught more of it. "Wrong again, eh, Greek?" strangers greeted him as they filed out of the stadium.

The year before, Jimmy made the Baltimore Colts a seventeen-point favorite over the New York Jets, in what has become the most historic of all the Super Bowl games. Before witnesses, in the middle of the week, Joe Willie Namath "guaranteed" that the Jets would win. He made the prediction at a banquet with a glass of Scotch in his hand. The game came three days later, and the Jets won, 16–7.

Jimmy was not there and did not watch it on television. The day before the game he underwent surgery for the removal of a stomach obstruction, a final repair of the condition that had troubled him during his years with Hughes. He was under sedation all day Sunday. On Monday morning a nurse walked in, flicked on his television set, and in his first conscious moments, just coming out of the fog, he heard Joe Garagiola on the *Today* show, saying, ". . . And even Jimmy the Greek was wrong."

When the Chiefs surprised the Vikings, Jimmy had missed twice, or so most people thought.

Well, we all have our own identity problems. Jimmy wanted people to understand that he was an oddsmaker. He did not pick winners. He was not a sportswriter trying to match wits in the weekly "guesspert" competition. He established favorites, odds, and point spreads — that is, the margin necessary to *equalize* the two teams.

Making the odds became a hobby for him, a kind of loss leader for his public relations business. He spent over $50,000 a year getting the information that went into the odds, and he gave them away — to the sports press, and to political reporters like Walter Cronkite, Harry Reasoner, and Jack Anderson. It kept his name out there.

It no longer vexed him when people jumped to conclusions about his work or his style. He got the feeling that some people expected him to appear in a frock coat and twirling a waxed mustache. He recalled when Howard Samuels, who organized Off-Track Betting in New York City, invited him there to pick his brains. Jimmy asked, "What time?"

"Why not Saturday night, in my office?" he suggested. "That's the best time."

Jimmy thought nothing of it, until he walked through the deserted lobby of the OTB offices in the old Paramount Building on Times Square. His footsteps echoed through the halls. Then he understood. All the other offices were closed. There was no one around who might recognize Jimmy the Greek Snyder, notorious Las Vegas oddsmaker and sinister influence. Jimmy only guessed what Howard must have expected. Maybe he thought he would arrive with four bodyguards carrying violin cases.

What he met was a businessman who happened to be an expert on odds and the science of probability, subjects he needed to better understand.

As they walked into Samuels' private office, Dick Aurelio, the deputy mayor under John Lindsay, quietly stood aside. After maybe fifteen minutes, Aurelio glanced at his watch and interrupted, "Howard, I have to go. Whatever you want to do with this guy, it's okay." With that, he was gone.

Jimmy agreed to act as an unpaid consultant. His projections on the OTB handle for the first three years proved to be off only one and a half percent. His estimate of their operating cost was low by only a point. He should have remembered that it always cost more when the government ran something.

Howard Samuels and Jimmy hit it off instantly. There was no more secrecy. They stopped at his apartment, had dinner later at "21." The next week he put Jimmy on display, proudly, in a press conference in the OTB offices.

Jimmy was impressed with Samuels. In 1974 he had everything needed to be elected governor of New York — distinguished looks, wealth, brains, and exposure — except for one thing. He could not get the nomination.

Everything in life is a betting proposition. You can get odds on whether you will wake up tomorrow (don't worry, you're a heavy favorite). Jimmy quoted odds on games, fights, elections, races, the Academy Awards, California falling into the sea, and when the cherry blossoms would bloom in Washington, D.C. He never made them on matters involving life or death, although he did once, in 1960, bet on Caryl Chessman going to the gas chamber. He was a 4-to-1 favorite to go, and he did.

It is possible to quote a price on any situation. The biggest gamblers in the world are insurance companies. The first time Jimmy ever boarded a plane, Pittsburgh to Baltimore, in 1937, he stopped at the insurance counter. He asked the young lady standing there how it worked.

"Well, sir," she said, "you get $5,000 of life insurance for twenty-five cents."

Mural of Jimmy's father's store, The White Star Meat Market, painted in the 1980s in Steubenville, Ohio. The mural denotes exact location where the store once stood.

— Synodinos family picture

North Carolina estate that Jimmy loved.

— Tommy Manakides

Childhood home where he first began gambling. The house is still standing in Steubenville, Ohio.

— Rosemary E. Antol

Jimmy at the innocent age of five.

— Jimmy Snyder

Ramparts *magazine illustrates Jimmy in his first front-cover feature in May of 1973.*
— *Ramparts Magazine,* Berkeley, California

Picking the odds for the Joe Frazier–Muhammad Ali heavyweight fight.
— Jimmy Snyder

THREE-IN-ONE SECTION
1. Schedule, Starting Time
2. Scores The Past 3 Years
3. Opening Las Vegas Line

SCHEDULE AND STARTING TIMES - bottom team is home team unless neutral field is specified. All starting times are Eastern Time.

PREVIOUS THREE SCORES - * indicates Home. (—) no game played that year.

NOTE: IN A COUPLE OF WEEKS WE'LL PUBLISH OUR FAMOUS "COMPUTER-IZED RATINGS" FOR ALL GAMES SCHEDULED AND TOTALS FOR THE PROFESSIONAL GAMES. WE WANT TO LET 'EM PLAY A COUPLE OF WEEKS BEFORE FIRMING UP THE NUMBERS FOR THE 1991 PUBLICATION.

	Opening Vegas Line	1990	1989	1988		
College Football, Wednesday, August 28th at East Rutherford, NJ						
GEORGIA TECH / PENN STATE 9:00	2½	—	—	—		
Thursday, August 29th at Anaheim, CA						
FLORIDA STATE / BYU 9:00	14	—	—	—		
Saturday, August 31st						
MIAMI-FLA. / ARKANSAS 12:30	21	—	—	*18 / 16		
BOSTON COLLEGE / RUTGERS 1:30	2	*19 / 14	7 / *9	*6 / 17		
HAWAII / WYOMING 2:00	6	*38 / 17	15 / *20	*22 / 28		
MISSISSIPPI / TULANE 3:30	3	*31 / 21	32 / *28	*9 / 14		
EAST CAROLINA / ILLINOIS 4:00	13	—	—	—		
PITTSBURGH / WEST VIRGINIA 7:30	4	*24 / 38	31 / *31	*10 / 31		
NEW MEXICO / TEXAS-EL PASO 9:05	3½	*48 / 28	7 / *26	*0 / 37		
Pro Football, Sunday, September 1st						
TAMPA BAY / N.Y. JETS 1:00	39 / 2½					
DALLAS / CLEVELAND 1:00	2½ / 26					
SEATTLE / NEW ORLEANS 1:00	37 / 4					
ATLANTA / KANSAS CITY 1:00	42 / 7					
PHILADELPHIA / GREEN BAY 1:00	2 / 45					
MINNESOTA / CHICAGO 4:00	36½ / 2					
SAN DIEGO / PITTSBURGH 4:00	35 / 5					
CINCINNATI / DENVER 4:00						
PHOENIX / L.A. RAMS 4:00						
L.A. RAIDERS / HOUSTON 4:00	43½ / 2½					
MIAMI / BUFFALO 4:00	41 / 7					
NEW ENGLAND / INDIANAPOLIS 4:00						
DETROIT / WASHINGTON 8:00						
College Football, Monday, September 2nd						
MEMPHIS STATE / USC 4:30	17½	—	—	—		
Pro Football, Monday, September 2nd						
SAN FRANCISCO * / N.Y. GIANTS 9:00	37 / 2½					

College Pointspread — 1990
(ALL VS. THE SPREAD)
(BOWLS INCLUDED)

THE BEST ...

	W	L	T	PCT.
North Carolina	8	1	0	.889
Temple	8	2	0	.800
Texas	9	3	0	.750
Georgia Tech	8	3	0	.727
Minnesota	8	3	0	.727
Washington	8	3	0	.727
Cornell	5	2	0	.714
Dartmouth	5	2	0	.714
Stanford	7	3	0	.700
Florida	6	3	0	.667
South Carolina	6	3	0	.667
Virginia Tech	6	3	1	.650
Colorado State	7	4	0	.636
Southern Mississippi	7	4	0	.636
Virginia	7	4	0	.636

THE WORST ...

	W	L	T	PCT.
Tulsa	0	7	0	.000
Georgia	1	10	0	.090
Princeton	1	6	0	.143
Arkansas	2	9	0	.182
Navy	1	4	0	.200
Clemson	2	8	0	.200
LSU	2	8	0	.200
West Virginia	2	8	0	.200
Harvard	2	5	0	.286
Wisconsin	3	7	0	.300
USC	4	9	0	.308
Iowa State	3	6	0	.333
Vanderbilt	4	7	0	.364
Washington State	4	7	0	.364
Wyoming	4	7	0	.364

The Greek picks his professional and college winners of the week in 1990.

— Sport Reporter Football Sheet,
Stars Sport Corporation, Lynbrook, NY

Best Bet: 'MALIBU BLUE' in the Ninth
Best Value: 'DUSTY DONNA' in the Fourth

FIRST RACE: **Senor Cielo** was sharpened in hot-paced 6 furlongs on wet Monmouth strip returning from layup, should benefit and figures to shake loose. **Traskwood** drops back to optimal distance after meeting tougher going long, logical favorite. **Senator To Be** was a good third in quickly run 7 furlongs behind Crackedbell at Saratoga Aug. 12.

SECOND RACE: **Drug Lord** has run well in four lifetime starts, freshened during Spa for this and sharp recent blowout. **Starters Dee Lite**, second time gelding, finished fast late for third returning from layoff at Spa Aug. 15; dangerous rival. **Alex's Ice Castle** was used hard early and held gamely in wake-up placing last time out.

THIRD RACE: **Quiet Enjoyment** held very well to just miss when third in good-figure well-meant Spa debut; makes amends with similar try. **Hoover Dam** finished fast too late after altering course in well-meant debut Aug. 12; should improve quickly. **Noactor** set live, pressured pace when third to promising Pine Bluff at this distance in second, improved start. **Familiar Flair** finished well late after early trouble in well meant debut.

FOURTH RACE: **Dusty Donna** placed gamely despite indecisive handling in lone Spa start, likes this track, makes amends. **Speed Minister** entry. **Speed Minister** drops significantly turning back into sprint, mate **Ballynoe** raced dully in slop following clearly-best two-turn allowance win previously. **Ciao Ciao Bambine** raced dully behind on wet track last time but prior was gamely placing in top-figure key-race try vs. tougher.

FIFTH RACE: **Mountain Madness**, entered right back off game placing while racing in-close through late stretch, should like added ground and appears nicely placed. I. R.

Raasie, up from Calder for live outfit, finished strongly in 2 of 3 turf starts. **North Branch Kid** returns to claimer off dull allowance sprint for Monaci and is turf bred both sides; wake-up possibility. (On dirt: **I'll Take A Stand**).

SIXTH RACE: **Honest Ensign**, back from Monmouth and returning to proper class, likes this surface, best takes this easily. **Long Trek** placed gamely in two-turn non-winners of 2 at Saratoga last out, back at proper level. **Big Daniel** raced dully on off turf at Monmouth now returns to optimal conditions over preferred track.

SEVENTH RACE: **Safflower** raced very wide in both two-turn attempts at Saratoga but one-turn prior here was first-rate wide-rally placing; another chance. **Miss Fapp** made fairly promising turf debut when third in first distance try last out; logical favorite with normal improvement. **Dreaded Credit**, freshened to await this, has blinkers removed for turf debut; bred both sides. (On dirt: **Aly Chic**).

EIGHTH RACE: **Screen Prospect** won recent return from long layoff like top-class filly; controls pace, and the race, with similar try. **Meadow Star**, needing no introduction, draws rail off two-month absence for first vs elders. **Queena** seeks fourth straight for McGaughey; packs 123.

NINTH RACE: **Malibu Blue**, back from California, figures to outrun these throughout. **My Hawaii Trip** gained conditioning from recent turf route vs. winners, back where she belongs. **Wiggles Law** drops into claimer first time.

TENTH RACE: **Roanoke**, pointed toward this, is suited nicely by conditions and has run well over track. **Chief Honcho** finally gets away from In Excess, figures to sit good trip. **Marquetry** is versatile and style suits this oval.

Snyder handicaps the races at the Belmont Track in New York.

— Today at Belmont, John Pricci,
New York's *Newsday*

Original cartoon by Jim Berry, signed by President Nixon.
Reprinted by permission of NEA.

— Jim Berry – NEA

'HELLO—JIMMY THE GREEK? I WANT TO GET SOME ODDS . . .'

Kissinger political cartoon by Pat Oliphant. Copyright © The Washington
Star; *reprinted with permission* Los Angeles Times Syndicate.

– Los Angeles Times Syndicate

Joking with close friend, the late Howard Cosell.

— Jimmy Snyder

Celebrating with his wife, Joan, at the Pierre Hotel in New York City.
— Jimmy Snyder

CBS-TV's NFL Today Show *team.*
From left to right: Brent Musburger, Phyllis George, Jimmy the Greek, Irv Cross.
— CBS file photo

The meeting between Rev. Jesse Jackson and Jimmy in a Washington hotel, after his remarks about black athletes.

–Tom Reed, Associated Press

His favorite photograph, taken in 1990 while visiting Las Vegas, Nevada.
— Tommy Manakides

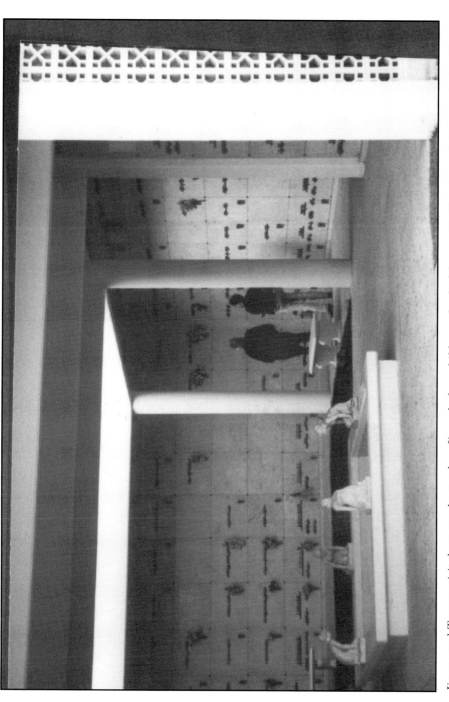

Jimmy and Tommy visit the mausoleum where Jimmy's three children, who died from cystic fibrosis, are laid to rest in Las Vegas, Nevada.

— Achilles T. Manakides

Daughter Vicki giving poker advice to her father.
— Tommy Manakides

Discussing last minute preparations for Las Vegas in the Greek's Durham, North Carolina office in 1995, with Tommy Manakides.
— Tommy Manakides

The Greek compliments Nick Manakides on his famous southern barbecue.
This photograph, taken on May 23, 1995, is the last picture ever taken of Jimmy the Greek.

— Tommy Manakides

Tommy Manakides, Al Davis, and Bob Stupak attending National Football Foundation College Hall of Fame, where an annual scholarship in memory of Jimmy the Greek was established for Las Vegas High School in May of 1996.
— Achilles T. Manakides

Father Illia Katri and Al Davis converse following Jimmy's memorial service at St. John the Baptist Greek Orthodox Church in Las Vegas, Nevada.
— Achilles T. Manakides

"Give me a dollar's worth," Jimmy said, reaching into his pocket. Those were the best odds he ever had — 20,000-to-1.

Insurance companies employ highly trained mathematicians, known as actuaries, to compute the percentages in any situation. With precise formulas, they arrive at rates based in part on age, job, and health. Jimmy's own formula was not scientific, but it always worked for him:

Knowledge x Energy x Intuition = The Odds.

Whether it was the Super Bowl or the World Series or a presidential election, the formula held up. *Knowledge* was the information he collected. *Energy* was the money and the time he spent analyzing all the key elements, in the same way a broker analyzes the stock market. *Intuition* was how he personally reacted to the intangibles, what kind of "gut feeling" he had when he looked at the whole picture.

Intuition is often the most important factor of all. A computer can absorb the raw material, perform the tasks of knowledge and energy, and spit out a price. However, it will not have the full picture, because computers cannot handle the intangibles: a team's mental attitude or a politician's charisma. It starts there, with that visceral feeling, the one you get when you look at a game and you think, "The line ought to be six. Now why do I feel that way?" There is no such thing as a computer with a "gut feeling."

Jimmy knew that one learns by experience. When he figured a team wrong — he made a bad number — he looked at it, studied it, and asked why. Then he decided: it was the wide receiver, his speed. When Jimmy first began to handicap football, speed was the first item he considered. Then it was the quarterback, who came in with the T-formation, replacing the tailback (in the single wing) as the key man on the field.

Now he had two categories: speed and the quarterback. Then he discovered a third. He had a bet won when, suddenly, a cornerback slipped and fell and the other team completed a touchdown pass over him. Right then, Jimmy began to think about the cornerback and his importance to the team.

At the start of the 1974 season, Jimmy's system included nine categories: (1) team speed, (2) defensive secondary, (3) quarterback, (4) front defense, (5) running game, (6) kicking game, (7) special teams, (8) home field, and (9) intangibles, which included those cases where he may be aware that one team had a better game plan.

It is a continuing process, slow changes over a period of years. It was only in 1966 that Jimmy added the special-teams factor. Suddenly, his numbers on Cleveland and Green Bay were wrong. He could not understand it. The game has to play to the number; their games were not. He kept checking his figures, his categories, and it finally dawned on him. Blanton Collier and Vince Lombardi were beating people with their specialty teams, at a time when some coaches considered such units to be cannon fodder. Later, George Allen and Don Shula came along, taking pride in their special teams.

By the end of the 1974 season, Jimmy added a tenth category: discipline. He gave a point or two for that, based on information that came to him about player attitudes and habits, how they practiced, their off-the-field behavior, racial problems, and what he saw for himself in the stadium and on the TV screen.

Jimmy used to lump this under coaching, which fell under intangibles. (Lombardi, Shula, and John Madden of Oakland were the only coaches to whom he awarded points, on their own, as a factor in the game.) Discipline commands more attention now, in an age when some coaches are permissive, some players militant, and some teams caught in the middle. You seldom give points for coaching, since most coaches are equal. What you do is take off points for *bad* coaches, such as Otto Graham, when he was with Washington, Joe Kuharich at Philadelphia, and Joe Schmidt at Detroit.

All of this came under the heading of research. When it was done, Jimmy named his favorite by the number of points he thought would equalize the game for the public. The points are there, at least in part, to assure the fairness of a friendly wager. For instance, take the 1969 Super Bowl. To Jimmy, the Colts by seventeen figured to be the number that best reflected what the fans believed to be the difference between the two teams. As it developed, the number went a little higher in Baltimore and New York, moving as high as twenty. The NFL sentiment was strong in both cities, and the Giant rooters — who detested the upstart Jets — were betting the Colts big.

The Jets were regarded as somewhat of a fluke, an average team, with only the third best record in its own league, carried by a theatrical but gifted quarterback. The AFL was not exactly held in universal respect. Its champions (Kansas City and Oakland) had been badly beaten by Green Bay in the first two Super Bowls.

In most of the country the number on Super Bowl III held at seventeen, which meant that almost an equal amount of money was being bet on each side. It also meant that Jimmy's opinion was correct.

As an oddsmaker, whether he is right or wrong is determined *before* a game starts by how the public reacts, not by a final score. Jimmy did not expect people to understand that. When he named a betting favorite, they related this to picking a winner, which explains why he sweated out every result. He was human. He liked being right, "in the public's mind" too.

In a way, he was like an umpire. An oddsmaker only draws notice when the fans think he has blown one. Nothing in his life prepared him for the overnight fame — notoriety — that came with the Jets' victory over the Colts. This was the game, remember, that earned him the "Bonehead of the Year" award in Dallas.

There is yet another factor that goes into the weighing of the odds, and that is what the public believes. Jimmy had, on rare occasions, made a number that went against his own instincts because to do otherwise would have created an unrealistic number and the fans would scurry, trying to place a bet. That was what he tried to avoid.

The Joe Frazier–George Foreman fight in Kingston, Jamaica, was a prime example. Jimmy thought Frazier was ready to be taken. He was not training well, tended to get high blood pressure in camp, and at the time might have had trouble passing the California physical test. Jimmy also knew he was overconfident, and that Foreman was the type of fighter who could hurt him. Foreman had a punch like a mule. Frazier's style, always coming straight in, was like giving Aaron a waist-high fast ball.

Jimmy made Frazier a 3-to-1 favorite, and this was why: Joe was the champion. He was undefeated. In the eyes of the public, he *was* the favorite. One of the first rules of the craft is you have to make a figure the public believes is right too.

The same condition applied to the comeback of Muhammad Ali. Few would remember this, but the day after Foreman belted out Frazier, Jimmy made Ali a 6-to-5 favorite to beat George and regain his title — if they fought within a reasonable time. Two years elapsed and the boxing picture turned upside down. Ali had his jaw broken by an unknown, Ken Norton, then struggled to win return matches from both Frazier and Norton. Foreman demolished each of them in two rounds or less. Ali was over thirty now and could not recover the skills that were dulled by a three-and-a-half-year exile. In the minds of the public, Foreman figured to be an easy winner.

Now an emotional thing happened. Jimmy made Foreman the favorite, but established the price as 11-to-5, which told the fans the fight would not be that easy. Nevada bookies carried Foreman at 3-to-1, and the big gamblers backed him.

The little people wanted Ali to win. It was one of the craziest things in sports. It had only been a few years since Ali was widely denounced as a traitor, a menace, and a threat to the American way of life. To others he was a braggart, a pest, and a clown. He made people angrier than the IRS did.

Jimmy rarely knew of a more popular victory in sports than his, a comeback that saw him win the world heavyweight title ten years apart. If Jimmy had been betting then, he would have taken Ali and the odds himself. He thought for sure he would win if the fight went past five rounds.

It is not what you would call an exact science. Sometimes your judgment is right for reasons that turn out to be wrong. That was the case in 1973 with Secretariat, winner of the Triple Crown, an unbeatable horse if there ever was one.

Jimmy had an informant whose life was horses, who practically slept at the track. He told Jimmy what few people knew then, that Secretariat had an arthritic condition in his left knee. If he did not work out three or four days before a race, to get rid of the stiffness, he could not run at top form on race day.

Sure enough, Secretariat did not work out the week of the Wood Memorial in 1973. Later, Jimmy learned why. There was a loose horse on the track when his handlers took him out. When they saw the other horse, his trainer and jockey pulled him off the track immediately. All they could do was get the horse hurt, and you do not take risks with a property worth $6 million. Jimmy's man was there. He had the binoculars on them. He never saw the loose horse, and they assumed the problem was the knee. In an interview before the race, Jimmy said Secretariat would get beat and he did.

After that, Will Grimsley of the Associated Press asked Jimmy about the Kentucky Derby, and Jimmy told him Secretaiat would go to the post as a 3-to-2 or 7-to-5 favorite. Jimmy told Will that the price was too short in Nevada, where the books were quoting Secretariat at 4-to-5. This offended the trainer, Lucien Laurin, and when Secretariat won handily, it pleased him to say, "Jimmy the Greek was wrong." He was not wrong. He never said Secretariat would lose, only that Nevada odds were wrong. The track odds proved him right. He was a super horse, the Mickey Mantle of the paddock. But he was not, because of his arthritic knee, a consistent horse to bet on, such as Native Dancer or Tom Fool.

Jimmy had reference numbers for the odds themselves. He read them the way some people read poetry. Writers have described Jimmy as "Oddsmaker of the Nation" and the "Wizard of Odds": calculating, measuring, comparing, filling up the pages of a notepad with his own equations. It was an addiction.

When Jimmy had his office in Las Vegas, he kept the sports wires. On weekends, when he watched the scores come in and checked the ticker, it was to him like a doctor taking a pulse.

Chapter 15

The Psychology
of Politics

GIVEN THE SLIGHTEST EXCUSE, people will bet on anything. The professionals will tell you that what they bet on most is not professional football or the Kentucky Derby or the World Series. It is politics. More money, big money, is wagered on a national election than any sports event you can name.

It is the biggest Super Bowl of all.

In the memory of living bookmakers, only one presidential election ever went against the odds. The year was 1948 and the underdog was Harry S. Truman. The election took a turn on a variable too ridiculous to mention, if not for the fact that Jimmy had the evidence cold.

The boys who set the price and the scientists who made the polls missed something: a mustache — on Tom Dewey's face. Because of his thin mustache, Jimmy won a suitcase full of money in what has since become the most famous of all presidential elections.

It started in a way that had nothing to do with anything. Jimmy was at home in Steubenville, dressing to go out on a date. As he studied himself in the mirror and adjusted his tie, he said idly, "I think I'm going to grow a mustache."

Jimmy's older sister, Mary, who lived with him at the time, was across the room. "Jim, don't do it," she said. "Girls don't like mustaches."

"I don't know about that," Jimmy said, heading for the door.

He forgot about it until a few days later. The kid who ran his errands left his usual supply of out-of-town newspapers on Jimmy's desk. This day there was a New York edition on top with a picture of Governor Dewey making a speech, with his hand chopping the air. That was not what caught Jimmy's eye. He stared at his mustache, a neatly manicured little mustache. Instantly in his mind echoed the words: "Girls don't like mustaches."

He thought, "That's impossible."

Dewey was as high as 30-to-1 to turn Truman out of office. It was a cinch. No one gave the feisty Missourian a chance.

That same photograph of Dewey appeared in more of the next day's newspapers. *Damnit,* Jimmy thought, *everybody assumes Dewey will win, but how do they know?* Of the voters, 52 percent were women. What if Mary was right?

Jimmy decided to find out. His first move was to call the priest at Holy Name. "Father," Jimmy said, "I need three women."

There was a slight hesitation. "For what reason, my boy?"

"I want to hire them to stand in front of the A & P store," Jimmy said, "and I want them to ask every woman who comes out one question: Do they like men with mustaches?"

"Jimmy, my boy," he said, "have you taken leave of your senses?"

Jimmy assured him it was all in the interest of science, and the arrangements were made. Among them, for a fee of $15 apiece, the ladies questioned 500 shoppers. Over the years, Jimmy has often regretted not saving the sheet of paper on which their figures appeared. It would have made a fine political memento, a piece of history. The breakdown told him exactly what he needed to know: 347 said they did not like mustaches; 122 said they did; 31 said they did not care as long as it was on a man.

Jimmy's mind began to spin. He always looked for a long shot. Anyone can find a favorite, but this is what makes a bettor's pulse race. The real carbonation is in finding an edge on a long shot.

Jimmy sent out the ladies (he had already begun to regard them as his "crew") and in a matter of days they had the figures. The technique they used was not sophisticated. He had them vary the places they went — grocery stores, an expensive dress shop, men's stores, and a store in an African-American district.

The question was point blank: Will you vote for Truman or Dewey?

It was dead even in one precinct. In the other, Truman led, 48 percent to 46 percent, with the rest undecided.

Jimmy was astonished. If a pivotal state like Ohio could be a toss-up, then someone made a giant miscalculation. This election was no cinch.

That night Jimmy got a ticket on the *Spirit of St. Louis* when it came through Steubenville, and he headed for New York. He had $11,000 in cash in his pocket. They loved favorites in the big cities, especially in the Big Apple.

Jimmy's old friend, Harold Salvey, who was loaded and living in Florida, came to New York to place Jimmy's bets. That was the kind of friend he was. He was willing to act as Jimmy's beard even though he heatedly disapproved of his tossing money away in such a hopeless cause. Two nights before the election, Harold was still trying to dissuade Jimmy. He had stopped off in Washington, visited with some important Democrats, and walked away with four tickets to the party's Victory Ball — if Truman won.

"But even *they* don't think he has a chance," Harold said.

"They just might be surprised before it's over," Jimmy said.

"You stick to sports, Greek. That's your game. You're just throwing your money away."

"Look, Harold," Jimmy said, "this is no 20-to-1 shot. This is pick 'em."

"Well," he said, shaking his head, "if I can't change your mind, we'll drop by Lindy's tonight and get it down." Lindy's was a sports and show biz haunt on Broadway, and some of the town's biggest bookmakers were patrons of the corned beef and cheesecake served there.

Harold quickly put out the feeler that he wanted to bet $10,000 on Truman at the best price he could get. In no time at all, they had the most popular table in the joint. They were offered odds of up to 22-to-1. Finally, Harold placed all of it with one fellow at 17-to-1.

Jimmy said nothing about his taking the shorter price, but Harold read his thoughts. "This guy pays off," he said.

Salvey was no debutante when it came to matters of finance. He was a part of the *original* Miami syndicate, a group of six men who controlled all the gambling in Miami.

The next night, election night, they had dinner at the Little Club, where Johnny, the Philip Morris midget, worked. You remember: *"Caalll for Phiilllip Moorrris."* They were ordering and Johnny, in his red-and-black uniform, walked among the tables, calling out the latest election results. Dewey was ahead. Across the table from Jimmy, Harold grinned. He was getting caught up in the excitement of the play.

"Johnny," he said, "you got a dollar in your pocket?"

"Yes, sir, Mr. Salvey," the midget said. "What for?"

"Tomorrow night, when we come back for dinner, you sign that dollar and give it to me, and if Truman has won, I'll give you a thousand-dollar bill." He pulled one out of his wallet and held it in front of Johnny's nose. Jimmy thought the midget was going to wet his pants.

"You got a deal," Johnny said. "I'll take those odds."

When they said good night, Dewey was still leading, but not by the margin that had been projected, and Jimmy glowed with confidence. Salvey was staying at the Waldorf Astoria, and Jimmy was across the street at the Beverly. At 6:00 A.M., Jimmy's telephone rang.

Harold's voice was a whisper. "Greek," he said, "you were right. You won."

"Yeah, I know," Jimmy said.

At 4:00 A.M. Jimmy called Ohio and learned that Truman carried the state. He knew then he had carried it off — they both had. The Greek won $170,000 betting against a candidate who looked like the little man on the wedding cake. Jimmy went to bed happy as a warm pup.

Harold picked up Jimmy's winnings the next day and brought them to his room. He had a total of $180,022, including the $10,000 he put up and the change in his pocket. It was the most money, in cash, he had ever won. His next bet was on the U.S. government. He slipped the money, most of it in hundreds and five hundreds and a few thousand-dollar bills, into three brown envelopes, wrapped them separately, went to the post office, and mailed them home to himself, each package insured for $100.

The odds against it getting lost in the mail, with any amount of insurance on it, were tremendous.

Later, they went back to the Little Club for dinner and Harold paid off Johnny. Harold, who loved an upset and the unexpected, was jubilant over the outcome. Jimmy's own pleasure was nearly as great as the midget's.

What that election proved to him was the power of the women's vote. It is beyond numbers. Long after Jimmy stopped backing his opinions with money, through his later role as an analyst for the likes of Jack Anderson and Walter Cronkite, this was the key to their research. It is what separated them from the pollsters. Jimmy's trade secret was that 70 percent of the people they polled were women. Suppose they polled 1,000 voters. His crews were instructed to include 700 women.

That might sound ridiculous to some, but his instincts told him it was accurate. He began with a basic fact: Women represented 52 percent of the vote. In most cases, if the husband is undecided, his wife will sway him. She is the one who has been to the coffees and the rallies and sized up the candidate on television. It was once the other way around. In all the years since 1944, this has been the single most important change in election style. The husband is either too busy or too preoccupied. The wife knows the issues and her mind, once made up, can rarely be changed.

When you poll the woman you not only have her vote but her husband's thinking as well. One clue to the trend can be found in letters to the editor, which are dominated by women during the heat of a political season.

This frame of reference led Jimmy, in late 1971, to establish Ted Kennedy as a much bigger underdog to Nixon than anyone else projected in the early line for 1972. He based this on a poll they took in which 67 percent of the women said they would vote against the youngest of the Kennedy brothers. After Chappaquiddick, there was simply a lingering suspicion and uneasiness, especially on the part of women over twenty-seven, that Ted was unable to overcome.

Jimmy believed Kennedy was wise to withdraw from the race, and he had no doubt that the burdens of the family obligations weighed heavily on his decision. Ted had led a mercurial life. He was the most open of the brothers. He lived a little, took a drink, enjoyed a wager. Jimmy happened to know that in 1960 he bet $25,000 at the Cal-Neva Lodge in Lake Tahoe on John Kennedy to win the presidency. The bet was placed with Wingy Gruber, one of the bosses at the Cal-Neva Club, but it ended up with Jimmy. Even if Ted denied it, Jimmy was rather proud of him. A fellow should bet on his brother, right?

The playboy image dies hard, but tragedy and responsibility have changed and tempered him. It was never in Jimmy's nature to see people only as percentages. He often wondered what Ted Kennedy must feel. Here he was, a senator of the United States, with two brothers murdered in high offices. Jimmy could picture Ted getting up in the morning and thinking, "By God, this is the day I'm going to run for president." Then he hears a car backfire in the street and he thinks, "What the hell do I want with it?"

In one of the first columns Jimmy ever wrote on politics, in the *Las Vegas Sun* in 1963, he described Ted Kennedy as "the shining star in politics." He wrote that of the three Kennedy brothers Ted had the most exciting personality, and he predicted he would be president someday.

Jimmy always figured his time would be in 1980 or later, when he edged past fifty and showed gray in the temples. He believed women have a tendency to more easily accept and to trust a man with gray in his hair. His prediction has yet to be proven.

Jimmy discovered the cult of female voters in a quirky way in the fall of 1948. Much of everything else he learned about politics came from Jack Nolan, one of the great men in his life, an attorney who, at the time, was the political boss and best-known gambler in Steubenville. All of this should give a small idea of how wide open the town was.

Nolan was about 5'4, Irish, plump, partial to big cigars and fast horses. There were 11,000 voters in Jefferson County when Jimmy first met him, and he figured Nolan knew at least 9,000 by name.

Whenever anyone ran for a state office in Ohio, from governor down, they came to see Jack Nolan — a measure of his power. It was 1940, a few weeks after the Democratic Convention in Chicago, when Nolan asked Jimmy to come to his office.

Nolan was strong for Franklin Roosevelt, who was seeking a

third term against Wendell Willkie. "Jimmy," he said, "what are the odds on Roosevelt?"

"They're betting two and a half to one," Jimmy said.

"Can you place a bet for me?"

"If you want me to."

"How much can you bet?"

"A substantial amount."

"Can you bet a quarter of a million for me?"

Jimmy tried not to gulp. "Yes, sir," Jimmy said. This was the most powerful man in the state. Whatever Jimmy had to do, he was not going to tell him no.

"You come up tomorrow . . ."

"Mr. Nolan," Jimmy interrupted. "I can bet it, but I don't have that kind of credit. You'll have to put the money up. But if you do, I'll see to it that the other party's money is also guaranteed."

"All right," he said. "Come by tomorrow and I'll have the money for you."

The next day he handed Jimmy five cashier's checks, each drawn for $50,000.

As a matter of form, Jimmy began to clarify the bet. "You're betting $250,000, to win $100,000. You've got Roosevelt. In case of death to either candidate previous to the election, the bet is off. In the event —"

"Stop talking, Jimmy," he interrupted, smiling, "and get it down."

Jimmy started out simply to offer Nolan a little professional courtesy. He made his living gambling. It was his *career*. This was when he kept an office in the National Exchange building. Jimmy had, by the way, just turned twenty-one.

That night, before he placed Nolan's bet, there was a major news break. John L. Lewis, the pugnacious leader of the United Mine Workers, came out for Willkie, after supporting FDR for eight years. Republican money showed instantly and the price fell to 10-to-6.

All of a sudden, Jimmy could bet Nolan's roll on Roosevelt with a chance to win back $135,000. The money was covered in Pittsburgh, through the help of Slim Silverheart (the greatest gambling name Jimmy had ever heard). Roosevelt won in a breeze. Willkie carried only ten states.

A few days later Jimmy was in Nolan's office, returning his five cashier's checks, plus the $100,000 he won. Jimmy kept the extra $35,000. He did not think of it as stealing. If the odds had shifted the other way, he would have had to make good the difference.

"Jimmy, you did a great job," he said. He counted out $5,000 from the pile and handed it to him. "For your efforts, here's five percent. Is that fair?"

Jimmy did some fast thinking. He was now $35,000 ahead, on *Nolan's* money. This was no time to get greedy. "Tell you what, Mr. Nolan," Jimmy said. "This election must have cost you a bundle. Please take my five percent and donate it to the Democratic Party, on my behalf."

A tear came to his eye. "Jimmy," he said, leaping from his chair, "God bless you. That's a very thoughtful gesture. If you ever need a friend, you have one in Jack Nolan."

Jimmy never met a man who better understood the psychology of politics. One year his candidate in a mayor's election, a railroad man, was a lopsided underdog. There was no way he could win, or so everyone thought, except for Nolan. He knew a way.

"Jimmy," he said, "do me a favor. Go up to Sixth Street tonight and offer to bet any amount, at even money, on my man to win the election."

"I'll bet you myself," Jimmy said, laughing. "I'll take that up there and get faded like crazy."

"Don't worry about getting faded. That is the way we're going to do it. You take this." He handed Jimmy $2,000. "And there's more if you need it. You'll get some takers, but then it will dry up. You'll see. Now please do as I say."

That night Jimmy stopped at the street corner on Sixth, outside of Charlie Greenberg's joint. "All right," Jimmy barked, "I'm betting even money on the railroader, any amount."

In no time at all, Jimmy had a crowd around him. "I got $200," yelled one guy. "I'll take $300," another chimed in. Almost as quick as a finger snap, $1,100 was gone. Then, just as Nolan predicted, the action stopped cold. "Come on," Jimmy said, waving a fistful of dollars, "I've got the Democrat, even money. Who wants some more?"

No one did. The next day it was all over town. By the end of the week the railroader became the betting favorite at 6-to-5. He closed at 9-to-5 and won in a cakewalk. Nolan had turned the town around. He convinced them his man was going to win. Psychologically, everyone wants to vote for the winner.

Jimmy figured they were even now. He used Jack's money, Jack used Jimmy's reputation. It was quid pro quo.

Jack and Jimmy became partners in a half-mile racetrack in Steubenville that they planned in due time to convert into a dog track. There was only one small problem: dog racing was illegal in Ohio. Jack was working on an annual coincidence, in which the law would close them down each year at the end of their ninety-day season, and they would remain closed until it was time for next year's opening.

They were still working on it the Friday night before the Democratic Convention of 1944. Jack called to say goodbye. "I'm off to Chicago," he announced, his voice filled with the fever he always contracted at that time of the year. "I'll be at the LaSalle Hotel."

"Okay, partner," Jimmy said.

This was to be a special convention. Jack was to nominate a congressman named Ferguson, from Ohio, for the vice-presidency. Roosevelt, having dumped Wallace, had thrown it open to the floor.

One of Nolan's theories, incidentally, was that you never bet on a candidate after his party's convention. You waited until the other party did its act, when spirits and loyalties were pumped to a high. One of the last things Jack said to Jimmy was, "We're not going to get our money down on Roosevelt yet. We'll wait until all this cools down. When the Republicans have made their speeches, that's the time."

Jack did not live to bet again on FDR, who won a fourth term over Dewey. That night before he was to nominate Ferguson, he turned on the shower in his room, was scalded by a blast of hot water, and died of a heart attack en route to a hospital. Had Nolan lived, and with Ohio's support, Ferguson might have been on the ticket instead of Truman. When Roosevelt died less than a year later, Ferguson would have been president.

With Jack's death Jimmy lost a friend and a mentor, not to

mention a dog track. His interest in politics began with Jack No-lan. It always excited Jimmy more than any other subject. It had all the drama, detail, color, and meanness of sports — but the stakes were out there where the meter did not register.

His interest was purely as an analyst, as a spectator. Only once in his life did he ever actively involve himself in a political campaign, and that was for the best of reasons: revenge. In 1963, when he was forced to close his Vegas Turf and Sports Club by the Justice Department, he had three opportunities to sell, to pay off his debts and walk away with a little dignity. The office of the then-governor of Nevada, Grant Sawyer, disapproved of each of the prospective buyers. Jimmy was broke and into bitter times.

Jimmy took it upon himself to work for the election of Saw-yer's Republican opponent, Paul Laxalt, whom he had never met. He went to the hotels and casinos and talked to the captains on each shift. He knew most of them from Steubenville. There was a kind of Steubenville ex-students' association in Las Vegas, maybe 400 of them who learned the gambling business there. The captains talked to the dealers, and the wives of the neigh-bors, and they got out to vote.

Laxalt won. When they met for the first time, a few weeks before the election, Laxalt remarked that he had heard about Jimmy's efforts. As Rick said to Louie at the Casablanca airport, it was the start of a beautiful friendship.

Jimmy made an election bet in 1960, on the Kennedy–Nixon race, and lost. He was settled in Las Vegas by then, and arguing politics almost daily with Wilbur Clark, who owned the Desert Inn and helped put Las Vegas on the map. Wilbur was a silent partner of Jimmy's in the Vegas Turf and Sports Club, but when it came to elections he loved to test him.

That year Jimmy did not think John F. Kennedy could even win his party's nomination.

"He's a living cinch to get it," Wilbur said.

"I'm not so sure," Jimmy said. "He has to beat Johnson and Stevenson."

"I'll bet you $25,000," Wilbur said, waving a hand. "You can pay me when you get it."

Jimmy should have known better. Wilbur had the surest instinct of anyone he knew when it came to elections. He could *feel* the winner; he also knew John Kennedy, a personal touch that made his opinion even stronger. Kennedy had stopped in Las Vegas once. In those years, anybody important enough to have a Social Security number stayed at the Desert Inn, and Wilbur had his picture taken with the young senator. From that moment on, he was one of Wilbur's favorites.

The morning after Kennedy won the West Virginia primary, Jimmy walked into Clark's office.

"Who do you think just called me?" he asked.

"Who, Wilbur?" Jimmy said, innocently.

"The next president of the United States," he said, "that's who."

To make a long story short, Jimmy lost the $25,000 bet on the nomination. As the election neared, his figures indicated it was a toss-up. Kennedy was a big favorite. After famous television debates he moved out at 2-to-1, then 11-to-5, and was now holding at 2½-to-1. No matter how he figured, it kept coming out a toss-up, a photo finish.

Wilbur disagreed. "Kennedy's a cinch," he said. "A living cinch."

"Wilbur, I've gone over this thing a hundred times and I'm telling you, this election is a coin flip."

"If you really think so," he said, his eyes lighting up, "I'd like to make a bet — a big one. I'll bet you $100,000 and lay two and a half to one."

"Okay," Jimmy said, "your 100,000 against my 40,000. And if it's my last $40,000, I'm going to take it, because I know this race is even money."

"You might think it is," Wilbur said, "but I think it's ten to one."

In other matters of chance, Wilbur Clark could not pick his nose. He had horses, but they won when he did not bet them and lost when he did. In the casino he was a cipher, but he had this *feel* for politics.

"Are you going to lay this off, Jimmy? Or are you going to keep it all yourself?"

Jimmy never lied to Wilbur. "I'm keeping it myself."

Wilbur nodded. "All right," he said, "you'll be paying me off at $10,000 a month for four months."

Jimmy laughed. "I paid the $25,000 that way," he reminded him.

On election day they began to get the results from the eastern states. Kennedy was leading, but according to Jimmy's state-by-state breakdown, everything was developing the way it should. In some states it was even closer than he anticipated. Wilbur just kept grinning.

"I told you," he said. "Jack's a living cinch."

"Listen, baby," Jimmy said, "it ain't over yet. You got a long way to go."

"If you want it," he said, "you can have twenty-five to one for another thousand dollars."

"Damned right I want it," Jimmy said, "and on this one we'll pay off tomorrow."

"I'm glad I thought of it."

Jimmy just shook his head. "Wilbur, believe me, you're overlaying it."

The next morning they still did not know who was president. Nixon came in strong in the Midwest and in the West, just as Jimmy figured. Jimmy had a chance at winning $125,000, and the TV boys were still hedging.

Jimmy called Wilbur. "Mr. Clark," Jimmy said, "would you call this pick 'em?"

"Pick 'em, schmick 'em," he said. "Get my money ready."

It never occurred to Jimmy that he might lose. When the votes were in, Kennedy won it, by a plurality of fewer than 150,000 votes of the nearly 70 million cast.

For the next four months Jimmy worked for Wilbur Clark — at $10,000 a month. That whole year went to Wilbur Clark.

Jimmy at least felt vindicated in one respect: His figures were correct. By the time the 1964 election rolled around, even Lyndon Baines Johnson was aware of Jimmy's figures. In October of that year, he was to appear in Las Vegas on a Sunday, on a campaign swing through the western states. To coincide with his visit, Hank Greenspun, the publisher of the *Las Vegas Sun*, suggested Jimmy publish his state-by-state analysis for the weekend paper.

Jimmy was ready for him. According to his forecast, Johnson would win forty-four states, Barry Goldwater would take four, and two were undecided. As far as Jimmy was concerned, the election was off the board. When he wrote that Johnson should be 10 million-to-1, it made headlines in other newspapers around the country.

Johnson was flying into the city when Howard Cannon, the senator from Nevada who was in the traveling party, handed him a copy of the *Las Vegas Sun*, with Jimmy's column prominently displayed on page one. Johnson, who liked favorable polls only slightly better than his left eye, was euphoric. "We spend all that money taking our own polls," he said, "and for a quarter I can find out all I want to know in the Las Vegas paper." Then he turned to Cannon, "Does this fellow Snyder know what the hell he's talking about?"

"He'd better," the senator assured him, "because it means whether or not he eats."

Johnson folded the paper and put it in his coat pocket. "Well, Howard," he said, "if he's right, we've got to send him a button."

Completing the term of the slain John Kennedy, Johnson wanted desperately to be elected by a margin convincing enough to establish his own presidency. He won with what was then the largest popular vote and the widest popular margin in the nation's history.

A few days after the election, Jimmy received a small box in the mail from the White House. In it was a gold LBJ lapel pin.

Politicians, of course, do not respect neutrality. If you print results favorable to their cause, they react with gratitude, as though you somehow recognized the rightness of their position. Polls are a pure and simple form of research, and Jimmy's system differed from those used by the Harris or Gallup agencies. They based theirs on national percentages. Jimmy found that method faulty. He broke his down state by state, according to electoral votes. That was where the elections were won. A candidate could win a state by three or three million, but he would still get the same number of electoral votes.

In 1968, when the other polls had Nixon and Humphrey too close to call, Jimmy made the number on Nixon 4-to-1. He predicted that he would get 300 electoral votes. He got 301. On election night, Walter Cronkite's people at CBS kept phoning to check Jimmy's figures, and he stood by them. The only state he really missed was Texas, where George Wallace slipped in. Jimmy's people had contacted 164 political writers in Texas, and 163 thought Nixon would carry the state.

The work, in retrospect, that pleased Jimmy the most took place that year, in 1968. It was a tough year to be right. The nation suffered continuing spasms of guilt over the deaths of Dr. Martin Luther King, Jr., and Bobby Kennedy, a war that would not end, and riots on college campuses. It was a bad year for politics. It was a bad year for everything.

At least ten days before any convention, Jimmy correctly predicted all six places on the three presidential tickets: Nixon and Agnew, Humphrey and Muskie, Wallace and LeMay.

As early as 1966, Jimmy described Richard Nixon as the strongest candidate of the Republicans. Even his publisher, Hank Greenspun, thought he was crazy. They bet a box of cigars on it. It was obvious to Jimmy that Nixon was picking up brownie points all over the country. The Republicans had been butchered in 1964 with the Goldwater candidacy after a bitter convention fight against Rockefeller. Nixon was the only one out in the field fighting for the party's candidates in the midterm elections. There was no way Goldwater's people would let Rockefeller have the nomination. George Romney had eliminated himself with his famous "I was brainwashed" quote after a trip to Vietnam, and Jimmy saw no one else emerging.

Picking Spiro Agnew as Nixon's running mate was something else. He listed him among six possibilities, including Jimmy Rhodes of Ohio, Gerald Ford, Chuck Percy, John Volpe, and Romney. It was clear that the Nixon ticket would be best served by a vice-presidential nominee from one of the midwest or border states. Nixon's strength was west of the Mississippi and in the South.

Rhodes, Romney, and Agnew were either uncommitted or leaning toward Rockefeller, with the convention two weeks away. Jimmy decided that the fellow who jumped first, and declared his support of Nixon, would get it. Within a day or two, Agnew, displeased by Rocky's indecision, announced his support for Nixon.

Jimmy's next column in the *Las Vegas Sun* declared that

Spiro Agnew, governor of Maryland, would be Nixon's choice as vice-president — and Nixon had not even been nominated yet. The ironic thing was that until he landed on the ticket in Miami, Jimmy did not even know Agnew was Greek. It never crossed his mind.

Picking Ed Muskie was a little easier. If you paid any attention to the speeches of Hubert Humphrey — it is surprising how many people did not — you would have detected certain flattering references to the gaunt senator from Maine. Muskie was a New Englander, and a Catholic, a good balance for the ticket. Jimmy projected Humphrey as the favorite from the start (100-to-1 after the death of Robert Kennedy). Had Bobby Kennedy lived, Jimmy believed he would have been persuaded to accept the second spot on a Humphrey–Kennedy ticket.

As for Curtis LeMay, the darkest shot of all, as George Wallace's American Party choice, that one was a tip. The night before he accepted Wallace's offer, LeMay called his old friend, Charles Barron, the retired air force general who was then an executive with the Sands Hotel. Jimmy had good information going for him.

By and large, the people in politics are not much different from those in sports. You project them to win and they interpret this to mean you are on their side. The reverse is equally true.

During any election, after any poll, Jimmy received his share of crank calls. Two out of every 100 that came into his office in that 1968 election were from Wallace supporters. Jimmy made the odds 500-to-1 that Wallace could not be elected, even though he had anywhere from eleven to sixteen percent of the vote at different times and people speculated he could throw the race into the electoral college.

One day, Jimmy's secretary buzzed his line, her voice a bit mused.

"It's somebody from the South," she guessed. Jimmy picked up the phone.

"Yew Jimmy the Greek?"

"Yeeesss."

"Yew sumbitch. What raht you got sayin' Guvnah Wallace is 500-to-1? What the sheet do yew know 'bout it? Would yew care to make a wajuh?"

Jimmy explained to the gentleman how the odds and the projections worked. Patiently, he told him that it was impossible for the governor to win the election, even if he forced it into the electoral college.

He said, "I tell yew what ahm gonna do. Ahm comin' up there with a hunnert thousan' dollahs and we'll see what kind of gambler yew are."

Jimmy said, "Sir, I don't gamble. It's against the law, you know, to bet on a presidential election."

"Well, then," he said, "yew just a lot of bullshit."

Then Jimmy got angry. "Sir, I'll tell you what. For me to cover your bet would be illegal. But if you'll bring the money here, you bring it to the state of Nevada, and I'll see that it gets covered." He hung up.

Dee Coakley, Jimmy's secretary, stared at him. "Mr. Snyder," she said, "do you know how much money that is, $100,000 at 500-to-1 odds?"

"That's all right, Dee," Jimmy assured her. "If he wins the bet I'll just make him a partner." Of course, neither the caller nor the money ever showed.

Chapter 16

Odds on Nixon and Impeachment

ON THE WALL IN Jimmy's Las Vegas office hung a framed cartoon by Jim Berry. It showed John Mitchell leaning over the shoulder of Richard Nixon. "I don't care what Gallup or Harris says," read the caption, "tell me what Jimmy the Greek says."

It was the original cartoon, inscribed by both the artist and the thirty-seventh president of the United States. Herb Klein, Nixon's press secretary back in the Ike days, later his "communications" director, mailed it to Jimmy. Klein was Jimmy's contact with the White House.

Jimmy could have been the greatest oddsmaker in the world, and he believed he was — and he would not have wanted to quote the odds in the spring of 1972 that Richard Nixon and Spiro Agnew would resign from the two highest offices in the land, shamed and broken men.

Jimmy was often asked, almost amusingly, if polls influenced elections. As events of that period unfolded, he suspected they did have a great deal of influence. Backing up just a bit, to July of 1970, Jimmy had a meeting in Chicago with Jack Anderson, who wanted Jimmy to establish odds and provide the polling for his syndicated political column.

"Greek, we've followed you closely and, damnit, you're always right," he said. "I want you with me. And we'll pay."

Jimmy made Jack a counterproposition. He would furnish

the polls to him exclusively, but his odds would continue to be available to any newspaper or any newsman asking for them. That was a rule he would not bend. Even when he later agreed to write a column of his own for Publisher's Hall Syndicate, it was on the condition that he would not hold back the odds. In other words, if a paper in opposition to one that carried his column called and asked for a number, he was free to give it to them. That represented one hell of a concession in the publishing business.

There was one other thing. He would not accept Anderson's money. He never accepted money for any work that involved politics. This was to avoid the risk of being compromised. Let's face it, he already had a touch of larceny in him.

Jack said, "However you want it. But let's do something on the potential candidates in 1972 as quickly as possible."

Jimmy said, "I'll have one for you in sixty days."

Two months later, Anderson released their poll. It showed Edmund Muskie comfortably in front for the Democratic nomination. More than that, they established Muskie as a 7-to-5 favorite over Nixon to win the presidency. The figures left no question; Nixon could be beaten. The stock market was in trouble. Unemployment was still rising. The war in Vietnam had widened, causing more grief. In May, Kent State had exploded.

Not long after Anderson's column appeared, Jimmy ran into Herb Klein in Los Angeles. He seemed cool. "Herb," Jimmy said, "don't be peeved with me because I made President Nixon an underdog to Muskie. That's the way it figured. If anything, I was light. The odds could have been a little higher."

What Jimmy did not know, and had no way of knowing until much later, was the wild reaction that poll caused in and around the White House. A Nixon aide later testified before the House Judiciary Committee that the Dirty Tricks Squad was organized soon after, to stop Ed Muskie, harass his campaign, and neutralize the lead that the poll — Jimmy's poll, in Anderson's column — showed him holding over President Nixon. Dirty Tricks begot the plumbers, and the plumbers begot Watergate.

Jimmy really did not want any of that on his conscience. It did, however, raise a point people missed throughout the long ordeal of Watergate. Time and again people asked, why? Why did they do it, when Nixon could have beaten McGovern by staying in bed (which he practically did)?

It was the Muskie candidacy, not McGovern's, that caused the Committee to Re-Elect the President (CREEP) its nervous moments, and led the president's men to bury him in the saddest political scandal the country has ever seen. They wanted to head off Muskie's nomination, if they could. All the funny games were first directed to that cause.

It started with a form of espionage not unfamiliar to the American political system. Somewhere along the line, it burst out of control. Money was spent; lies were told; power was misused on a scale the American public had never before imagined.

The phony letters, the fake stories, the sabotaged schedules — who can really measure how much those damaged the campaign of Ed Muskie? There is no question that the people at CREEP wanted McGovern, and McGovern they got.

It is a law of politics that whenever you match two candidates who are middle-of-the-road, the election will be close; for example, look at Kennedy and Nixon and Nixon and Humphrey. In fact, even though events were running Nixon's way by 1972, had either Muskie or Humphrey been the Democratic nominee, the race would have been tight. It is when a party selects a candidate from the edges, the far left or the far right, a Goldwater or a McGovern, that it gets stomped.

The first presidential sampling of Jimmy's seemed to have been more widely read than *Confessions of a French Secretary*. In December of 1970, Jimmy was in Washington, and Senator Cannon from Nevada invited him to drop by. He said someone wanted to meet him. He led him through the halls and downstairs and finally opened an office door. Sitting there behind a large desk was a statuesque figure, the lanky senator from Maine.

Ed Muskie smiled and thanked Jimmy for having made him the favorite. Jimmy started to explain that the numbers, not Jimmy the Greek, did that. Before he could, he said, "I want you to know we printed 50,000 copies of the Anderson column, mailed them out, and raised nearly $400,000."

"Well, that's fine, Senator," Jimmy said with a grin, "but where's my end?"

They chatted about the upcoming Democratic primaries

and Jimmy was startled to hear Muskie say the important one was in Florida.

"What's important about it?" Jimmy asked.

"I've got to win it to knock Hubert out."

"Senator," Jimmy said, "neither one of you is going to win down there. Wallace is going to win it."

He flashed Jimmy a tolerant smile and said, "Ohhh, we're going to win it, all right."

Jimmy said, "Senator, you better get up to New Hampshire. Play the ones you got. Stay cool in Florida."

Jack Anderson had told Jimmy that, whatever else they did, he needed the Florida outcome badly. In January of that new political year, Jimmy's staff got on top of it. Florida was a beast of a race that discouraged most of the other pollsters. There were eleven candidates. They called it in the exact order of finish, right down the line, with almost the exact percentages. It was Wallace, Muskie, Humphrey, with Jackson a close fourth. Anderson went out of his skull.

Jimmy had refined his research considerably since 1948, when he picked Harry Truman to win on the basis of Dewey's mustache. They broke down their polling into three categories: issues, image, and support. Under them were twenty-seven criteria. For example, they had Nixon 100-to-1 over McGovern (it could have been more) on a line that looked like this:

NIXON		McGOVERN
	Issues	
10	Foreign Affairs	2
10	Business	2
7	Military	1
9	Law and Order	7
7	Busing	3
7	Economy	6
7	Welfare	7
8	Farm Subsidy	10
7	Federal Spending	7
3	Revenue Sharing	3
6	Vietnam	4
81		52

Image

10	Recognition	8
9	Politician	4
7	Credibility	3
7	Charisma	5
7	Intelligence	4
9	Religion	8
49		32

Support

10	Foreign Support	1
8	Financial	3
10	Republicans	½
4	Democrats	6
10	Big Business	2
6	Jewish-Americans	4
6	Independents	3
6	Labor	4
5	Youth	5
3	Minorities	6
68		34½

No president was ever elected with a larger mandate than Richard Nixon appeared to have, from every corner of American life. If ever a man's fortunes seemed to be ascending, if anyone's future ever looked golden, it was Richard Nixon's. By the time the election was over, Jimmy the Greek was known as President Nixon's favorite pollster, and occupying the second highest office in the land was another Greek. Jimmy's future did not look so bad, either.

Then came the self-destruction of Spiro Agnew. Jimmy had already established him as the favorite for the Republican nomination in 1976. There was no doubt in anyone's mind that he would head the party's ticket. He was the living embodiment of the great American dream sequence. Nowhere else in the world can a fellow fall out of bed one morning and find himself a star, and having achieved that, disappear as quickly or completely.

Jimmy's information was that Agnew resigned for reasons other than his tax problem or the charge that he accepted graft from Baltimore County contractors. Jimmy was told that he was willing to fight that, and felt he could win. But he had attended certain motel parties while he was the governor of Maryland, and did not want to put his family through the gossip that would result.

Has there ever been a more ill-fated pair in the history of the American government? Agnew's downfall coincided with the rough beginnings of Watergate and, suddenly, the country felt as though it were on a road never traveled before, taking us we knew not where with no comfort station for miles.

Jimmy did not think he felt much differently from most Americans during that time. He excluded the partisan or the idealogue, who always prefers someone else. Most of the public wanted to believe that their president was not guilty of anything.

Jimmy's own feelings were complicated by the fact that he met Julie Eisenhower, through friends at the *Saturday Evening Post*, and he was quite fond of her. He had, however, kept his distance from the president, for reasons that had to do with the integrity of his polls. He tried hard to avoid the appearance of taking sides.

At a party in Minneapolis held in Jimmy's honor, he met Hubert Humphrey. This was shortly after he made McGovern a 2-to1 favorite for the 1972 nomination. He arrived late from a speech in Youngstown, and all the guests rose when he walked into the room. "Well," Jimmy cracked, "I'm glad to see the senator has arrived to find that he's a two-to-one underdog."

Humphrey grabbed Jimmy's hand and pumped it. "Jimmy," he said, "at this moment I know your odds are absolutely right. But I'm going to upset them, because I intend to work hard enough to win it."

Jimmy said, "Senator, I hope you do."

A few weeks later Jimmy was sitting in the box of Bob Strauss at the convention, when Humphrey appeared on the floor. Everyone converged on him. After a while, he looked over and noticed Jimmy sitting alone. Jimmy waved at him. Suddenly, he realized Humphrey was walking over to shake hands. He was not sure that was a good idea at the time, so he bounced out of his seat and met him halfway. He wished him luck and told him — and he believed it — that he considered him one of the great Americans.

Jimmy had enduring affection for Humphrey. He was one of those politicians who overdosed on goodwill and good humor, qualities that the people consistently reject. He believed he would have been a superior president.

At the time, there was no reason to believe that Dick Nixon would not be. He winded down the war in Vietnam, opened a bridge to Russia and Red China. The stock market recovered. The campuses cooled down.

Watergate was characterized by Ron Zieglar as "a third-rate burglary," and not many rose to argue with that. It attracted only scattered paragraphs in the papers. No one paid much attention to it.

But all through 1973 it would not go away. It was like living in London right after the war. Every other week some damned half-buried bomb, some forgotten war souvenir, exploded in your yard. The first inkling of unrest in the Nixon administration became evident to Jimmy when Pete Peterson resigned as secretary of commerce. He said, "I got tired of clicking my heels." Jimmy did not know what he meant at the time. Later, when the stories about Haldeman and Ehrlichman began to surface, he understood.

The first time anyone was curious enough to raise the question, Jimmy made the odds 1,000-to-1 that Nixon would not be impeached.

Art Buchwald, among others, had a dollar on that. He gave a few of his other writer friends — Shana Alexander, Pete Axthelm, and John Merryman — odds of 100-to-1 for a buck that Nixon would finish his term. He had them sign their dollars for his collection, a practice he picked up from Harold Salvey the night he bet the midget.

Then in January of 1974, as soon as the football season ended (first things first), Jimmy decided to take a hard look at Watergate. He could see it turning uglier, but he had the gut feeling that Nixon would survive; although, he could no longer rally the country with his dramatic travels. "Nixon," Jimmy told his friend, "is plus six abroad and minus twelve at home."

Jimmy put his office to work finding out what Congress thought about impeachment. It could no longer be ignored. The speculation leaped with every new disclosure, with each move:

the eighteen-minute gap in the tapes, the firing of Archibald Cox, the transcripts, and the sparring with Leon Jaworski. For the first time in centuries people stopped talking about sex.

They polled Congress. It was 91 against impeachment, 64 in favor, with 105 undecided. That projected 50-to-1 that Nixon would not be impeached.

For months, Jack Anderson and Jimmy argued constantly. He knew that Jimmy felt some sympathy for President Nixon. Jack was convinced of his guilt, and certain that Nixon's presidency was doomed. Now, Jack Anderson, from a moral standpoint, was damned near a saint. He was Mormon, had nine kids, did not smoke or drink, and Jimmy had been around him enough to know that away from his wife he never looked at another female. He probably had more information in his files than the FBI, but Jimmy never knew of him to use it maliciously. He did not knock people for mischief. He would not hurt anyone intentionally, unless it involved an act or deed that affected the way the government worked. He was totally honest.

With Jimmy, Jack knew it was a case of math, not politics. Just a month before the last tape showed — the "smoking pistol" tape — Jimmy insisted it was still 2-to-1 that Nixon would not be impeached.

"Jimmy," he said, "you're crazy. You're dead wrong."

Jimmy looked beyond the obvious. By then, he was a slight underdog in the Congress, but there were three other factors that figured into Nixon's future: (1) he could be censured, set down by Congress, for ninety days, (2) he could volunteer to step aside for an indefinite period, (3) he could resign. Jimmy did not say whether or not he was guilty, but when you added the four "possibilities" it boiled down to simple math: 2-to-1 that he would not be *impeached*.

Jimmy stopped quoting odds in public. For months Watergate had been a rich new vein of material for nightclub and television comics. One joke had Nixon calling in three immortal ex-presidents to confer with him. Washington advised him not to tell a lie. Jefferson urged him to follow the constitution. Lincoln suggested that he go see whatever was playing at Ford's theater.

When the jokes stopped, Jimmy stopped. It became much too serious. A man's existence was at stake. His family was demonstrating, almost daily, a larger capacity for public suffering. In such cases the odds often became a part of the results. As a matter of policy, Jimmy did not set odds on moments of urgency or life-and-death situations.

He was still in touch with Herb Klein, who had been squeezed out of the White House some time before by Haldeman and Ehrlichman. But President Nixon called him back when the trouble got thick. Herb was the guy who supervised the preparation of the transcripts, who put the books together. The Wednesday before it all blew up, Jimmy asked Herb, "How about these tapes that are going to Jaworski? Will they kill Nixon or what?"

Herb said, "No, there isn't anything on there they don't already know."

Klein believed that, Jimmy was sure. But in Jimmy's business, you were only as good as your information, a point he frequently made. He was certain Nixon would quit if it appeared he lacked the votes in the Senate to turn back impeachment. The day the last tape was exposed — and with it Nixon's early knowledge of the cover-up — he still had thirty-nine senators who favored acquittal, enough to win. It did not matter now. They found the smoking gun, without which Wiggins and Sandman and the other Republicans on the Judiciary Committee insisted there was no case.

A few hours before the news broke on television, Jimmy received a phone call from Julie Eisenhower's publisher at the *Saturday Evening Post*, Dr. Cory Cervas. She was sobbing, almost incoherent. "Jimmy," she said, "I want you to send a telegram. Tell the president not to resign. This cannot happen. It must not happen."

Jimmy could not think of anything to say. He knew there was nothing he could put in a telegram that would change anyone's mind. She kept insisting Jimmy should send the wire: "He mustn't quit. He mustn't. Jimmy, we still have time."

Jimmy knew she reflected what Julie felt, what she must have said to her a few minutes earlier. All Jimmy could say was, "Cory, I'm sorry. I'm so sorry." She was still crying when he hung up the phone.

It was all over. Within the hour, Jimmy heard from two

close friends, Jack Kemp, the Buffalo congressman and former quarterback (and in 1996 Bob Dole's vice-presidential running mate), and Senator Howard Cannon. Jimmy did what he was sure millions of Americans were doing that afternoon. He turned on his television set and listened to a statement by Wiggins, Nixon's staunch defender in the House, calling for the president to resign. A few moments later, a television newsman read the letter of resignation that carried the signature of Richard M. Nixon. The date was August 8, 1974.

Jimmy reflected on the bitter irony of politics, of life. Two men who might have been president, Ted Kennedy and Spiro Agnew, were out of the picture (Kennedy for now, Agnew forever), and a man who had been president had left in dishonor.

In a curious way, Jimmy's reputation as a political analyst benefited from the career of Richard Nixon: through his close defeat to John F. Kennedy, his comeback from the political tombs, his election in 1968, and his landslide victory over McGovern.

Jimmy was not a moralizer, and he had no profound point to offer from all of this. If he learned anything, it was that politicians are the biggest gamblers of all. No one ever gambled for higher stakes than Richard Nixon.

Chapter 17

The Tracks: What You Know Won't Hurt You

LATE IN 1953, NOT LONG after Jimmy's Saudi Arabian fiasco, he was hanging around New York, when a friend introduced him to Charlie White. He was an Atlantic City bookmaker, an intense little man with the look of custom tailoring. When he dressed for an evening, he used three different colognes.

"Greek," he said, "I've heard about you, that you know how to bet, how to book, everything."

Jimmy blushed attractively and said, "I haven't been active lately. I'm looking for oil. I've been away from betting."

Charlie had a proposition. He was barred from the track at Atlantic City, but had some action going the next day and needed someone reliable to handle it. Jimmy planned to go out anyway and was obliged.

He handed Jimmy an envelope containing $6,000 in hundreds. He said to watch for a certain jockey, in three races, when his horse was in the paddock. "If he takes off his cap to smooth his hair with his hand, you bet him $1,000 to win and $1,000 to show. If he doesn't take off his cap, don't bet the race."

Jimmy stared at him. "You've *got* to bet it," he said, "either way."

"What do you mean?" Charlie asked. "How can you bet it either way?"

"Look. If he doesn't take off his hat, he's telling us he

doesn't think his horse can win, right? Then that eliminates one mount. Now, it depends on the price of the horse. If he's sitting on anything up to a six-to-one shot, and he doesn't give us the signal, I think we should bet the favorite because his chances are now improved by fifteen percent."

"How do you know that?"

"Here," Jimmy said, taking out a pencil. "It's simple. Six plus one equals seven, and seven into 100 is almost fifteen." Jimmy was amazed that an experienced bookmaker did not know percentages, but he figured he may have been testing him.

"All right," he said, "do it your way. But keep an eye on him. Watch him every second he's in the paddock. He knows somebody will be watching him."

"Do you want me to wear anything special?"

"No," he said, "that doesn't make a difference."

Now this, Jimmy thought, *is a great system. The jockey doesn't know him. Jimmy doesn't know the jockey. The jockey doesn't know who he is signaling, or who is looking for it.*

The next day at the track Jimmy checked the prices on their jockey's three mounts: they were 6-to-1, 4-to-1, and 5-to-2. His first appearance was in the third race, and when he moved into the paddock, Jimmy was on the bridge between the grandstands, looking down. The jockey never moved. Jimmy went to the favorite and placed the bets, including $200 of his own, which constituted most of his worldly assets.

The favorite won and paid $5. He was ahead a couple of thousand with Charlie's money and won $300 for himself.

On the jockey's next race the cap came off and he brushed back his hair, and Jimmy bet everything. His horse dropped from 5-to-1 to 3-to-1. He charged out of the gate like the Light Brigade and won it, wire to wire, and paid $8.

For the last race, Jimmy was on the favorite, the 5-to-2 shot. His eyes never left him in the paddock. He edged up in the saddle, fixed the stirrups, and adjusted the bridle. Jimmy leaned over the rail of the bridge. The jockey went under Jimmy without touching the cap.

It was like candy for the soul, Jimmy thought, and he had somebody else's money on top of it. Charlie instructed Jimmy to bet $1,000 to win and show on each race, but if ever a guy should plunge, Jimmy thought, this was it. He did not really know him well enough to take the chance. At least if they lost, he had the tickets to show him. He pressed the bet.

With the favorite out, he went to the second choice, a 3-to-1 shot. On the way to the $100 window, the price dropped to 2-to-1, and the horse their jockey was on moved to 4-to-1. It looked as though other people had the same information he had, which made it all the stronger.

Everything was all right until the eighth pole, with Jimmy's horse in front by two lengths. Now who do you think came roaring up? Yeah, the jockey whose horse was not supposed to win. That did not keep him from trying. He was beating the hell out of his horse, laying the whip to both sides, and closing fast. Jimmy was about to croak. The finish was a photo . . . but they won.

That night Jimmy went to Charlie White's house. His eyeballs did a pirouette when Jimmy handed him his winnings, around $15,000, and a breakdown on the bets and payoffs for each race. He pressed a bonus of $1,500 into Jimmy's hand and asked for a favor. "I got all these betting slips here," he said, nodding at a cardboard box on his desk. "You got the winners of today's races, you know what they paid. Do my bookkeeping for me, Greek, just tonight, as a favor."

When Jimmy finished the books, he told Charlie that he cleared about $22,000 for the day, including his own bets.

"How about staying on?" Charlie asked. "You stay, you got $200 a day and a piece. Everybody knows Charlie takes real good care of his people."

Jimmy found out later that Charlie struggled to read and write. Jimmy thanked him, but told him he had other plans. He did not even stick around for a party he was having that night in his home, and a lot of beautiful ladies were going to be there. Charlie was a lady-killer.

Two days later, back at Jimmy's apartment in New York, there was a knock at the door. Two fellows walked in, blue suits and rotary club faces, flashing a badge. They were the FBI. They asked if Jimmy knew a Charlie the Blade, a bookmaker in Atlantic City.

Jimmy thought fast. "I knew a Charlie White," he said.

"How do you know him?"

"I'm a handicapper," Jimmy said. "I offered him a deal for my services, but he thought the price was too high."

After a few more questions they left, and that was the end of it. How long the FBI had been trailing Charlie, or why, Jimmy did not know, nor did he care to know. Years later, Jimmy heard that Charlie had opened a successful gambling house in London, with George Raft, the actor, briefly involved.

Jimmy always considered the racetrack a kind of sanctuary. He never bet the horses professionally, as part of his livelihood. Racing was his recreation, his therapy. Other guys went out and got drunk. Jimmy went to the track. It was his spa, a place to relax and have fun.

Jimmy felt a grace and leisure, a mellowness, around a racetrack that was not present in other sports. Horses took your money just as fast, and that was the trick. It helped your enjoyment if you assumed from the start that, sooner or later, the track would end up with your money. It was fun, and it was not hard-core gambling, *if you did not bet more than you could afford to lose.* Of course, it did not exactly dilute your pleasure to win.

Some of Jimmy's gayer afternoons were spent in Miami, when his ex-father-in-law, old man Miles, had his horses running there. One morning Jimmy rode out to Hialeah with him to time a workout of Rush Act, a gelding he owned. Rush Act had finished out of the money his last six starts, but there was a reason for it. The old man caught his trainer playing games with his horses. He changed trainers, and no one really knew how to handicap Rush Act. Now he was down to $7,500 claiming races, and entered the next day at seven furlongs.

In the workout, he breezed three-quarters of a mile in a minute, $12^2/_5$. The computer in Jimmy's head began to whir. The horse was ready, and the next time he was a cinch to be at least 20-to-1 on the morning line, off his record.

Rush Act opened at 40-to-1. As Jimmy watched that mercury thermometer at Hialeah, he went to 60, 80, and finally 100-to-1. Jimmy's adrenaline pumped. The favorite was a horse named Johnny J., owned by a clique out of Canton, another wide-open Ohio town. Johnny J. was 6-to-5, and a couple of bus loads of tourists from Canton were betting him like crazy. Quietly, Jimmy began buying tickets on Rush Act, $20 across, $10 across, $5 across. To condense a long story: Jimmy made a fairly substantial bet, maybe $200 across the board. His price came down only a little, so he bet another $50 across.

By the time the field went off, he was 35-to-1. Johnny J. broke in front and led until right at the wire, when Rush Act (apt name) came in to win. Jimmy let out a yell that turned every Flamingo in Hialeah white. The horse paid $77 to win, $30 to place, and $13 to show. It took Jimmy *four* days to cash in all the tickets at the $2, $5, and $20 windows. It was one of the most memorable periods of recreation he had ever known. He won close to $20,000.

Around that time, old man Miles claimed one of Alfred Vanderbilt's handicap horses, Speed to Spare, and was running him at Tropical Park, with Don Meade, the jockey.

Meade was a lively character, who had an unusual, wild riding style. In close quarters he was known to use both the whip and an occasional half-nelson. Don led the nation's riders in winning mounts in 1941, but was later suspended in Florida for betting on horses that happened to be competing with his own.

If Don Meade wanted to ride a particular horse, no one could ride it better, especially if he came out of the gate with a speed-burner. Jimmy went down to the saddling path with Mr. Miles, who was a beautiful old fellow, but so tight he squeaked.

"Don," the old man said, "you got a good horse. You've got a good chance to win."

"I'm sure I do," Meade said, "but it would be nice to have something going for me."

With Meade there was no bullshit. Jimmy loved him for that. Jimmy waited until Miles stepped away and he whispered to Meade, "I'm betting $2,000. You got a piece of mine." His face was expressionless. Jimmy wanted Don Meade on his side. The old man did not seem to understand him, but Jimmy read him perfectly.

"You're going to get $750," Miles said when he came back. "Ten percent of the purse. I think that's pretty good." Jimmy kept his eye on Meade. Finally, he nodded, just once, without looking at Jimmy.

Meade broke Speed to Spare in front and had him three

lengths in the lead coming into the stretch. He started to short-en his stride, but Meade held him together to win by a half length. The win was worth a grand to the jockey, plus his ten per-cent of the purse. Don Meade may have been the best rider ever lifted onto a horse.

Bookmakers were not always so sporting. What you have to accept is the fact that bookmakers do not like for other people to make excessive sums of money, at least not on bets they book. They maintain that this leads to inflation, gout, and other un-pleasant human conditions. Whenever possible, to shelter their own losses the boys indulged in a practice known as "laying off."

The best Jimmy ever knew at this art, as it applied to race-tracks, was Jimmy Carroll of St. Louis, the cradle of horse books. Sid Wyman and Charlie Rich had large offices there, furnished somewhat sparsely with a desk and a couple of chairs. In those days, people could wire their bets to St. Louis, and many did. Jimmy Carroll was the official price maker on horses at the time, though not the extravagant gambler many assumed he was. Carroll would take a sizeable wager but would dump a percent-age of it into the racetrack pool to lower the price on the horse he booked, thereby reducing his risk.

No one really knew what Carroll was doing, but by accident Jimmy discovered one day where, and how, he managed to lay it off. Jimmy knew a trainer named Red at Oaklawn Park, in Hot Springs, Arkansas, who was a heavy bettor. He did not run horses for the improvement of the breed or even to win purses. He ran them to bet. He phoned Jimmy one afternoon at his of-fice in Steubenville.

"Greek, I got some horses down here, and they're ready to run. Can you bet for me? If they knew it was me it would kill the price."

"How much are you thinking about?"

"Up to $3,000 across," he said.

"That's no problem, Red, so long as I get the total bet. I don't want you giving it to me and then to somebody else too."

"You got it all," he said.

If you're running a betting stable — that is, betting your own horses — the object is to get the biggest possible price. If you give out the horse to everybody, you are just not helping your cause.

The fewer people who know about it, the higher the price. Jimmy phoned Jimmy Carroll in St. Louis. He agreed to take up to $5,000 across the board from Jimmy. He also assured Jimmy that he would not dump any of the bet into the track itself.

"But," he told Jimmy, "I want the bet at least half an hour before post time."

A few days later Red phoned in the morning from Hot Springs with a horse. Jimmy waited until the afternoon, half an hour before the post, and called Carroll. Jimmy placed the $5,000 across. After the race, Red called, boiling mad.

"We won it," he said, "but I only got two-to-one."

"What the hell happened to the price?"

"Within a couple minutes to post," said Red, "the horse was six-to-one. All at once $3,000 hit across the board — just like that, three-three-three. The horse only paid $6, $3.20 and $2.40. Greek, the son-of-a-bitch musta dumped it. What do we do now?"

Jimmy did not want to go off half-cocked. "Let's give him another chance," Jimmy said. "Maybe it was somebody else."

The next time Red phoned, he had a long shot. They went through the same procedure. His horse lost by a head on this one, but the money showed again. They got a poor price for place and show. When Red told Jimmy about it, he knew for sure that Carroll dumped the money at the track.

"I'll have to find somebody else to take the bets," Jimmy said.

To his surprise, Red did not agree. "No, stay with Carroll one more time," he said. "I've got an idea."

Jimmy decided not to argue with him. They were his horses and his money. Besides, Jimmy knew Red as a cunning fellow, slightly unpolished, but not easily used. A few days later he called with another horse.

"Do it just like you always do," he said. "Only this time see if you can get down for another thousand dollars across."

Jimmy asked Carroll if he could press the extra thousand for him. "Make it six across," Jimmy said.

"We can handle it," Carroll responded.

This time Red was late in calling back. Jimmy was curious. An hour and a half after the race, Jimmy's phone rang. Red was laughing.

"What happened?" Jimmy asked.

"We won it," he said, between whoops. "We got $18 to win, $9 to place, $6.80 to show."

"No money showed?"

Jimmy had to wait for a moment while Red composed himself. "*Nobody* showed," he finally bellowed.

Then he told Jimmy the story. It seemed that across the street from the entrance to Oaklawn Park was a drugstore. A couple of clerks from Carroll's office parked there in between races, waiting near the phone booth. Carroll would call, give them their instructions, and they would trot across to the track and bet whatever he told them.

This day the scenario was a little different. Red staked out the store and was ready for them. When the runners started across the street, a car swung up to the curb and three guys piled out. One of them shouted, "Hold it right there." He flashed a badge and ordered the two stooges into the car. They drove aimlessly around Hot Springs for an hour, during which time Carroll's men offered the cops a bribe — $100 apiece, probably — to let them go. They took the money and finally shoved them out the door, knowing the race was long since over. The phony cops, of course, were hired by Red, but you would never know by looking at them. They had the dark suits, the plain brown shoes that needed a shine, the Dick Tracy hats. One way or another, justice was served.

Jimmy's theory of winning consistently at the races consisted of two steps: research, and backing a great horse. If you are one of those people who thinks he has a system that cannot lose, the track will send a car and meet you at the airport.

In the years when Native Dancer and Tom Fool were running, Jimmy practically supported himself by betting on them. He placed big bets. He once put up $50,000 on Tom Fool to win $10,000, that was how sure he was.

In 1959 he could have nearly retired from what he stood to win on Sword Dancer in the Kentucky Derby. He took odds of up to 15-to-1 in the Winter Book at Caliente, on down to 3-to-1, and by the day of the race he bet a total of $20,000 across. In the stretch, Sword Dancer lost by a nostril in a photo finish to Tommy Lee. Though Jimmy made out on place and show, clearing

$90,000, he figured to win fifteen times that much. The kicker was, while Sword Dancer went on to be chosen Horse of the Year, Tommy Lee won only one more race in his career, an overnight in California.

All of which recalls the old horseplayer's lament: "I hope I break even; I need the money."

It takes patience to develop a great horse. It does not happen in two or three races. When it happens, though, it can be money in the bank for anyone along for the ride. Of course, inside information is the coin of the racetrack — and sometimes even that can backfire.

In 1949 Jimmy was at a dinner party in Fort Lauderdale, attended by Jimmy Jones, son of the legendary Ben, the trainer for Calumet Farm. The year before, they won the Triple Crown with Citation. Now they had the Winter Book favorite for the Kentucky Derby in Blue Peter.

At the party that night, Jimmy Jones let a bomb drop. "Blue Peter won't be ready for the Derby," he said. "He hasn't been running up to expectations."

Fred Hooper had a horse called Olympia, and with Blue Peter out of it, Jimmy knew Olympia listed as 10-to-1 in the Winter Book, loomed as the favorite. The price figured to drop to maybe 3-to-1.

"We'll have Ponder ready," Jimmy Jones said, casually, "but it will be June before he's even close to his best stride." Jimmy sympathized with Jones, but when he said that, he mentally scratched Ponder. After dinner Jimmy could not get back to Twenty-third Street in Miami Beach fast enough, rubbing his hands all the way. Everyone there had an opinion on the Derby. Twenty-third Street was a supermarket for people wanting to bet horses. That night Jimmy must have laid $15,000 on Olympia for the Derby, with odds of up to 12-to-1.

Jimmy watched the odds on Olympia drop with the inner contentment of a man who put his money in gold bullion shortly before the market crash of 1929. Olympia went to the post as the favorite, at 4-to-5, with Eddie Arcaro in the saddle.

Olympia broke out in front, stayed there for a mile, and finished sixth, barely in time to hear the last chorus of "My Old Kentucky Home." You will never guess which horse won: Ponder.

Ponder paid $34 to win, and Jimmy did not have so much as a bus token bet on him. It is trying to understand such matters that will keep a horseplayer's brain, and also his belly, lean and hard.

But to demonstrate how racing luck really works, one of the best days Jimmy ever had at the track was a day when he forgot to take any money. He went to Gulfstream Park with a friend, Peter Van Vaks, and while he bought the tickets, Jimmy dropped off the car at the valet parking. It was not until he was inside that he realized he left his cash on his dresser at home. Pete was already off, wandering through the stands, blocking an aisle someplace.

Jimmy reached in his pocket and scooped up the change and counted it. He had $2.80, enough for a $2 bet in the first race. English Bid was the horse's name. He won and it paid $50. A trainer Jimmy knew, F. W. Martin, had three horses running that day. Jimmy happened to land on the first two, then he parlayed everything on Martin's horse in the last race. This one came in and paid $9. At the moment, Jimmy's physical tone was splendid. He just cashed in and took the package home.

When Jimmy walked in, Charles, who worked around the house for him then, was waiting at the door. "Mr. Snyder," he said, "you forgot your money."

"No, I didn't, Charles."

"Oh, yes, you did, sir."

Jimmy reached into his pocket and pulled out a roll that would have choked a rhino. It contained $7,000. "Then where," Jimmy said grinning at him, "did this come from?"

Charles scratched his head. "I don't know, Mr. Snyder, but the money you had here, it's still here."

When Jimmy went to the track, he was not pulled by the betting. A light lunch, a little wine, good company, fast horses, and slow judgment was his idea of a day at the races. He enjoyed challenging the board, knowing that in the long run he could only finish second.

There were many other times in the years that followed that he wished he had forgotten to take his money.

Chapter 18

Nick the Greek
Wanted a Peek

"THE GREATEST EXPERIENCE IN life is winning a bet, and the second greatest is losing one." So said Nick the Greek, many times.

There was a kind of faded elegance about Nicholas Dandolos in the final years of his life. He was like a once-rich European aristocrat, living in an empty mansion. The servants were gone. Drop cloths covered what was left of the furniture. The electricity was turned off, but he still dressed for dinner every night.

He was Nick the Greek, once the biggest name in gambling, and, in a way Jimmy did not always enjoy, an important figure in his life. He was the stereotyped movie gambler with a smooth, almost oily charm, complemented by a mean, suspicious mind.

He died broke in 1966 at eighty-three, owing Jimmy money and hating him too. By then he hated the world, because it would not let him be Nick the Greek forever.

Jimmy spent most of his first fifteen years in Las Vegas trying to outgrow being confused with Nick by strangers, but the professionals never confused them.

"I bet $50,000 on a football game once," Nick boasted one night sitting at a card table.

Jimmy let it pass; but a bookmaker named Pittsy Manheim did not. He winked at Jimmy and turned toward Nick. "Hell, that's nothing, Nick," he said. "I know a Greek who once bet a *quarter of a million* on one game."

The boys at the table laughed. Nick glared at Jimmy and the space above his collar reddened. They were not from the same generation, but their roots were one. Jimmy respected Nick at one time — Greek children are raised to honor their elders. But to him, Nick was a counterfeit. He had been a Greek with notoriety, one of the few – *once*. He did not like the idea of anyone moving in on his territory.

Jimmy was quite sure that Nick the Greek's fame did not hurt him at all when he came along, and he could never take that away from him.

His legend enveloped Jimmy. It even prompted him to make Nick a business offer in 1951, five years before Jimmy moved to Las Vegas.

Jimmy was friendly with the Goulandris family, the Greek shipowners. (The six richest men in the world were Greek.) Jimmy was trying to persuade them to build a hotel in Vegas, which was just starting to boom. The Sands was not finished yet. It was that long ago. They looked at the land where Caesar's Palace now stands. The idea was for Nick to be the front man for the hotel, the general host. Nick the Greek was a name that said "gambling" like a neon sign.

Jimmy suggested to the Goulandris family that Nick deserved a hefty salary, plus five points in the hotel; that is, five percent of the profits. Over the years, it would have been worth millions. For Nick it was not enough. "I can get more points than that," he told Jimmy, "from any gambling house in zee vorld. Forget it, kid."

That killed the deal — and a five percent cut Jimmy would have collected too. Maybe, deep down, that is why Jimmy did not try harder to get along with him after he settled in Las Vegas.

They first met in 1950, in Florida, where Jimmy was in the oil business with Ray Ryan and was swapping football games with H. L. Hunt. Nick breezed in one day with Tom Whalen and Murph Calcatura, friends of Jimmy's out of St. Louis. They brought him out to Jimmy's home that winter and introduced them. Jimmy was fascinated by him. Nick told stories by the hour. He recited poetry. He had a deft touch with a phrase and said things like: "I would rather fall from a mountaintop than die of boredom on the plain."

They drank good wine together. Memory can be a con man, but that night Jimmy recalled wanting to like him. It was not that he needed his patronage. It was not a schoolboy thing, the student hoping for the professor's approval. There was just a certain amount of honest admiration for the name, for a fellow who prospered at the business of living by his wits. (Jimmy was out of it at the time, engaged at what he considered to be a witless profession of trying to take oil out of the ground.) He was, more or less, the original Greek.

It was remarkable to watch him in action. He attracted people who begged him to play with their money. It was the legend and the charm and, no doubt, the idea of sharing winnings with Nick the Greek. He was beautiful with women. He made Omar Sharif look like a truck driver.

He was at the peak of his fame then. He had an entertaining personality, and he bowed to ladies and kissed their hands. This and other odd mannerisms led to a popular belief that he was a cultured article. He also had a reputation, in the trade, for running games that were less than pure. In the old days he often traveled with two or three other guys, moving into a town and maneuvering a poker game with the local star or the local money. The star seldom had a chance. Two or three players against one represents almost impossible odds. Whenever one of them had a good hand, he got help in raising the pot against the town pigeon. That was how Nick went around winning all those big pots.

Not that he won them all, but he was invariably promoted as the big winner. He may actually have been among the best, once. When Las Vegas hit its stride, he was in games that were on the square with younger, sharper cats who knew the percentage on every card that turned up.

Jimmy always suspected that Nick's skills and his nerve never really caught up with his publicity. A magazine writer once described a scene in which Nick, sitting with kindred spirits in a parlor car of an eastbound train, passing through a light drizzle, made a bet on which raindrop would hit the bottom of the windowpane first. The bet was for around $500. By the time it reached print, the figure was up to $50,000.

In Miami, at the racetrack one day, Nick got Jimmy alone.

"Jeemmmy," he said, in his thick, old-country accent, "you got to do me favor. I got to play Ray Ryan again."

Nick and Ryan, it developed, had been in a poker game in Las Vegas, a $250,000 freeze-out. In a freeze-out, you cannot quit until you have *all* of the other guy's money. Under the rules, if you quit, you forfeit $50,000 automatically. There was not anyone who wanted to kiss off a fifty-grand forfeit. That night Ryan won it all, the $250,000, but Nick had another reason for wanting to play him again.

"Ryan had a peek on me," Nick insisted. "From behind me, he vas getting signals."

Jimmy later learned that Nick played poker like a sucker. He never looked at his cards the way a real player should: low and quick and turn them down. He held his cards high, fanned out. Nick was convinced that Ryan had a peek on him; that is, a conspirator read Nick's cards and tipped Ryan off. Jimmy knew Ryan better than that. Nick and Ryan never had another freeze-out, which did not exactly surprise Jimmy. Neither of them would play unless he thought he had an edge. But at least Ryan used his own money. Nick always had somebody else put up the bankroll.

A couple of days later Nick asked Jimmy to help him cheat Ryan. He not only wanted Jimmy to arrange the game, he wanted him to cheat. What he had in mind, he soon made clear, was for Jimmy to give *him* a peek on Ryan, for half the winnings. "It vould be easy, Jeem," he pointed out. "He ees your friend, and everyvun knows you are honest man."

Sure, Ray trusted Jimmy enough to open his hand to him. The rest would have been a cinch. A certain card, a certain signal — you light a match, touch an ear, a hundred ways of doing it. Jimmy refused, informing Nick that he found his style of larceny a bit crude, and he intended to tell Ryan (which he did). Nick was offended. "I vas mistaken," he said. "I thought you vas a gentleman."

That was the beginning of the tension between them. At the time, Nick the Greek was sixty-seven and on his way down. The old ways did not work anymore, but he could not let go of the past. He was getting bankrolled less and less. His judgment grew more erratic.

In a curious offshoot to all this, Nick was arrested by the FBI in 1963, along with two or three others, on charges of conspiring to extort money from Ray Ryan.

The problem was, to some people Nick was still a kind of elder statesman, and they believed him. He kept yelping that Ryan owed him; he still thought he was cheated. Word got around, and one day a couple of young tough guys set out to collect on Nick's behalf. They held Ryan for maybe a day, but Ryan was cool enough to get some people on the phone who could straighten it out. In the meantime, they made the error of driving across the Nevada line into California, and the FBI got interested. Later, the charges against Nick were dropped, but the two young guys who muscled Ryan were put away for a year or so, as Jimmy recalled.

Back in 1959, about the time Jimmy settled in to Las Vegas and resumed gambling, he could not avoid Nick. They sat in on frequent card games and their contacts were polite. Then one night, at the Fremont, they were playing lowball poker. Jimmy never really liked cards, but when he moved to Las Vegas he knew he had to learn to play at least one game well, because it was practically the town sport. (It was like an executive learning to play golf.)

Jimmy picked lowball. You take the five lowest cards of the six dealt — two down and one up, then three more up, one at a time. He went into a complete study of it. He even put lowball hands on a computer in Santa Monica. He learned the value of the hand according to what was in the pot.

This night they were playing 160–320; the minimum bet was $160 on the first three cards, $320 on the fifth and sixth. The betting got to Nick, who had a nine up, and he raised it $160. Jimmy was to the left of him, the last man, with an eight up and a deuce-trey in the hole — the better hand in three-card. His hand actually called for a raise, but he decided to slow-pay it, figuring Nick might try to steal the ante. Jimmy just trailed in.

On the fourth card, he drew a nine. Jimmy got a jack. Now Jimmy was low, because Nick had the two nines. Jimmy bet $160. Nick saw it. On the fifth card, Nick caught an off card, a six. Jimmy caught an eight, which gave him two eights with the jack up. Over their heads, the cigar and cigarette haze was so thick a plane could not land in it. Not a facial muscle moved at the table.

Nick had the two nines with the six up. He appeared to have the better hand now, because it looked as though he could be low with a nine against Jimmy's jack. He laid another $320, the maximum. There was now nearly $7,000 in the pot. On the last card, he caught another nine, for three nines and a six, and Jimmy caught a second jack to go with the two eights. Now Jimmy could throw away one of the jacks, which left him with two eights for low. The best Nick could do was to throw away one of his nines, which left him with two nines for low. Jimmy had him beat. Across the table, the dealer nodded at Jimmy.

"Jimmy, you're low," he said.

Beside Jimmy, Nick shook his head. "I'm betting another $320 and raising $320," he growled, biting his cigar. Around the table, a couple of chairs scraped.

Jimmy did not want to embarrass him. In Greek, he asked, "Do you know what you're doing?"

"Bet your hand, punk," Nick snapped. "Who you think you are? Who you think you play vit?"

Jimmy shrugged. "You asked for it."

Deliberately, Jimmy slid three black $100 chips and two $10 chips toward the pot. Nick matched them, pushing his chips to the center of the table. "I vill keep raising you," he said, "vit all I got."

Soon it was all out there, nearly $13,000. They were down to the cloth. Nick turned over his other cards, but he still had the two nines. Jimmy turned over his: two eights for low.

"Jimmy wins," the dealer announced.

Nick jumped to his feet. "I vant a house decision," he shouted. "I'm low. Jimmy not low. I vant a house decision on this."

The dealer called over Paul Wyerman, one of the Fremont managing partners. "Paul," said Nick, showing him his cards. "Lowball. Who vins?"

"Well, Nick, Jimmy has the two eights, you got the two nines. Jimmy wins."

Nick whirled toward Jimmy, his chair clattering to the floor. "You bastid," Nick snarled. "You punk bastid."

Jimmy walked away. He was not going to lose his temper with him. Hell, he was older than Moses. If anything, he felt sorry for him. He saw Nick as an almost comic figure, hustling other people's money in the casino. It was his one sure way of showing profit. He was in for half of what he won; in the meantime, he pocketed whatever he could steal while he was playing it.

If Jimmy's name had been Jimmy the Italian, or Jimmy the Hungarian, it would not have bothered Nick. But to lose to some hot dog named Jimmy the Greek wrecked him.

Beating Jimmy was his obsession. There was no pretense now of being sociable. From then on, they were bitter enemies. A few days after the lowball scene, Nick challenged Jimmy to a series of freeze-outs, $25,000 each, the money on the table. Jimmy beat him first. Nick won the second.

The third game (this happened over a three-month period) took place at the Fremont the night of the first heavyweight title fight between Floyd Patterson and Sweden's Ingemar Johansson. Their competition had not gone unremarked in Las Vegas, a town that dotes on the eternal triangle — two players and a pile of money.

Nick was winning, with Jimmy down to about $7,000, and he could not conceal his glee. He grinned. His eyes danced. A little tobacco juice stained the corner of his mouth from the cigar he was chewing.

The fight was coming on soon, and Paul Wyerman brought over a radio. They were in the middle of the ring introductions. Across the poker table, Nick sat back, shifted his cigar, and threw Jimmy a long look. "What price the fight?" he asked.

Jimmy said, "Six-to-one, Patterson."

"Who you like?"

"I don't care," Jimmy said, "as long as I get the price."

In his head, Nick was counting the money on the table. He wanted to clean out Jimmy as quickly as possible. "You got $7,000," he said. "I give you six-to-one, you got the Swede."

Jimmy nodded. "We're betting for the whole pile or damned near." Nick had $43,000 in front of him. He kept out $1,000, and they moved all the checks to the center of the table.

No one really knew what to make of Johansson. He was a blonde, dimple-chinned playboy whose training camp featured Swedish beer and a cupcake named Brigit. By contrast, Patterson lived like a monk. Jimmy liked the price and he thought Floyd had a chin made of fine crystal.

Johansson put Patterson away in the third round, using a combination he called "toonder and lightning." The world had a new heavyweight boxing champion, and Jimmy rebuilt his holdings into a fast $49,000.

Nick was down to that last grand. In no time Jimmy took that too. Nick was tapped out. With gamblers, such a condition is only temporary. As test pilots love to put it, "There's always another dawn."

"Vait, vait," he said, "I come back. I go to the Sands and get money. Ve keep playing."

Jimmy stacked the chips and handed them to Paul to be cashed. Jimmy shook his head. "Not tonight, Nick. Let's make it tomorrow. We've had a long day."

Jimmy stayed away from the Fremont all that week. Nick showed up every night, looking for him. That was fine. Jimmy wanted him to be steaming. This went on for a couple of months. Jimmy always meant to give him another round, but he heard other music and never played freeze-out again. Jimmy had won the rubber game and finished $25,000 ahead.

The months and the years rolled on. They were slow, painful ones for Nick, a fine old clock running down. He was always a handsome guy, tall with wavy black hair and a chiseled Grecian profile. Now he was fleshy, stooped, his face lined and his disposition always crabby. He still walked into a room as though someone had blown a trumpet. He played the role, still Nick the Greek, and though Jimmy hated to admit it, he felt a grudging admiration for the old man.

A year or so after the freeze-outs, when Jimmy was operating the Vegas Turf and Sports Club, Nick dropped in to see him. "Jeeemmy," he said, "I got a proposition."

"What is it?" Jimmy asked, wary of it already.

"I got a couple of Japs in Los Angeles," he said. "I tell 'em how to bet. I have 'em call you on baseball. You know, I say, bet on Vashington against the Yankees. You don't have to lay no three-to-one [the Yankees were big favorites in those days]. You lay 'em seven-to-five, you cut the price way down. They don't know no better. They bet $10,000, $15,000."

It was a scam. Jimmy believed he was probably bullshitting altogether, trying to set him up. Whatever the odds, he had a free ride for, say, a $10,000 bet. If the Senators won, he stood to collect $14,000. If they lost, he probably did not intend to pay off anyway. He would just tell Jimmy his Japanese friends cheated him.

Jimmy had to fight back the hairy bear in him that stirred when he knew he was being used. He took a deep breath and said, "Nick, I don't do things that way. I have to quote my prices the way they are."

Nick gave him a look that would exterminate head lice. Then he turned and walked out.

Nick was irrepressible. Six months before he died, he was still scheming. This was 1966, during Jimmy's own cold attic period. He had been sat on by the Justice Department and the IRS, was not gambling, and had to scrape to meet the $600 monthly payment on his federal fine. That is how low he was.

A good deal of sympathy existed for him around Las Vegas then, and at the hotels and casinos he was still accorded special courtesies. No matter where, he was allowed inside the velvet ropes that always marked off the *big* poker games. He was allowed in, even though he no longer was in good condition to play. He would sit next to Sid Wyman or any other high player, it made no difference.

Nick knew this. He also knew Jimmy was in bad shape. One day he phoned him. "Jeeemmy," he said, with his standard opener, "I got a proposition."

It developed that Nick had lined up a wealthy sucker from Tucson for a poker game, and he wanted Jimmy to sit next to the fellow and spy on his hand. Any time the two of them were in a big pot, Jimmy was supposed to tip off what the other guy had. "Everybody know we don't speak," Nick said. "It vill be perfect."

"Nick," Jimmy said, "all I know is that you owe me $5,000," and he slammed the receiver down.

Jimmy made him a loan when the Turf and Sports Club was still going strong. He could not explain why he gave him the money, knowing they detested each other, and that it was damned unlikely he would ever see a dime of it again.

A few months after the phone call, Nick the Greek was dead. Jimmy felt nothing — not elation, sadness, or regret. He only wondered if now, at last, people would stop calling him

Nick. (The answer was no. In November of 1974 Jimmy was at the desk of the Madison Hotel in Washington, getting his key, when a party of maybe four slightly tipsy couples moved through the lobby. They stopped, whispered, and sent over one of the husbands. "We just made a bet," he grinned foolishly. "My wife says you're Nick the Greek."

"She loses," Jimmy said slowly. "My name is Jimmy Snyder."

The morning after Nick died, Jimmy got a phone call from Hank Greenspun, the *Las Vegas Sun* editor. Hank was fond of Nick and had pushed him in the early boom years as a sort of public relations front for Las Vegas.

"Jimmy," he said, "I think you should be one of the pall-bearers."

Jimmy almost choked. "You have to be kidding," he said. "Nick and I never got along, you know that. We were enemies."

"I don't care what you were. At least be at the funeral."

Jimmy attended the services and when he arrived at the Greek Orthodox church, he lit a candle. That was it. Jimmy believed that a guy who was a pain while alive did not miraculously become a saint just because he died.

Chapter 19

Gambling: There Are Few Good Systems

PERIODICALLY, PEOPLE ASKED, "Jimmy, why did you start gambling?" This came up a hundred times and it always stumped him. To him, it was like being asked, "Why did you start breathing?"

A lot of considerations went into the answer; some of them were, possibly, unconscious reasons. His environment was one. He grew up in Steubenville, where it was wall-to-wall gambling. Basically, his attraction to gambling was the challenge of matching his wits against the other guy's. It was his information against another's, and if his research was better, he won.

That is why he never cheated anybody. There was no fun in cheating to win. It took the challenge out of it. The great thing about gambling was the satisfaction in the aftermath of a win. When you steal money, what do you have except the money?

Some of Jimmy's friends accused him of having a total disregard for money. It is true he made a single football bet of $250,000, a sum many men spend all their lives accumulating to put in a savings account and live off the interest. When Jimmy was a kid starting out and betting one of his first bookmakers, Chuck Deemer in Steubenville, Deemer would say, "Greeek . . ." He always stretched out the name and repeated it twice to get Jimmy's attention. "Greek, you got to take it easy. Always remember to pinch your last bet. Hold something back for tomorrow." When Jimmy liked something, he bet it *all*. Let tomorrow take care of itself.

What few people noticed was this: When Jimmy made a big bet, it was because he was *winning*. When he was losing, he cut his bets back.

That was the key to his philosophy as a gambler. The size of the bankroll had nothing to do with it, except to scale the size of the bets. His usual custom was to make single, double, and triple bets. If he had a ten percent edge, say, he bet a single unit. If his edge was fifteen percent, he doubled it. Over that, he placed a triple bet. On occasion he bet it all, but experience taught him, as Chuck Deemer said it would, that the smart gambler managed his money.

If Jimmy's units of play were ten, twenty and forty, and he won, over a period of weeks, he moved it to $20,000, $40,000 and $80,000. If he lost, he cut it back to $5,000, $10,000 and $20,000.

Part of that philosophy is what separates the gambler from the sucker. When heads comes up four times in a row, the professional gambler will bet it comes up again. A team that has won six in a row will win seven. *He believes in the percentages.* The amateur figures that heads cannot come up again, that tails is "due." He will bet that a team on a losing streak is "due" to win. *The amateur believes in the law of averages.*

This is one of the main reasons Jimmy was never supportive in the concept of legalizing gambling, especially on professional sports. The average American public as a whole does not have the discipline to stop when losing.

Just assume that a person has $200 he wants to gamble. If gambling were legalized, he could take that $200 and place his bet. If he lost, he would bet $300 to try and recoup his loss and make a little extra. He would lose. Now he is down $500. He has just lost his car payment. Instead of stopping there, he bets his last $400 in an effort to just break even. He loses and has now lost his grocery money.

If you do not believe this is true, take a look at Las Vegas. How do you explain the incredible growth of massive hotel-casinos like the Mirage, a 3,000-room hotel-casino with an erupting volcano and tropical rain forest? How about the Excalibur, a

4,000-room hotel-casino built by Circus Circus; or the MGM Grand Hotel and Theme Park and Mirage's Treasure Island? The addition of these resorts alone contributed more than 10,000 hotel rooms to Las Vegas in 1994. The MGM Grand Hotel and Theme Park alone cost $700 million and provided 5,000 rooms to the Las Vegas tourist. That alone should tell you how much money these casinos are gaining from the American public.

Another reason Jimmy never supported the idea of legalized gambling was to protect the athlete. If gambling were legalized, athletes could be bribed easily. The way it is right now, the athlete makes so much in comparison to what an individual can bet, that he would be crazy to take that chance. In addition, the athlete gets medical care and retirement policies.

If an individual wanted to place a $50,000 bet today, he could do it — but he would have some difficulty getting it down. Any effort to bribe an athlete would most likely be unsuccessful because the money he would attempt to bribe is nothing to the athlete. Also, for a $50,000 bet, it would not be worthwhile to the bettor to pay the athlete the price he would expect to throw a game.

If gambling were legalized, an individual could place a million-dollar bet. Then it would be worthwhile to the athlete to throw the game for, say, $75,000. He would not even have to throw the game; he could just stay home sick. You would not even need a quarterback. You could just take the center, or even the referee.

With legalized gambling, every play, fumble, pass, and call would come under scrutiny and suspicion. A man would place a bet for $300 and would cry out "fix" at any call.

Legalized gambling would kill the little man. The big bettors would determine the outcome of the game. Games would no longer be played by the athletes. The athletes would be played by the game. Essentially, more money would be wagered, and the rich would get richer and the poor would get poorer. That would be detrimental to the American economy.

It is healthier overall, Jimmy believed, to just leave things the way they are. It is better to let the gambler research the odds and make an educated bet. It is more the challenge than the money that drives the gambler. Everyone, including the gambler, is always in search of an easy way out. Since no present one exists, it is a much better solution to let the gambler continue in his never-ending search for an edge. That does not hurt anyone.

From the time Jimmy started betting at age fourteen, he always looked for an edge. When he bet against Chuck Deemer, he made him change almost every rule on the board. Jimmy sat up at night thinking of new angles. One day he bet $1 to place, on a horse, "if-come a dollar to win." Chuck took it. Jimmy made thousands of bets after that, but he remembered this particular horse and rider: White Legs with Paul Keester at Arlington Park, Chicago. White Legs won, and when Chuck added up his payoff he had a fit. "You can't do this," he said. "It's not right."

"You didn't have anything on the board that says I can't if-come it," Jimmy said.

"But it's not right."

A new rule went up on the board.

In searching for the eternal edge, the three biggest betting sports are football, baseball, and horse racing.

FOOTBALL

In making a football bet, Jimmy always had to believe he knew something about the game a lot of people did not know. The point spread on a game is a reflection of the opinion held by the general public, the great mass of bettors. It is the number designed to get the most action, to split opinions right down the middle. Jimmy would perhaps look at one team's strength and see that it was matched head on against the other's. Maybe Alabama's strength was running. Notre Dame was number one in stopping the run, and Alabama could not pass. This would lead him to bet on Notre Dame. But it was tough to bet on the Irish, because they are a national team with hordes of backers who like to back them with money. This led to Ara Parseghian's retirement, which he said was spurred by a 14–6 victory over Navy. "After the game," he said, "you would have thought we lost." Yes, he *did* lose — or the people who bet on Notre Dame did. The Irish did not beat the point spread.

Jimmy missed one of the biggest killings possible, betting on Notre Dame, because he was greedy. This was August 1946, and the previous year Army humiliated Notre Dame, 46–0, with Blanchard, Davis, and Arnold Tucker. But the Cadets had been playing against students. Now Frank Leahy held tryouts before letting anybody on campus. He had virtually a pro team. Jimmy went to Mel Clark's in Chicago and asked Charley McNeil to quote him a money line on Army–Notre Dame.

Charley said, "Okay, I'll give you a point line. How much do you want it for?"

A "point line" is nine-five and one-two, or six-five and seven-five, only a point difference between what they are laying and what they are taking. Jimmy thought, *Oh, Jesus, if he's going to give me a point line that means he's going to make it under two-one.*

Jimmy said, "Okay, a point line under two-one is what you're talking about."

Mac said, "Yeah, but the regular speed if I go over two-one. How much?" He did not know who Jimmy was going to bet.

Jimmy said, "Oh, twenty or thirty." Mac said twenty was enough, but Jakie Summerfield, his partner, said, "That's okay. Let him bet thirty. We'll put it up now and do a lot of business on this game."

So Mac made it two and a half and three. Jimmy could lay 3-to-1 and take Army or take 2½-to-1 and take Notre Dame. He took the Irish for $30,000 from Jakie and Mac, and some other fellows around Clark's that day laid it to Jimmy for ten more. He finished up betting $40,000 (to win $100,000).

When the game rolled around that fall, it came up dead even. The week of the game, Army came up a half-point favorite, and Jimmy pressed his bet for $25,000 more on Notre Dame. The game ended, 0–0, with the ball on the 50-yard line. Back in August, if Jimmy had taken any points at all, instead of being greedy for the odds, he would have won the whole bundle.

On many occasions when Jimmy had information about a game, he made damned sure "his team" got hold of the same information in some way. With his contacts on the campuses, through an assistant coach or a player or an ex-coach who saw the practices, Jimmy knew how one team was preparing to play the other.

Before one bowl game in 1959, he learned of a certain

team's game plan, offense and defense, and had a complete report on their practices. He called one of his scouts, who had a good friend on the other staff. He gave him the information and the scout relayed it. The coach knew he could believe him. Jimmy liked the favorite to beat the point spread, anyway, but this was additional insurance.

His team, the favorite, scored two touchdowns in the first quarter and another in the third. The other team did not get on the board until the fourth quarter.

How immoral or unethical was this? The coaches were doing it themselves whenever they could. When Army used to "upset" Michigan every year, it was because Red Blaik had a guy who watched Michigan's practices. Every night at West Point, Blaik knew what happened that day at Ann Arbor. Jimmy knew this, because Herman Hickman was on Blaik's staff then and told him about it.

There are two reasons Jimmy quit gambling. One, it hurt his credibility as an oddsmaker, and two, the laws are bad. It is against federal law to make a phone call across the states for purposes of betting or even conveying betting information. He should know.

Consequently, you cannot gamble like you could in the days when you could match your wits against everybody in different cities, get different points, different ideas. You do not have the percentage going for you. If Jimmy liked a Chicago team and it was playing a team from Atlanta, he called Atlanta to bet on Chicago. If Fordham came to Pittsburgh to play Pittsburgh, Jimmy called Slim Silverheart at the Amorita Club in Pittsburgh to get half a point more. He did that once: got Pittsburgh and a half point in New York, and Fordham and a half point in Pittsburgh. It came out, 0–0, and he won both sides.

Today in Vegas, from one sports club to another, you will not find more than a half-point difference. On occasion, you can buy in early on the first line on Monday and find there is movement by Friday. Then you can buy in on the other side. Every experienced gambler knows this. It is called "catching a middle." The average bettor is either too lazy or too unaware to do this. All you are betting is the *juice*, the one point to win twenty. The wider the "middle," the more beautiful is 20-to-1.

BASEBALL

Football is a numbers game. Baseball is an odds game. If you get the right odds, it does not matter if Sandy Koufax is pitching. If it is 2½-to-1 and you get 3-to-1, you take it. You do not bet on the team; you bet on what the odds are.

Consider the 1974 World Series between Los Angeles and Oakland. Jimmy made it a toss-up. He sent it out 11-to-10 Dodgers just to make somebody a favorite. The reason they said 11-to-10 Dodgers was because the Dodgers got the most publicity. The World Series belongs to the public, not to the smart guys, the bookmakers. This is one betting proposition that runs away like crazy. The player, the outside guy, takes the team he *wants* to win. Jimmy's opinion was 11-to-10. With the bookies it went to 8-to-5 Dodgers, way out of proportion.

That used to happen in the heyday of the Yankees too. Everyone wanted the Yankees. They were not often disappointed.

Jimmy did not do well on one of the great series he should have because he was a Cleveland fan. That was his Ohio team. He was in the Hickory House Restaurant in New York. Between the Hickory House and Gallagher's in those days, 1954, you could bet a quarter of a million dollars because all the gamblers loafed there. It was still early and it looked like the Giants were going to play Cleveland, and Jimmy wanted something ahead of time. He ran into Manny Kimmel, one of the smart people of the world. He owned the Kinney Parking lots and finally sold. Jimmy bet Manny $11,000 on Cleveland to his $10,000. Jimmy knew the public was going to bet Cleveland because it had one hell of a pitching staff — Lemon, Wynn, and Garcia — and it got all the publicity. Cleveland opened a 7-to-5 favorite, but the public sent it to 9-to-5.

Jimmy went to the opening game, when Willie Mays made that catch on Vic Wertz in center field and Dusty Rhodes hit a pinch home run in the tenth inning. Al Rosen, Cleveland's third baseman, was hurting. Jimmy said to himself, "I'm in trouble. I'm going to go in and get rid of this." Because he originally made such a good bet, it was still 11-to-10 with Cleveland losing the first game, so Jimmy laid 11-to-10 on the Giants to get off. Now, no matter who won, he had to lose $1,000, but at least he was not going to lose $11,000. Because Jimmy liked Cleveland at the start, he stayed away from the Series altogether and the Giants won four in a row. Every day the public made Cleveland the favorite, and the last game was 8-to-5. The public kept saying, "The Indians can't lose another one."

Now, Jimmy did not like systems. He hated them with a passion, but there *is* one system that does exist in baseball, which he checked on and followed from a statistical point of view. As follows: *If a team has won four in a row, bet on it until it loses. If a team has lost four in a row, bet against it until it wins.*

This is how it works. There is a cycle of four in baseball with every team. They have four starting pitchers. There are a lot of four-game series. Four is the basic structure of baseball.

You will, from time to time, have a double bet going for you, when a team has won four or more in a row, and is opposing a team that has lost four or more in a row.

A great advantage in this system is that you cannot get hurt with it. What happens is, you will find yourself overlaying almost a nickel a hundred on these games, or two and a half percent of a hundred, because the bookmaker increases the odds. Instead of a 13-to-10 favorite, the team that is winning will be 7-to-5. Instead of the losing team being a 3-to-2 underdog, they will be an 8-to-5 underdog. Sometimes even the guy making the odds will hold them down. It is amazing that otherwise smart-betting men do not realize this. They bet the other way.

Of course, in baseball, you are often betting on or against a certain pitcher. You study them, learn their habits, file away odd pieces of information, and look for trends. Warren Spahn, through most of his great career, had problems in the early innings — on those days when he had any problems at all. Jimmy always liked Spahn, but that became one of his gimmick bets. He would take odds that the other team would score on Spahn in the first inning.

In 1947, Jimmy had already picked the Boston Braves as a team on the move. (They won the pennant the next year, even though they appeared to have only a two-man pitching staff.) The Boston battle cry was Spahn and Sain and a day in the rain. In June of that season, Jimmy stumbled into one of the most unusual betting opportunities he *thought* he had ever known.

The Braves were in Cincinnati for a series with the Reds, a mediocre team kept alive by one great pitcher, the late Ewell (The Whip) Blackwell. He won twenty-two games that year, sixteen of them in a row, with a sidearm motion that came by way of third base and drastically increased the laundry bill for the National League hitters. They were forever flinging themselves into the dirt, as the ball snapped over the plate for another strike. "The Whip" was a joy to watch.

This night was even better, because Jimmy watched him from the next table, in a club across the river in Covington, Kentucky, where all the gambling was. Three of them were having dinner: Nate Linnett, Sleep-Out Louie Levinson (who owned the 606 Club, where they were), and Jimmy.

Sleep-Out was the best of company. He knew the lyrics to every song written, or so it seemed. He was a great gambler, ambidextrous, and could throw a silver dollar against a wall with either hand and make it land on its edge. Once he stopped a craps game, took two wheel balls off the table, and they played marbles for $5,000 a shot. He beat Jimmy too. Louie rolled them and Jimmy played fat-lady style, like a jerk. He lost $25,000.

When Blackwell walked into the club with a knockout on his arm, light brown hair and built, Sleep-Out got excited. They sat down at a table just behind them. "My God," he said, "get a load of the barracuda with Blackwell."

Jimmy had never heard that expression before. It meant, in the deep, natural sense, a man-eater. Sleep-Out said, "He may not know it, but there won't be anything left of his pecker when she gets through with him tonight."

Blackwell was to pitch the next night, June 18, 1947, against the Braves, who were starting a right-handed pitcher named Eddie Wright, one of the pitchers they used on days when it did not rain. The Reds were favored, Jimmy knew, by 11-to-5.

Jimmy's mind began to whirl. "Sleep-Out," Jimmy said, "will she take money?"

"Doesn't everybody?"

Jimmy reached into his pocket and fished out four $50 bills. He said, "Look, sooner or later, one of them has to go to the restroom. When it happens, catch her alone and slip her the $200. Tell her all she has to do to earn it is give you a report on what she did with Blackwell and what time she left him, nothing more. If she takes him to bed, how many times. Now get this straight. You're not paying her to *do* anything. She's not getting paid to sabotage Blackwell. Make that goddamn clear."

Sleep-Out nodded, but Jimmy made him repeat it back to him, every word. He was an intelligent fellow, but Jimmy wanted nothing said that might later sound like an attempt to fix the game. Jimmy told him the barracuda was to call them, no matter what time it was that she and Ewell parted company.

After a while, she got up and headed for the powder room, and smoothly, Sleep-Out rose and crossed her path. When he returned to the table he said it was all set. Now, keep in mind this was in 1947, and $200 was not candy, and all she had to do for it was to make a phone call.

At 8:15 the next morning, the phone rang in Jimmy's suite at the Netherlands Plaza. It was Sleep-Out: "Well, the barracuda just called. She left him fifteen minutes ago. *Five* times."

Jimmy was not wide awake yet. "What do you mean, *five* times?"

"She says she went down on him five times."

Jimmy said, "Let me get this straight. Are you telling me, she said she took him off five times?"

"Greek, that's what she said, and there's no reason for the girl to lie. She doesn't know what information we wanted, or why, and we already paid her. Why would she lie?"

"My God," Jimmy repeated, *"five times."* Jimmy was impressed, if only from an aesthetic standpoint, forget the gambling angle. Twice, maybe three times might not mean that much. But those extra two turns, Jimmy figured, had to take something out of a guy. Most fellows who get off five times in a night would wind up in a jar at the Harvard Medical Laboratory.

It began to look to Jimmy like a six-inning game. Between the three of them — Sleep-Out, Nate, and Jimmy — they bet $100,000 on the Braves. In those days, with black market money still in circulation, gambling was the national pastime. You could call five places in Covington alone and get down $100,000 in an afternoon.

Jimmy seldom anticipated a baseball game with more glee. That night, before a home crowd that cheered every delivery,

Ewell Blackwell pitched the only no-hit, no-run game of his big league career. The victory was the ninth of his string of sixteen straight, and the Reds breezed, 6–0. In his next start, against Brooklyn, "The Whip" came within two outs of a second straight no-hitter. Jimmy was grateful he had no inside information riding on that one.

HORSE RACING

Jimmy was reminiscing one day about Jack Nolan, the political boss of Steubenville when Jimmy was growing up. Nolan liked to bet big at the racetrack, and would bet a horse $10,000 to win and $20,000 to place. A friend interrupted Jimmy's story. "Is that a good system?" he asked. Jimmy almost shouted his answer: "There is *no* good system to bet horses."

Horse racing was a different thing to Jimmy. Even though the track finished up with all the money, racing was his recreation, his first love. In his opinion the moment you looked at a racetrack as a place to make money, rather than a place to have fun, you were going to get hurt.

There were occasions, what were called "spot" plays, where you could have the parimutuel odds working in your favor.

He was at the track when Riva Ridge won the Belmont. For some reason or another, Riva Ridge never got the credit he should have gotten, as good of a horse as he was. Jimmy would have rather bet on Riva Ridge than Secretariat, Penny Tweedy's next horse.

Riva Ridge was actually overlaid most of the time he ran. Secretariat took the country by storm and his prices were far shorter than they should have been.

This particular day in the Belmont, Jimmy started looking at the board where Riva Ridge was 3-to-2 to win and he looked at the place price and, to his dismay, he was 13-to-10 or 7-to-5 to place. He said to himself, "Oh, gosh, that will change." New York tracks today get a tremendous impact from the Off-Track Betting shops around the city, with major dollars on a big race. Most of the OTB players played Riva Ridge to win, and the "pie-in-the sky" bettors played the long-shot horses to place. A price of 3-to-2 to win and 13-to-10 to place was something like a 300 percent overlay. He should have been 3-to-5 to place, returning sixty cents on a dollar. Here he was returning $1.30 to a dollar.

Jimmy had $5,000 in his back pocket, so he gave it to a friend, Mike Pearl, and sent him to the $100-place window with instructions to buy fifty tickets on number three (Riva Ridge). The horse paid $4.60 to place, and Jimmy won $6,500, more than double what the horse should have paid. He *had* to go for the overlay.

When Jimmy went to the racetrack in his latter days, he did not follow the horses. He did not go to take a racing form and try to figure it out, except on a big race. Nor did he go to handicap the claiming races and the allowance races. He handicapped the high-stake races, because it was all there. There were too many intangibles in the other kind of races.

There is a way of playing so you do not experience the worst of it. He wanted to overcome the seventeen or seventeen and a half percent take-out by the track and the state, at least for the $50 or $200 he bet per race.

The handicapper at the racetrack should know more about these horses than anybody, right? That is why he is hired. He makes the morning line, and that line is right there in the track program.

What Jimmy did then, a minute or so before post time, was compare his odds in the program with the odds on the board. Then he bet two horses:

1. The horse that was an overlay on the handicapper's line.
2. The horse who had the money for it.

Jimmy bet, say, $50 on one and $30 on the other, the "money" horse. But it had to be a certain figure. If a horse was 3-to-1 in the handicapper's line and now he is 6-to-1 on the board, Jimmy had to take it. If another horse was 4-to-1 in the handicapper's line and now it is 2-to-1 on the board, he knew there was a lot of money bet on it.

This saved him the time of studying, because he knew the track handicapper did all the studying. So, if it goes from 3-to-1 to 6-to-1, the handicapper has been there since the racing started. This is just a logical way of playing. It does not mean you are going to beat the track. It is a way to have some fun — because you have always got a "live" horse, one with a lot of money going for it and you have got an overlay. When those overlays win, you really get your money back.

These are first, second, and third choices only. He did not look for a money horse being the favorite, like a horse going from 3-to-1 to 8-to-5. He meant about a 10-to-1 shot coming to 5 or 6-to-1. Or a 6-to-1 shot coming to 3-to-1.

If you like favorites, the stakes races are the only places to play. They are solid. Jimmy bet thousands and thousands of dollars on Native Dancer and Tom Fool. They were horses you could trust. He would get 3-to-10 or 1-to-2 or 2-to-5, but that is forty cents on the dollar. Where else can you make forty cents on the dollar in two minutes?

Chapter 20

Casino Gambling:
For Entertainment Only

JIMMY WAS NEVER TURNED on by Las Vegas; otherwise he could have owned interests in a dozen hotels when he first came out. He hated casino gambling. He believed it preyed on the weakness of people.

Gambling, specifically casino gambling, was a disease. Forget about Jimmy the Greek, and the small percentage of guys who made a living at gambling because they were smart enough to research it.

Nobody makes a living betting in casinos.

He believed the minute you viewed casinos as anything more than entertainment or a way to pass time, you were predestined to financial doom.

Casino gambling was never his game, but it was more to his taste in the heyday of the Mounds Club in Cleveland, and the other great old casinos that belonged to another America. It was the America of black Packards, evening dress, and orchestras with violins. They were still going strong until the late 1950s, these casinos tucked in the woods or on a hill, somewhere back off the highway.

The Mounds Club was like a castle, completely surrounded by a high iron gate. You had to identify yourself to a guard, and you could not get in without a reference. Inside it was elegant and tasteful, like the homes of people who have been wealthy for

215

a long time and have no further need to prove it. Basically, there was no French whorehouse decor, just expensive lamps and chandeliers and old leather furniture. There would be one big act, say, Hildegarde or Joe E. Lewis, and it was the beginning of an idea that came to flower in Las Vegas. The Mounds Club was among the first to pay top money for entertainers, up to $10,000 a week, starting in the 1940s.

It was accepted routinely that, for such places to operate, they had to have the sheriff on their side. That was just part of the overhead and no one thought much of it, either way. The big politician in the area usually had a cut too. When his side lost an election, someone else took over.

The times and ambitious lawmen eventually wiped out the grand old gambling houses. Jimmy never subscribed to the theory that the casinos were linked or backed by a national syndicate, what conspiracy fans have sometimes called "The Organization." These were casinos, not take-out taco parlors. You did not franchise them. They were owned by tough men who bought whatever big money could give them, and some had reputations several pages long. As a rule, the casinos were privately owned by men who did not believe in chain stores.

Crime always struck Jimmy, an observer of the passing scene, as notoriously disorganized. If it was not disorganized, and there was "organized crime," it would run the country. There is not much to keep your business from growing if you do not mind killing people.

In the matter of simple larceny, gambling has a long tradition, although the advantage keeps shifting. In Nevada, gambling was legalized in 1931, because the state had little other income, and in the early stages, cheating was rampant. In those days, around the time Hoover Dam was being built, they erected tents and operated games of chance inside, the mice running into the holes, three-card monte, all the hustling carnival stuff.

Casino gambling grew out of that era, and for a long time, no one could or would do much about improving it. Almost anyone who wanted a license could get one. The state *wanted* them to come in; it needed the investment and the people gambling would bring. The governors had no jurisdiction.

All that began to change in the mid-1960s, during the sec-

ond term of Governor Grant Sawyer, and continued under Paul
Laxalt. They cracked down, cleaned it up, created order and dis-
cipline, and appointed impeccably honest men to the Gaming
Board to keep it that way.

Today the pendulum has swung the other way. What the
house has to do is protect itself. The cheating is done by the customers. They mark cards, copy the dice, slip a gadget into the
slots. Millions of dollars each year are stolen from the casinos.
Any day, you can visit the sheriff's office and see on his wall a
roguery of cheaters, identified by their specialties — slots, craps,
or cards. They are on posters, like the FBI wanted list, only these
people are gambling cheats.

A hotel will allow a one percent leakage for thievery by their
own dealers, in the course of the year. But the casino people are
always looking for it. They have what they call the catwalk and
the peep-hidden mirrors, through which someone is looking
down at all times at the dealers. A fellow needs super quick
hands to get away with anything, and he will never last. In time,
he is caught, fired, and if word circulates that he is a thief, he will
not work again. No, they do not break his fingers. That went out
with high-button shoes.

The boys were more likely to go into business for themselves
and do a little skimming, in the days when they could play where
they worked. Today state laws forbid any employee from gambling in his own casino, including owners, dealers, bellhops, and
entertainers — especially entertainers. In the first place, no owner
wants his star to gamble, in the belief he does not perform as
well when he is *losing*. The owner does not want his money; he
wants his talent, which brings in other people's money.

The late Joe E. Lewis used to blow at the tables whatever he
earned on the stage, usually $7,500 to $10,000 a week. (In salary,
he was not up there with the heavies.) When he worked for Belden Kattleman at El Rancho, Belden tried to protect his pay by
calling the other casinos and asking them to limit Joe E.'s credit, or bar him completely. He did it because he loved him, everybody did, and wanted him to leave town with something in his
pocket besides lint.

Eddie Fisher was another who often ended up singing for
nothing, or a little less than that. But the grand champion was

Frank Sinatra, who played like a crazy man. The difference was that the Eddie Fishers had to pay off, and Sinatra's markers, most of them, were usually torn up. That, in fact, was what started the feud between Frank and Howard Hughes.

When Sinatra played the Sands, before it was sold to Hughes, he drew such enormous crowds that whatever he lost at the tables was canceled out. Playing for free, or next to it, was his bonus. He brought in the big gamblers.

Under Hughes this practice was discontinued, and Bob Maheu instructed Jack Entratter to inform Frank. Entratter was the entertainment director of the Sands, a booking agent on the side for a few select clients and a guy with the burly build of a one-time bouncer.

Jack was afraid to tell Frank, so he did not.

The next time Frank was in the casino, he was losing, and had reached whatever limit Carl Cohen, the casino manager, had placed on him. It was something like $25,000. Carl, of course, was under the impression that Entratter had advised Frank he would be playing with his own money.

Sinatra asked the pit boss for more chips and was told, in front of the table, "I'm sorry, Mr. Sinatra. I can't give you any more credit. I have to call."

It was like playing with gunpowder to put down Frank in front of other people. He exploded. Steam came out of his ears. Instantly, Carl Cohen appeared and tried to calm him. Sinatra got really nasty, with a torrent of hyphenated words, the mildest of which was "cock-sucker." Then he heaved a room-service cart through a glass partition, turned to Cohen, and squared off. Now *that* was a bad move. Carl shot a right hand to the side of the face, point blank, and decked him. It was instant anesthesia, the only way Carl knew how to end the scene before it got even more out of hand.

That was how Frank Sinatra happened to drop the Sands and move over to Caesar's in 1970.

Now, it is part of his charm that Frank would not dislike a man just because he hit him. Chances are he would like him no more or no less than before. Jimmy's understanding was that Sinatra did not stay angry at Cohen, who slugged him, or Entratter, who deceived him, but Howard Hughes, who cut off his credit.

Carl Cohen did not exactly fit the gambling stereotype, if there was one. He was a refined and educated man, who spoke half a dozen languages. Sid Wyman was another who did not buy into the image. In Las Vegas, Wyman was one of the gods when it came to running a casino. Big and heavyset, Sid had a kind of corporate smoothness. He was also a fine storyteller out of his own experiences.

He was playing poker in the Dunes one night when one of his staffers came over and said, quietly, "Sid, one of your busboys is very ill. It looks like he's got cancer. He's going into the hospital and we're all pitching in. You want to put in something?"

Sid looked up from his cards. "Whaddaya mean, put in something? Here," he said, scribbling a name on a score sheet. "Call this doctor in Los Angeles, and send him there and tell him to bill me for whatever he needs. I'll take care of him."

Sid had never met the boy. Jimmy doubted he even remembered his name, but a year and a half went by, the bills came in, and Sid paid them all.

One morning — that is, by his clock — Sid ordered breakfast from room service. It was around 3:00 P.M. A bachelor, he always ordered breakfast at whatever hour he met the day. It depended on when he got to sleep, and what he had to do.

The waiter wheeled in the cart and set up the table and Sid barked, "Take $5 for yourself off the dresser." He signed the checks, but made it a point to pay his tips in cash.

The waiter hesitated, then said, "Mr. Wyman, if you don't mind, this one is on the house."

Sid snapped, "What? You so rich you won't take my money?"

"No, sir," the waiter said. "I'm Rico, Mr. Wyman. The guy you sent to California a year and a half ago. I'm well now and I just came back to work, and I got no other way to thank you."

Gratitude always made Sid nervous. He muttered something like, "Gee, that's great, kid," and watched him back out of the room. He had never seen him before, did not know his name, and had probably spent $15,000 on him.

When Jimmy told this story in his column in the *Sun*, Wyman, who was probably one of his five closest friends, did not speak to him for three weeks. It was not all modesty, of course.

He was deluged with phone calls and sad letters from people wanting handouts.

Men like Sid Wyman and Carl Cohen — along with the likes of Benny Binion, Eddie Torres, Al Benedict, and Charles Rich — were part of a breed of executive gamblers who learned the ropes young, grew up with it, and became businessmen, not adventurers. The adventurers were the gamblers, hustlers, and con men.

Casinos provided a gathering place for all of them, and the conglomerate of these men who used their wits to earn a living was Jimmy the Greek's main attraction to the casinos. As Jimmy reflected on those years, he realized how many of them left imprints on his life, in one way or another.

One of the premier con artists of his time, and perhaps anytime, was a gremlin of a man named Swifty Morgan. This was one of the great hustlers of the world. In fact, Swifty *was, is,* the Lemon Drop Kid, transferred to print and made immortal by Damon Runyon in his Broadway classic, *Guys and Dolls.* Bob Hope later played the part in a movie.

Runyon's fictional Kid was unpolished, corrupt and irrepressible, no more so than Swifty, who had balls of brass. He spent all of his life looking for an angle, and somehow he usually found it. In 1949, at Joe's Stone Crab in Miami Beach, Jimmy saw Swifty try to sell a gold wristwatch — hot, of course — to a man whose name was J. Edgar Hoover.

Jimmy was having dinner with Herman Hickman, the Yale football coach, when Swifty walked in and headed for their table. Jimmy was a benevolent customer of his, a buyer of ties, watches, cuff links, whatever he was hustling. Swifty sat with them only a moment when his eyeballs, which were always working, spotted Hoover a few tables away. "I'll see you guys in a few minutes," he said, pushing back his chair. "I got a bigger pigeon over there." He nodded in Hoover's direction.

Hoover was in town to watch the ponies run at Tropical Park. J. Edgar was hip, bright and, at times, convivial. He was not then the stern old grouch he was pictured to be in later years.

Swifty sat down, uninvited, pointed to the watch on Hoover's wrist, and shook his head. "Hoover," he said, "why don't you get rid of that piece of shit and buy yourself a really fine watch? Man of your stature, you ought to be wearing something in *gold.*" Whereupon he produced a gold watch and put it on the table. "Now, here's one that will give you some class."

Hoover turned it slowly in his hand. He nodded. "Give you a hundred dollars for it," he said, firmly.

Swifty looked at him with wounded eyes. "Goddamn, J. Edgar," he said. "Look at that watch. The insurance premium for that piece, alone, is higher than that!"

When Jimmy was living at the El Rancho in Las Vegas, Swifty dropped by for seven straight weeks to sell him a pair of French cuff links, at $100 a pop. They were well worth the money, or would have been, except that Jimmy did not wear French cuffs. Jimmy bought them anyway. He had to do something to help Swifty make ends meet.

By the time the eighth week rolled around, Jimmy was begging for mercy. "No, Swifty, no," Jimmy said. "Please, no more cuff links. I'm up to my ass in them already."

Swifty gave him a look of complete innocence. "Who said anything about cuff links? I just brought you a jewelry box to keep them in." The price tag was $100.

The last time Jimmy saw Swifty he was still going strong, living in a suite at the Beverly Wilshire, though he needed a wheelchair to help him get around. He was eighty-three, a stocky, rumpled little man looking for a good bridge game.

Swifty had great connections. Jimmy believed that Frank Sinatra helped pay his bills. Joe E. Lewis chipped in for years. Once or twice Jimmy tided him over, between capers. Swifty's biggest caper, one he boasted as his "claim to fame," landed him in a French jail for six months.

For $300 he rented a complete wardrobe — tails, top hat, gold-tipped cane, studs, and pocket watch — and walked into a plush Paris gambling house. He took a position near the *chemin de fer* game, and waited until a big play came up. There was $60,000 on the table. When the dealer asked for bets, Swifty raised his gold cane (it alone rented for $50) and said, *"Banco, m'sieur."* He was covering the table.

The dealer looked at him, and took it all in — the tails, the cane, and the watch, even a diamond ring he had borrowed. The bet was on. Swifty lost. When they discovered that he could not pay, did not have a cent on him, the gendarmes were summoned and Swifty went to the bastille. Still, it was not a bad gamble — six months against $60,000.

Jimmy heard him tell that story one night to Cheesecake Ike, during an argument over who was the better con man. Ike had not worked a single day since he was twenty-nine. Swifty recited his story about yelling *"banco"* for $60,000, and admitted he had made one mistake. He went first. That immediately makes you an underdog.

Cheesecake Ike curled his nose and gave him a look that passed for contempt. "You poor, phony, cheap little bastard," he growled. "Why, I laid down to Dunhill's for more than that in cigars." Jimmy moved on, leaving the two philosophers to argue it out.

Ike became one of the elder statesmen in Las Vegas. He would spend his years there, as many old gamblers do, the way retired seamen so often hang around the docks. You could always find him at the casinos, in the side rooms where the cards were played, or at the California Turf and Sports Club. It was a lifestyle he grew accustomed to love.

No account of famous con men Jimmy ever knew would be complete without one more reference to Nate Linnett. Nate was tall, dark complected, with kinky white hair. He was handsome in a vacant way. Jimmy and he saw a lot of each other. He enjoyed Nate's company, though Nate was not a fellow easily trusted. He was in the room at Atlantic City, remember, when some of the boys set back Jimmy's watch and bet him on a long-shot horse, already knowing the outcome of the race.

Gambling was Nate's trade and he was candid about it; but he was less candid about some of his sidelines. He spent a long stretch in prison.

From time to time Jimmy lent him money, but always with the understanding that someday Nate would give him the full inside and unedited story of what happened in the most famous card game in the history of American crime. He was there. He sat in on the card game that led to the murder of Arnold Rothstein.

Rothstein was a romantic underworld character of the day, a bootlegger who did not drink, a gambler, loan shark, and diamond smuggler. The game was held in September of 1928, at an apartment on New York's West Side. Others at the table included Sam and Meyer Boston, Abe Silverman, George McManus, Red Bowe, and Titanic Thompson. All of them had big reputations as gamblers, bookmakers, or horse players.

The story circulated that Rothstein lost over $200,000 that night. On November 4, 1928, in room number 349 of the Park Central Hotel on Seventh Avenue, Rothstein was shot and killed by a gunman hiding behind a screen. The weapon was thrown to the street below.

George McManus, the brother of a New York cop, went to trial for the murder of Rothstein and was acquitted. Courtroom testimony brought out the fact that Rothstein, while losing $200,000 to the others, had won $51,000 from McManus at high card. Who killed Rothstein, and why, what happened at the game and later, remained a puzzle, the details known only to a handful of men who kept it that way.

Jimmy had heard, but never really believed it, that Nate fingered Rothstein. That is, he arranged to have him at that place at that time. Jimmy had planned to ask him if that was true whenever Nate released the details. They were going to sit down, with a bottle on the table, and Nate Linnett was going to spill the secret of Arnold Rothstein's killing. But Nate took it to the grave with him, as Jimmy knew all along that he would.

Jimmy last saw Nate on his deathbed. When he heard he was sinking he felt an urge to see the old rogue and not let him die unremembered in a hospital room in Las Vegas. He was well past eighty then, a hard eighty. Nate's wife, Dale, stood quietly at the foot of the bed as he visited. When it was time for Jimmy to go, Nate raised himself slightly on his pillow and motioned Jimmy to lean down. "Jimmy," he whispered, "I'm a little short right now. Medical bills and all. Could you lend me two grand for a few weeks until I can pay you back?"

It was all Jimmy could do to keep from laughing, right there in the hospital. "Tell you what, Nate," Jimmy said, taking out his roll. "I've got exactly $1,500 on me, and I'm going to give you half of it. And that way we're each gonna make $750."

They said their goodbyes and Dale walked out into the corridor with Jimmy. She was upset. "Jimmy," she said, "what did you do that for? Nate has plenty of money. He didn't need a loan. Let me get it back."

Jimmy patted her on the hand. "It's okay," Jimmy said, smiling. "I don't mind. Nate just had to make that final score."

To the end, Nate Linnett was a pro. Jimmy admired his competitive spirit.

Jimmy always had a grudging admiration for those whose larceny was of a gentle kind, who lived by their wits, who could maneuver you in a thousand creative ways. He was aware, however, that this opinion was not shared by many.

In fact, anyone who has not been back since the 1950s will not be convinced that Las Vegas has a heart. Before then, the town had the soul of a bus-stop joint. The people who ran the casinos cheated *everybody*, including each other. That is no longer the case. Those elements were bought out and chased out. Of course, the casinos never needed to cheat, and that is not because of house percentages. There is something more certain and magnifying than that: human frailty.

There are a select few in Las Vegas who make a living gambling, by betting on sports events or perhaps playing poker. These fellows occasionally go to the casinos and play the tables. *But they play the games for entertainment.* That is the oddity.

Jimmy was crazy about poker, but the only time he played was those four, five, or six times a year when Joannie and he had a war. In the wake of domestic argument, he played poker, in the biggest game he could find.

Sometimes he came home exultant, and sometimes he came home chagrined. That was all part of it.

If you work it right, Las Vegas can be the greatest place in the world for a vacation or a convention. The glitter is contagious. It has a greater concentration of big-name entertainment than anywhere in the world. There is year-round golf and tennis, and the world's most beautiful prostitutes go gliding by with a rhythm all their own — Sodom and Gomorrah, Sodom and Gomorrah, the rhythm goes. There is a hysteria in the air that leaps from player to player.

Oh yes, Las Vegas can be a lot of fun, and you can have a swinging time at the tables, if you can stick to two simple principles:

1. Never gamble with more money than you can afford to
lose. When that is gone, walk away.

2. Consider that sum of money as an entertainment expense, and gamble for fun.

The first rule is purely practical, dollars and sense. The second is important because it is psychological, and this rule helps you walk away with your own money and perhaps some of the casino's too.

A house percentage of, say, five percent means gamblers lose an average of $5 for every $100 bet. The truth is, it is not the house percentages so much that you have to beat. You have to beat *yourself*.

Those numbers are not the kind casinos can rely on if they are going to finance high-rise hotels and pay entertainers $200,000 a week, while charging $30 for a dinner show. So the players are obviously doing many things wrong.

Casino operators have their own language in discussing profit margin. They use words like "drop" and "percent." The drop is how much money is bet, as in "the handle" at a racetrack, and it is figured on a daily basis. The percent is what the house expects to make. This figure varies according to the game, but not according to the players. The casino knows it should average between nineteen and twenty-two percent at blackjack and craps. In other words, they have a calm anticipation that you, ol' buddy, will lose twenty cents on every dollar you bet.

Where do these extra percentages come from? They come from the average bettor who does not have the discipline to quit when he should. He will not walk away until he has punished himself to where it hurts.

That is the built-in advantage that keeps Las Vegas wheels turning. Most people lose ten times more than they win.

Jimmy said many times that no system was ever invented that can beat the casinos; but there is an exception to every rule. His wife, Joannie, had a foolproof system.

Whenever they went to the Strip to have dinner and see a show, she would ask him, "Jim, are you going to play the tables tonight?" If he said he might, she would say, "Well, here's $200 to bet for me." If he won, of course, she got it all. If he lost, she just took $200 off the dresser the next morning before he woke up.

Now that is a foolproof system.

Chapter 21

"The Greek's Grapevine"

IN THE FALL OF 1976, Mike Pearl, the producer of CBS-TV's *NFL Today* show, telephoned Jimmy.

"You know, Greek, we're thinking about adding you to our team on the show. I think you should come in."

Jimmy packed his $400 custom-made suit, his $175 alligator shoes, kissed Joannie and the kids goodbye, and took the first available flight to New York.

He met with Robert Wussler, then-president of CBS Sports, and after negotiations were met, he signed a three-year contract with a one-year renewal option earning $150,000 a year, plus a hefty expense account. With each consecutive season came a substantial increase in his earnings. He joined Brent Musburger, Phyllis George, and Irv Cross on *The NFL Today* show, and a pre-game-show format was established that would not soon be forgotten.

It was a perfect arrangement. Jimmy did the same thing he had done for years — predicted the outcome of games — except now he did it in front of a television camera. His only instructions were to make sure whatever he stated was true and to never give his numbers when he made his picks on television. That was a specification made by the network's attorneys.

Jimmy regarded this career move as an opportunity to transform his image of gambler into an oddsmaker. He was offered legitimacy on a platter and served it to the American people in the privacy of their homes. Although he had received a presidential pardon for his wrongdoing in 1974, he believed the stigma of having been a "felon" remained. He worked hard to rebuild his reputation. Self-respect and integrity were of great importance to him.

During a segment on the show called "The Greek's Grapevine," Jimmy reported what was going on in the entire spectrum of sports. In another segment, called "The Greek's Board," he discussed the day's games and predicted the outcome of future games.

Jimmy spent a great deal of time and money in preparation for the show that broadcast every Sunday afternoon. He had a staff in New York and one in Las Vegas that researched and compiled data the minute it hit the wires. He had nineteen full-time people on his payroll. It was their responsibility to put out spreads on basketball and college football and the odds on baseball; however, he alone made the line on all the NFL games. He used his own system, one he had developed years before. It included eleven categories on which he rated each team. He was convinced that no one spent more time or money in research than he. The work was continuous, twenty-four hours a day, seven days a week.

A vital part of his research included information. It was necessary to know what was going on behind the scenes. He needed opinions from many people, and privileged information. Through his forty years of oddsmaking, he had acquired a healthy network of sources and now relied on them more than ever. That is why he was always reluctant to share his sources. He probed to uncover sports gossip and inside information on the teams and their players. He believed his job was to create excitement for the show.

He broke the story that George Allen, who was then-coach of the Washington Redskins, would go on to coach the Los Angeles Rams. Allen called the set that Sunday and said, "Jimmy, where did you get that? I'm not going anywhere."

Jimmy said, "Yes, you are. You and Ed Bennett Williams aren't getting along. The two of you are going to split up, and Rosenbloom wants you." Jimmy added, "You're going to go to the Rams."

Allen said, "That would be great. That's close to home." He had a nice home there on a cliff overlooking the ocean. It was a beautiful place. He ended by saying, "Nah, I don't think so."

Nothing happened for a while, and every week Brent asked Jimmy, "What happened with Allen?"

Jimmy would say, "It's going to happen, just wait."

Then Rosenbloom called Jimmy. He said, "Listen, Cosell was on ABC this morning and said this would never happen. Well, I've made up my mind, without question. There is no way I'm going to let him be right over you. I'm going to hire Allen." They both laughed. Allen coached the Rams the next year but was fired before the first regular season game.

He was there for a total of three weeks. Jimmy picked up the phone and called Rosenbloom.

"What the hell are you doing? You waited all this time to get Allen and now you go and fire him."

Rosenbloom said, "All of a sudden I got up in the morning and it's Allen this and Allen that with the Rams. There's no more Rosenbloom Rams." He said, "He took my baby away from me. Next to my wife and children, the Rams are number one."

"Oh, I understand," Jimmy replied.

Jimmy and Rosenbloom were good friends. In fact, the day Rosenbloom drowned, they had planned to have dinner together that evening at Joe's Stone Crab.

Jimmy predicted that Chuck Knox, who was coaching the Rams with great success, would either go with Detroit or Buffalo. Knox signed with Buffalo.

He broke the story about Terry Bradshaw going into a television series.

He also revealed how Hollywood Henderson would end up at Houston, before Bum Phillips even talked to him. They had Hollywood on *The NFL Today* show and Brent asked Jimmy what his scoop for the day was. Jimmy said to Hollywood, "You got one more chance left in your career. You're gonna finish up in New Orleans under Bum Phillips within the week." Jimmy knew Hollywood was making really good money. He added, "When you go down there, don't think too much about additional money. Just take what they offer, and go ahead and play and clean yourself up."

Monday morning Jimmy received a telephone call from Bum Phillips, who was a good friend of his. "Jimmy, I don't know about Hollywood coming here. Where did you get that idea?"

On Tuesday, Bum signed him. You see, Jimmy had no inside information that this was going to take place. He simply knew that Bum had three linebackers on the injured reserved list and was in need of a good linebacker. Jimmy conveniently brought it to the attention of Bum, and he bought it. That was a coup.

One of the greatest stories he ever broke is one Brent Musburger would never forget. Howard Cosell, Al Davis, and Jimmy were having lunch one day at the Beverly Wilshire. Cosell had several drinks and he turned to Davis and said, "I swear to you that I will never go on television for ABC again."

Davis said, "You're full of shit. I've heard that before."

"I'm telling you, I am not going back. This is it," Cosell responded.

Jimmy just listened. Every year Cosell said the same thing and he never took it seriously. All of a sudden, Cosell slammed his hand on the table, and said, "Al, on Emmy's life, I tell you I am quitting."

Jimmy had known Cosell for almost thirty years, and he knew one thing for certain: Cosell loved Emmy, his wife, more than anything in the world. When he swore on her life, Jimmy took it seriously.

They were on the show a couple of weeks later and Brent asked Jimmy to comment on a Monday night game. Immediately, Jimmy's mind clicked and he said to Brent, "By the way, this is Howard Cosell's last year with ABC."

Brent said, "What did you just say?"

Jimmy said, "This is Howard's last year."

"How do you know?" Brent asked.

"I know, but I can't tell you *how* I know."

Cosell got angry. He called Jimmy the next day and said, "You shouldn't have said that."

Jimmy said, "Howard, you know I would never hurt you intentionally, but this *is* your last year."

"What makes you so sure?"

"You swore on Emmy."

"By God, you're right. You're ahead of all those guys. You're brilliant."

Sure enough, at the end of the year, Cosell quit ABC.

Jimmy went through a slump after that. He could not get another story. Then he broke the story that Chuck Muncie was going to San Diego. He knew the Saints were tired of Muncie and he most likely would be dealt with someone else. One of Jimmy's sources was an airlines executive in New Orleans. He gave him a call and asked him to research Charles Muncie in the computer to check for reservations to anywhere. Within a few hours he called back and said Muncie had reservations to San Diego. Jimmy took care of his source in the airlines with two C-notes.

Al Davis of the Oakland Raiders was also part of Jimmy's "grapevine," and was always a dear friend. Jimmy had great admiration for Davis. He made something out of Oakland. He made something out of nothing. He was responsible for the AFL merger with the NFL. He was the commissioner of the AFL and took all the right steps to create the merge. The two talked at least two or three times a week and kept in touch to the day Jimmy died.

In addition to his commentary on *The NFL Today*, Jimmy also covered some of CBS Sports' broadcasts of thoroughbred racing. He covered the Belmont Stakes, the Travers, the Woodward Stakes, and the Jockey Club Gold Cup.

In 1978, at the Washington D.C. International, he successfully picked the one-two-three finish of the race in exact order, by choosing a long shot, Johnny D., first, followed by favorites Exceller and Majestic Light. In the 1979 Travers he picked Smarten for first and General Assembly for second. Although they finished in the first two places (General Assembly was first), his big prediction was that the filly Davonah Dale, the 5–2 favorite in the race, would "fail miserably." Davonah Dale finished out of the money, beaten by twenty-five lengths.

In 1980 Jimmy forecast thirty-two underdogs on the show. Twenty-seven of them proved him right.

Jimmy continued to make speeches and do commercials. However, he was particularly careful to only agree to do those that enhanced his newborn image of an oddsmaker. He frequently turned down any that could have questioned his honesty, integrity, or credibility.

He continued writing his column in the *Las Vegas Sun,* which was syndicated and appeared in more than 300 newspapers around the country. His column, filled with sports gossip and his predictions of forthcoming games, was carried three times a week. Success overflowed when, during high-interest periods of the year, he entertained nearly 30 million readers.

In addition, he had half-minute radio spots in over 360 stations of the Mutual network five times a week. So, if you had not seen Jimmy the Greek on the CBS *NFL Today* show, seen one of his commercials, been a guest at one of his speaking engagements, or read about him in the newspaper, you probably heard him on the radio. Jimmy the Greek became a household name.

Brent Musburger was the host of the show, or the "quarterback." Though Jimmy and he had their share of disagreements in their twelve-year association, he believed Brent was important to the show. Playing the role of quarterback, he endured the immense pressure of calling the shots and handing off the ball to Jimmy, Phyllis, or Irv. The three were always in competition with one another for air time.

Because Brent was highly competitive and almost rigid, if he believed one of the team was not performing at what he considered to be their best standards, he gave them little air time. He would also find ways to test his colleagues. Like the time Jimmy viewed the monitor of the Raiders' games (he was one of the Oakland Raiders' biggest fans) and Brent asked him to comment on another game, one he was not closely watching. Jimmy was human. Sometimes his mind wandered while waiting to be called for air time. Brent toyed with Phyllis too. Sometimes she got off track, commenting about something that had little to do with sports, and Brent would ask her something he knew would catch her off guard.

Brent functioned like a machine. He was so focused on the success of the show and its ratings that he became somewhat inhumane at times. He meant well, but Jimmy and he were destined to lock horns.

The first three years were great. They actually became good friends. Things began to change after that. The pressure became more intense as Brent became obsessed with perfection. He appeared to the viewers as a calm, collected professional who never lost his temper. Off screen, he was a bit of a tyrant. After the show he reviewed the recordings time and again scrutinizing them for possible changes. If he did not like the way he gestured, he changed it by the next show.

On two separate occasions, Jimmy and Brent got into fist fights over their disagreements with the format of the show. One time occurred when the two were alone and Jimmy backed him up against the wall. The other time became well-publicized and was picked up and distributed by the Associated Press.

The fight happened in 1980 on a Sunday at a Manhattan bar. It originated over the amount of air time Jimmy received during the telecasts and his concern with the format of the show on that particular day. During the show, Phyllis did a piece with Steve Little's (kicker for the Cardinals) wife. Little was in an automobile accident that left him paraplegic. They also did a piece about Victor Galinder, an Argentinean boxer who died at an early age, and a segment about a player for the Washington Redskins who sustained an injury that resulted in a later death.

Jimmy was aggravated that so much negativity was reported in the same show. Though all of it was newsworthy, he believed the average viewer who worked hard all week long did not need all the gloominess. He was angered that his air time was limited for these stories. He figured the sports fan preferred seeing him for at least half of that time to lighten up the show. So when Jimmy and Brent discussed this, Brent said something he should not have, and Jimmy (who was sixty-one at the time) landed a punch to Brent's (thirty-nine-year-old) jaw.

Jimmy wanted to make sure he was not forgotten in the line-up. He spent great amounts of money and time putting together his end of the show, and he had a great deal he wanted to say.

Brent Musburger, on the other hand, apparently did not like all the attention and time Jimmy was getting. In a telephone interview with the Associated Press, Musburger said, "When you're involved in a fight with America's oddsmaker, it's rather depressing because you realize there's no way you're gonna be the favorite."

The next day they both regretted the fight. They feared what it would do to their relationship on the show. In fact, in the twelve years Jimmy was with CBS, he only recalled being nervous on two occasions: the first week he was on the show, and the Sunday following the fight.

Prior to the show that day, Jimmy sat in the dressing room with his daughter, Stephanie.

Stephanie said, "Calm down, Dad. Everything's going to be okay."

Jimmy could not even speak. He was horrified over what would happen if Brent made the smallest derogatory comment on the show.

Then Brent did the best thing possible to ensure things went smoothly. He came into Jimmy's dressing room and said, "You think you were mad at me? You should have seen what happened at home with those two guys of mine." Brent was referring to his two children. Jimmy adored Brent's children, and the feelings were mutual. Then he added, "They wouldn't speak to me for two hours. I said, 'What the hell is the matter with the two guys?'" His oldest son said, "Dad, how could you have an argument with our friend, Jimmy the Greek?"

That was enough to relieve the tension between them. Then Brent said, "Hey, you know I should pay you to do PR work for me. Before this incident, nobody even knew who Brent Musburger was. I was just that guy who sat next to Jimmy the Greek. Now *everyone* knows who I am."

The fight received so much attention, the two appeared on the show that day wearing boxing gloves. Brent said to the viewers, "Welcome to *The NFL Today*, or maybe I should say, *As the World Turns.*"

During that same year, Jimmy told Phyllis George Brown on the air that he hated her "fucking husband," who was then-Kentucky Governor John Y. Brown.

This is how it happened. Phyllis was on the set one day, prior to the show airing, and Jimmy was in the corner. She turned to Jimmy and said, "You don't love me anymore."

Jimmy said, "Yes, I do, Phyllis."

She came back about five minutes before the show aired and said, "No, you don't love me."

Jimmy said, "Phyllis, I adore you. It's your fucking husband I hate."

They had the microphones on and it aired.

John Y. Brown came down to the network and unsuccessfully tried to have Jimmy fired. Phyllis and Jimmy were separated for a year. Jimmy came in at 10:30 A.M. to tape his three-minute segment with Brent, and then left. Then Phyllis would come in and tape her segment. He was never on the set at the same time with Phyllis.

Jimmy and John Y. Brown had known each other for a long time. Jimmy had worked for Brown in 1971, when he owned Kentucky Fried Chicken and later Lum's restaurants. They had a dispute over a business deal that ended their friendship when Brown did not pay Jimmy $66,000 that he owed him. Brown made millions with Kentucky Fried Chicken and never paid Jimmy his money. Jimmy filed a lawsuit against him in an effort to collect the money, but later dropped it because Phyllis, who left the show for a couple of years, had returned. When she came back, he felt the conflict would hurt the show too much.

Jimmy was the one responsible for getting Phyllis George and John Y. together. At the time, Jimmy and John Y. were close friends. John Y. was getting a divorce from Ellie Brown, who Jimmy believed was one of the most beautiful women he ever met.

John Y. was upset about the divorce, and a light bulb went off in Jimmy's head. He decided to fix up John Y. with Phyllis. He believed they would make the perfect couple.

Jimmy said to John Y., "How would you like to go out with Phyllis George?"

He said, "Are you kidding? That would be the greatest thing, Greek. Goddamn, you're my friend, you're my friend."

Jimmy said, "Well, get your ass on up here."

They went out and liked each other. Then Phyllis was swept off her feet by Bob Evans, and they were married. It did not take them long to split up.

The minute Jimmy learned they were having problems, he got on the phone with John Y. "Now's the time. She's getting a divorce. You'd better be at her front door with roses and champagne if you want her, and you'd better move fast."

The rest is history.

They always got along great. Jimmy's memories of her were favorable and kind.

Jayne Kennedy was on the show for a couple of years during the time that Phyllis was gone. Jimmy and she got along well. She was gorgeous, there was no question about it. Everyone was after her except for Jimmy. In fact, she even mentioned that to him one time.

She said, "Everybody's on the make for me, but you've never tried."

Jimmy said, "I like you and you're married. And if there's anything I do, I respect a married woman. But don't think I wouldn't be after you under other conditions."

The reason she left CBS was because NBC offered her a part in a syndicated show. She wanted to do both, but was forced to choose between the two and she took the syndicated show (which unfortunately failed). When she left, Phyllis returned to the show.

Irv Cross was a good kid. He always minded his own business and never complained. Jimmy liked him, and they got along beautifully. Then, again, how could you not get along with someone who smiled all the time?

There is much to be said about the chemistry that evolved through the combination of Jimmy, Brent Musburger, Phyllis George Brown, and Irv Cross. This unique mixture could not be duplicated. The first year of the show before Jimmy was a part of it, CBS barely beat NBC in their competing *NFL Live* show. In fact, the ratings were almost dead even. When Jimmy joined the show, it was like everything came together; the chemistry clicked. From then on, the ratings rose to an impressive 7.0 and 8.0, and by far surpassed their competition, always beating them by at least two percentage points.

Jimmy believed the show was so successful because of this chemistry. Yet, he believed *he* was so successful because he was "down to earth." Brent Musburger was the professional, broadcast-major anchorman who coordinated the sports events and happenings. Irv Cross, the former Philadelphia Eagles and Chicago Bears defensive back, appealed to the athletes themselves. Phyllis George, former Miss America, attracted attention and offered a warmer, humane side to sports. But Jimmy the Greek appealed to the average person. He was not educated whatsoever in broadcasting; he had a tenth-grade education. He was not strikingly handsome; he was average. He did not possess the rock-hard physique of a former athlete; he was overweight and flabby. He spoke in everyday language and was a little rough around the edges. The Greek was never one to formally prepare scripts of exactly what he would say. He simply did his homework, researched, knew everything there was to know about a given topic, and he spoke. His manner was never one of a polished, smooth orator. In fact, it was his knowledge, not articulation, that "made him."

He was on the same level as the sports fan who gathered around the television on Sunday afternoons with a beer in his hand, watching the show. They liked him just the way he was. When Jimmy the Greek spoke, they did not see or hear him on the television: They saw and heard him in the same room. He was sitting right there in their own living room, having a beer with them.

Jimmy was aware of that. But what he did not know was that in the big world of television, a man must learn to choose his words with care.

Chapter 22

NFL Today:
SOS Tomorrow

JIMMY AWOKE ON JANUARY 15, 1988, prepared to spend the weekend covering the NFL Championship between the Minnesota Vikings and the Washington Redskins. He was at Duke Zeibert's, a popular Washington eatery, in the latter part of the morning taping a feature for *The NFL Today* show. When the camera malfunctioned, he sat down to eat. Jimmy the Greek never anticipated how much that lunch would eventually cost him.

It was Dr. Martin Luther King, Jr.'s fifty-ninth birthday and Ed Hotaling, a WRC-TV reporter, planted himself at the restaurant, seeking opinions of the progress of blacks in society.

He approached Jimmy the Greek and asked his view concerning progress made in the area of sports. The Greek welcomed him to the table. The interview went like this:

> HOTALING: Is there anything you still think we need to do or do you think we don't need to worry about civil rights anymore?
> SNYDER: Yeah. Pretty soon they're going to have to equalize it for the Blacks, for the Greeks, the Jews and for everybody. I mean let's make it equal for everybody. You know!
> HOTALING: Is it equal? What about sports?
> SNYDER: They've got everything, if they take over coaching like everybody wants them to there's not going to be anything

237

left for the whites. I mean all the players are black, I mean the only thing that the whites control is the coaching jobs. Now, I'm not being derogatory about it, but that's all that's left for them. The black talent is beautiful. It's great. It's out there. The only thing left for the whites is a couple of coaching jobs.

HOTALING: Yeah, but do we need to get more black coaches?

SNYDER: Oh, it's all right with me. I'm sure that they'll take over that pretty soon, too . . . . I don't want this on [referring to the camera] . . . . I'm just . . . there isn't much left for the white guys anymore.

HOTALING: Well, uh, actually there is.

SNYDER: Where?

HOTALING: Well, they can make big progress in basketball, for example, or in football. How can you improve height performance?

SNYDER: There's ten people, there's ten players on a basketball court. If you find two whites you're lucky, either four out of five or nine out of ten are black. Now that's because they practice and they play and practice and play. They're not lazy like the white athlete is.

HOTALING: Yeah, but you know another thing is the predominately white schools don't emphasize sports.

SNYDER: That's not the reason. The black is the better athlete to begin with. Because he's been bred to be that way, because of his high thighs and big thighs that goes up into his back, and they can jump higher and run faster because of their bigger thighs, you see. The white man has to overcome that. But they don't try hard enough to overcome it.

HOTALING: But it developed in certain sports that you have more prominent —

SNYDER: What, swimming? As that guy said . . . tennis, sure because you don't need the thighs, the thigh situation, as much as you need it in other sports, you see. In football and baseball and any game that you have to run a lot, I mean your thighs come into prominence, very much so, because that's what gauges your speed and your jump, in situations such as that, in basketball, your thighs the things that make you jump high. I'm telling you that the black is the better athlete, and he is bred to be the better athlete, because this goes back all the way to the Civil War when during the slave trading the big, the owner, the slave owner would breed his big black to his big woman so that he could have a big black kid, you see. I mean that's where it all started.

That is how the interview aired. What the networks, news-papers, and radio never mentioned was that the four-minute interview was the result of editing and splicing from an actual thirty-minute interview. Nevertheless, when it aired, Jimmy's problems began.

After the interview, he finished taping the segment for *The NFL Today* show and left Duke Zeibert's. He did not think anything about the interview. Within a few hours, Brent Musburger and Ted Shaker, executive producer of CBS Sports, viewed the tapes and talked to the CBS executives in Hawaii. Neal Pilson, president of CBS Sports, was on his way to Hawaii for network affiliate meetings when Jimmy gave the interview.

Jimmy was unaware that anything was wrong until he returned to the Washington Grand Hotel, where he was staying. It was approximately 6:45 P.M. and the interview had already aired on WRC-TV at 6:00 P.M. As he entered the lobby, he was bombarded with reporters. Then, an *NFL Today* production assistant approached him and said, "Shaker wants to see you, *now.*" He escorted Jimmy to Shaker's room, where George Veras, *NFL Today* producer, Shaker and several others from the show and network were congregated.

When Jimmy walked into the room, Shaker yelled, "What the hell's the matter with you? Do you know what you've done?"

Jimmy did not say anything. Everyone was gathered around the television watching the *CBS Evening News* with Dan Rather, which aired parts of the interview. Jimmy sat down and viewed the show with them. This was one of many shows that telecast similar segments.

When it was over, Shaker said to Jimmy, "What do you think about that?"

Jimmy was shocked. He said, "Ted, you don't understand, they did some major cutting."

Shaker said, "All I know is we're in big trouble." About that time, Gene Upshaw entered the room. Upshaw, who is black, was president of the National Football League Players Association and a former Oakland Raider player. He had just met with the press in the lobby.

He asked Shaker, "Why is everyone so excited? Why is everyone making such a big deal out of this?" His remarks were ig-

nored. Then Shaker called Jay Goldstein, a CBS Sports public relations person in New York, and they prepared a statement for
the press. Shaker read aloud the statement to those in the room:
"CBS deeply regrets the remarks made earlier today to a news
reporter by Jimmy the Greek Snyder. We find them reprehensible. In no way do they reflect the views of CBS Sports."

Jimmy said, "Don't use that word."

"What word?" Shaker asked.

"Reprehensible. Reprehensible means you're dead," Jimmy
said.

"That's *my* word," Shaker said.

CBS offered this statement to the media in the exact form
Jimmy had heard in the room. The words seared deeply in his
mind. He had hoped that, once given the chance to explain, this
whole misunderstanding would diminish. When CBS labeled his
words "reprehensible," he believed they condemned him to a
life sentence. He could never recover from that.

He immediately asked if he could appear before the media
to clear up matters. They said they had a prepared apology on
his behalf that a CBS spokesperson would read, but he was not
to have any contact with the media.

The spokesperson read the following apology: "I'm terribly
upset and sorry for my remarks and I offer a full and heartfelt
apology to all those I may have offended."

Shaker even had two production assistants follow Jimmy to
his room to ensure he spoke to no one.

The apology did not detain the efforts of the media. The interview was dispersed at breathtaking speed. It made the networks that night and front pages in the morning with more than
1,200 articles appearing around the country.

Jimmy was shocked that his comments were termed as racially offensive because he intended to appraise the African-
American athlete. He thought the white athletes would be the
offended race because he referred to them as "lazy."

As for his remarks about the physical build of black athletes
and their heritage being part of their athletic ability, he had read
about it in a January 18, 1971, *Sports Illustrated* article entitled,
"An Assessment of Why Black is Best," by Martin Kane. It discussed the claimed physiological differences between African-

Americans and whites. The article stated that researchers found that black Americans:

> ... tend to have a shorter trunk, a more slender pelvis, longer arms (especially forearms) and longer legs (especially from the knees down) than his white counterpart ... He has more muscle in the upper arms and legs, less on the calves.

In that same article, Lee Evans, a black Olympic gold medalist, said: "On plantations, a strong black man was mated with a strong black woman. [Blacks] were simply bred for physical qualities." Ironically, this remark is most remembered. The comment, originally spoken by an African-American with no reaction whatsoever, was only reiterated by Jimmy and was interpreted as racist.

Jimmy the Greek was also familiar with Frederick Douglass' autobiography, entitled *Narrative*, where slave breeding was openly discussed. Douglass told the story of a new slave owner who bought Caroline, "a large able-bodied woman about 20 years old." He further described how the owner rented a male slave and "him he used to fasten up with Caroline every night!" Douglas explains that Caroline was purchased for purposes of "breeding." It is true the point he expressed was intended to show how Caroline was bought to reproduce more slaves; however, Douglass noted her physical characteristics as "large" and "able-bodied," implying her offspring would produce the same qualities.

In addition, Malcolm X frequently mirrored the beliefs of selective breeding. He said: "They bred any kind of looking slave you wanted."

Therefore, the assessment Jimmy expressed was shared openly by the offended race.

Pilson called Washington the next morning and told Jimmy it would be in his best interest to resign.

Jimmy said, "What the hell did I do? There is only one more game left in the season. Why don't you say you're suspending me from the game without pay? Then everything will cool down before the next season."

Pilson said, "That sounds fair to me. That's exactly what we'll do."

Twenty minutes later, Jimmy turned on the television and heard Gene Jankowski, president of CBS Broadcast Group, reading the following statement to the press:

> In an interview yesterday, CBS Sports personality Jimmy the Greek Snyder made a number of remarks about black and white athletes which had patently racist overtones. CBS deeply regrets this incident and wishes to categorically disassociate itself from these remarks. . . . CBS has terminated its relationship with Mr. Snyder, effective immediately.

Jimmy was in disbelief. He learned he was fired via this broadcast. Jimmy could not understand why Pilson had not been honest with him when they spoke on the telephone just minutes earlier.

He later learned that Pilson, Jankowski, and Theodore Shaker had a conference call and unanimously decided to terminate him. After twelve years of loyal service, Jimmy wondered why no one bothered to tell him he was fired. He never even received a letter.

Ted Shaker, who offered him no support now, once thanked Jimmy for paying for the new extension on his house because the show ratings were so high.

Brent Musburger, host and managing editor of *The NFL Today,* called Jimmy's comments "shocking" and "unbelievable." He said he "fell off the chair" when he first heard the interview. Then he said on CBS network radio: "This suggests that we have a long way to go in trying to break down some of the old stereotypes." These were the first of several defamatory remarks Musburger made about Jimmy the Greek. In an article by Norman Chad that appeared in *The Washington Post* on January 23, 1988, Musburger said:

> We're probably guilty with letting him [Jimmy the Greek] get away with too much off-camera over the years. I've heard him be more anti-Semitic and anti-female than anti-black in some of his comments.

Even after Jimmy was gone, Musburger continued to bash him. Most surprising was Musburger's remark that appeared in *The New York Daily News* more than two years after Jimmy was fired from CBS. In Bob Raissman's "TV Sports" column in April 1990, Musburger called Jimmy a "fraud." The fact that Musburger did not support him was no surprise to Jimmy because they had not gotten along for quite a while. But the fact that he said untruthful things about him and continued adding fuel to the flames as late as two years after the interview was unpardonable.

When the Sunday following the interview arrived, for the first time in twelve years CBS aired *The NFL Today* show without its primary counterpart. The introduction still resounded with the announcement of Musburger, Snyder, and colleagues Irv Cross and Will McDonough. Editing Jimmy the Greek's name from the introduction interrupted the accompanying song. McDonough sat in that day as a temporary replacement of Jimmy, but there were no predictions before the NFC Championship.

Jimmy did not watch the show. It was too painful sitting on the opposite side of the camera. He found refuge at the racetrack.

Brent Musburger slid the network's apology into the format of the show to the viewers awaiting the kickoff of Sunday's National Football Conference championship game. He delivered four lines in explanation of the events and labeled Jimmy the Greek's remarks "regrettable" and "offensive." That was the end of CBS' discussion of some important issues Jimmy raised.

There was mixed response everywhere. Many people came forward to defend Jimmy the Greek. The biggest surprise was his support from the African-American population. Famous black leaders and athletes defended him: Bill Cosby, Jesse Barfield, Dexter Manley, and Roy Innis, chairman of the Congress of Racial Equality.

Jimmy met with Jesse Jackson on the Sunday of the NFC Championship game for more than an hour in his Washington hotel room, apologizing again. Following the meeting, at a nationally televised news conference, Jackson said he "didn't want Snyder to become a scapegoat for sports or for television networks which don't use enough black talent."

Ed Hotaling, the WRC-TV reporter who interviewed Snyder, criticized the rapid firing by CBS. He said that CBS should have kept him on to cover black-related issues.

Bill Cosby said CBS fired Jimmy the Greek because "the networks are always interested in getting the heat off. He said he was truly sorry . . . . He shouldn't lose his job over it."

At an awards dinner commemorating Dr. Martin Luther King, Jr., on January 18, 1988, Roy Innis said:

> Jimmy must have been reading Malcolm X. During the days of slavery, we were bred like chattel. It's wrong that they did that to us, but it's not wrong to talk about it. Jimmy the Greek spoke the truth.

He called Jimmy the Greek's firing "a tragedy."

Jesse Barfield, who was with the Toronto Blue Jays, stated: "Leaping, running — physiologically, we have an advantage."

Jim Rice, former Boston Red Sox outfielder, told *Miami Herald* that Jimmy was right in his remarks. "It's a gift. Raw talent," he said.

Fox Television's *A Current Affair* had Dr. Alvin Poussaint, a Harvard Medical School psychologist, on their January 20, 1988, show. In response to Jimmy the Greek's remarks, he said:

> Black Americans are a select group: They're very strong physically. The slave traders went over to Africa and they took the biggest and strongest blacks to work the fields and survive the journey to America.
>
> Jimmy the Greek wasn't being malicious. He was trying to explain why black athletes are so dominant. What he said was by and large complimentary to black players and their talent. He wasn't saying blacks couldn't be coaches or that coaching jobs should be reserved for whites.

In response to a plan Jimmy the Greek contrived to write letters of apology to black athletes, Jesse Jackson called it "admirable and the right thing to do." He added, "The man apologized. That's all a human being can do."

Jimmy sent letters to Clarence Thomas, then-chairman of the Equal Employment Opportunity Commission, Willis Edwards, president of the Beverly Hills-Hollywood Chapter of the NAACP, and over 300 various other African-American leaders and athletes. The following is the letter he sent:

> I regret that I have to write this letter, but it is necessary. Recently, I made some remarks on television that were offensive, not only to Black Americans, but to all Americans. It was not my intention to offend anyone, but I did. As a result, I embarrassed myself, my family, my friends, and my employer.

It would do no good to explain that I was actually trying to say something very positive about Black athletes — that they work hard, they are disciplined, they overcome great obstacles and odds to become great athletes, and they are highly motivated (I said, "hungry" in the interview). No positive explanation, however, can overcome the negative remarks that were made and the offensive way they came out.

Thus, the only thing I know to do as a human being is to say I am sorry, offer my regrets, and ask for forgiveness. In all honesty, more than the loss of my job at CBS, the thing that hurts me most is the loss of your respect for me. The job I can do without. I need my self-respect back. The only way I know to do that is to ask for forgiveness from the people I offended — Americans generally, Black Americans in particular, and Black athletes especially. That's why I am writing you — to ask for your forgiveness.

Jimmy received a letter of reply dated February 16, 1988, from Herschel Walker, then with the Dallas Cowboys (later with the Minnesota Vikings). This was one of many letters of support he received from African Americans. It read:

I wanted to thank you for your letter and to tell you how sorry I am that something like this had to happen. I think the shock was the reaction of the public, not what you actually said. I think people tend to make a lot more out of things than they need to. I am just sorry that as a result of this you lost your job. Please don't feel embarrassed or think that you have been disrespectful. I understand your situation and I am not going to judge you in any way differently than I have in the past. I forgive you and I will pray that your life will return to normal very soon. Best of luck to you. May God bless you.

Jimmy received over 4,000 letters, and not one African American said he was offended. In fact, CBS received so many letters, they eventually forwarded them to Jimmy the Greek's home address. An article in *The New York Times* on January 26, 1988, said: "the company has received 2,000 calls, letters, and telegrams since it dismissed Snyder, by far the most the sports division has ever received on any subject." The article added that response in favor of Jimmy the Greek "was about 75%."

Jimmy watched the *Oprah Winfrey Show* when she had ten athletes on as guests. Nine of them were black — guys like Dexter Manley — and nine to one said The Greek was right. What he said about slave masters breeding their big black men to big black women was part of their history, they explained.

Those who knew Jimmy well spoke up against any implication that he was prejudice. Paul Zimmerman of *Sports Illustrated* said, "I've known him for more than 20 years, and I've never seen any of the tell tale, giveaway signs of the closet racist — the offhand good-ol'-boy remark when there is no one around, the nasty slip of the tongue."

Irv Cross, Jimmy's colleague on *The NFL Today* show, who is black, told *Time* magazine: "They [Jimmy the Greek's remarks] don't reflect the Jimmy the Greek that I know, and I've known him for almost 13 years."

Jimmy paid for college educations for many poor black athletes. He gave them money from time to time, and bus fare for Christmas vacation and other holidays.

Public response was overwhelming. Four days after the interview, Fox Television's *A Current Affair* conducted a 900-number telephone poll that showed nearly 92 percent of the 128,702 people polled believed CBS erred in firing Jimmy the Greek. That is, 118,373 people said CBS should not have fired him, while only 10,329 said CBS did the right thing. Bob Hope jested that with those numbers, the Republicans should run him for president.

A public-opinion poll conducted by CNN asked the question, "Should Jimmy the Greek have been fired?" With over 7,000 people who responded, 6,202 said no, he should not have been fired. That was an amazing 89 percent support for Jimmy the Greek.

In retrospect, he said he felt that he erred in mentioning the "high-thigh theory" because it was just that: a theory. The biggest mistake Jimmy made on that Friday afternoon was not being racist or a bigot. He failed to clearly articulate what was intended to compliment the African-American athlete. He was never one to plan ahead or choose his words carefully. Therefore, his fumbled words interpreted a different meaning than the one intended.

His sense of timing was another disadvantage. On the birthday of Dr. Martin Luther King, Jr., as expected, blacks evaluate their progress made in equality. This evokes painful memories. Now add to that a major controversy that occurred nine months earlier when Los Angeles Dodgers executive Al Campanis said on national television that blacks lacked the "necessities" to manage in the major leagues. The remarks caused a firestorm forcing Campanis to resign. This created a movement focusing on placing blacks in coaching and managerial positions. The climate was restless and apt to destroy anyone who did not choose his words with special care.

Jimmy the Greek was never accredited for his openness to discuss racial issues when no one else would. He had the courage to discuss possible differences between the races. He believed that to say nothing was to leave things as they were. Only through discussion could differences be resolved. Many times following the interview he said that a man has the right to say whatever he believes because that is the American way. If what he says causes chastisement, then we lose a part of our unalienable rights granted to us by our forefathers.

When our freedom of expression is extracted in small portions, we hardly notice. But when that final portion departs with our dignity and integrity, we are enabled to see what was happening all along. It is then that we have to take on the judicial system and trust that the wheels of justice roll along freedom's path.

Chapter 23

Victim of Network Conspiracy

THE TELEVISION INDUSTRY IS in a class of its own. There is no "job security" or tenure. You go from one contract to the next wondering if this will be the one the network chooses not to renew. An employee may produce high ratings and years of faithful service, and attract leading endorsements and viewer loyalty. None of this holds any significance if a network is ready to get rid of you.

After he overcame the initial shock, Jimmy the Greek began to view things with clearer vision. The more he looked, the more he became convinced that he was a victim of network conspiracy. A number of things that formerly were difficult to understand now began to make sense.

He was convinced that long before he gave his interview at Duke Zeibert's, CBS had their own agenda: getting rid of him. It all began when they hired an independent consulting firm to come in and take a look at things. Upon viewing *The NFL Today* show, they strongly advised changing the format of the show. They suggested the show should divert from gambling and gossip; in other words, they should eliminate Jimmy the Greek from the team.

CBS apparently liked the idea because they almost did not renew his contract for the 1986-87 season. They finally decided to keep him on and not entirely for humanitarian reasons. It posed too great a risk *not* to renew his contract.

With strong viewer support and unfailingly high ratings, CBS had to provide a good explanation that justified letting him go, to Jimmy the Greek himself and to the public who loved him. They did not have one. Without a reason, they ran the risk of appearing they had failed to renew it because of his age. He was now seventy and the public would outpour with sympathy for him, not to mention the possibility of an age-discrimination suit and all the negative publicity that would surround a claim of this magnitude. Plus, they ran the risk of another network securing him, causing a possible drop in ratings to a competing show.

CBS renewed the contract for the 1986-87 season and the 1987-88 season. His final contract was his first one-year contract. All previous ones were made for two years or longer with an option-to-renew clause.

Next, they proceeded with an alternative: prodding him into leaving. They began to harass him about small things. Ted Shaker hounded him to lose weight. Neal Pilson began to demand a script of exactly what he was going to say on the show each week. Brent Musburger became more and more unreasonable.

The remarks annoyed Jimmy, and the conflict with Musburger was even more bothersome, but he endured. On the day he gave his interview, he gave CBS exactly what they wanted: a reason to fire him. When CBS labeled his remarks "reprehensible" within hours of the interview, that proved to Jimmy they were making no effort to restrain public reaction. Instead, they magnified it. "Reprehensible" is a strong word. There are many other word choices that would have effectively disassociated themselves from his remarks, but they opted for the strongest, and did so, against the will of Jimmy the Greek.

Their hastiness in firing him also intensified public reaction. He was fired the following morning — one day before his contract expired. They could have suspended him for the last game of the season, then refused to renew his contract for the next season. That still would have alleviated pressure, and it would have demonstrated respect for a loyal employee of twelve years. Or, if they wanted to keep him on, they could have suspended him for the last game of the season. By the beginning of the next season, the flames would have died down. Then they could have renewed his contract.

Jimmy believed that CBS fired him instead of suspending him for selfish reasons: to blackball him with other networks. They no longer wanted him for themselves, but they did not want someone else to have him, either. The swift firing made it appear that his actions were inexcusable; hence, preventing him from working for another network.

He was also not permitted to explain himself to the public on the eve of the interview. CBS was his employer up to that day and he obeyed their demand against his own intuition. With no explanation, matters were allowed to escalate.

When public reaction demonstrated overwhelming support for Jimmy the Greek, suspicion arose concerning his firing. Attorneys from all over sent him letters explaining his rights to sue CBS. Jimmy did not pursue any immediate legal action for several reasons. The biggest reason was that he experienced intense self-blame and embarrassment. Though most of the public was gentle and still loved him, he no longer loved himself. He was convinced that no one respected him anymore. He did not blame CBS; he blamed himself for everything. He retreated from public eye. For three years, in between hospitalizations for deteriorating health and depression, he basically lived at the Miami racetrack.

Another reason Jimmy did not seek legal action immediately was because he suffered from severe depression. Shortly after he was fired from CBS, he had an emotional breakdown and was treated for acute situational depression and severe anxiety at Duke University Hospital.

He also experienced a decline in health. Two days after he was fired from CBS, he was hospitalized for chest pains. By the end of the month, he suffered a heart attack and was hospitalized for two weeks. He was diagnosed with angina. This was the beginning of a succession of visits to medical clinics and hospitalizations. At the beginning of March 1988, he suffered chest pains again and was also diagnosed with an active peptic ulcer. At that point, he was given a stress test. The results of the test prohibited him from partaking in any stress-inducing activities, which included making calls to his business office. He was also ordered not to travel. In the three months that followed his firing, he was hospitalized three times.

In November 1988 he was admitted to Miami Heart Institute and diagnosed with chicken pox and acute shingles, the direct result of tremendous stress. For nine months he was in and out of Miami Heart, suffering from pain and itching caused by the shingles which his doctors confirmed were caused by the stress of the CBS occurrences.

It was not until the fall of 1989 that he was well enough to seek work. It was then he realized the extent of damage inflicted by CBS. First, at the age of seventy-two, who wanted to hire him? Now add to that an *unhealthy* seventy-two-year-old, and chances were even worse. Putting those issues aside, he was portrayed as racist. No one wanted to take a chance on him, even if the public loved him and his ratings were always there. The way CBS mishandled circumstances left him blackballed with all the networks.

Jimmy sought a football analyst position with ABC, NBC, Fox, and the cable networks. No one wanted him. Barry Frank, Jimmy the Greek's former agent, agreed: "I've talked to everybody in town [New York]," he said, "but no one will touch him [Jimmy the Greek]." The best example of the negative impact the CBS firing had on his career came from a conversation with Robert Wussler, then-president of the Turner Broadcast System. Wussler had originally hired Jimmy the Greek for CBS in 1976. When Jimmy asked him for a job in September 1989, Wussler said, "We'd love to have you, Jimmy, but CBS fucked you for everyone else."

When CBS fired Jimmy the Greek, he lost his secondary income as well. Long before he joined *The NFL Today*, he had his own public relations firm. After a while of being on the show, it became too much to maintain, because his time was no longer his own. He had to talk to newspaper reporters, make appearances, and attend meetings. In the meantime, he attracted major endorsements and speaking engagements that gave him an additional income of over $400,000 a year. He was involved in television promotions for Bud Light beer, Burns Automobile in Chicago, *USA Today*'s "Beat the Greek" contest, and Trump Castle Hotel and Casino. Between his primary and secondary incomes he was making over $800,000 a year, not to mention a hefty expense account valued at $300,000 a year. When he was fired, he lost it all. In addition, Jimmy the Greek lost all his speaking engagements, approximately fifteen to twenty lectures a year. Because of the condition in which he was left, resuming his prior position of a public relations man was out of the question.

Finally, on January 15, 1991, three years following the incident, Jimmy contacted the American Arbitration Association and filed a "demand for arbitration against CBS and other CBS executives, employees, NBC-CBS's affiliate station and Ed Hotaling," the one who interviewed Jimmy. The demand alleged "Defamation of Character, Disparagement, Injurious Falsehood, Breach of Contract, Interference with Contract and Interference with Economic Advantage." He sought damages in excess of $10 million:

- $5 million from CBS and various CBS Sports employees for the humiliation suffered and their criticism, defamation, and disparagement;
- $600,000 for income loss due to breach of contract;
- $600,000 for economic harm as a result of character damage suffered;
- $5 million for loss of secondary income, which included endorsements and speaking engagements, as well as compensation for having been blackballed; thus, destroying his career, health, and life;
- reimbursement for expenses, penalties, and legal costs.

His suit for age discrimination stated: "CBS used a non-work-related incident as an excuse to fire him because he was getting too old." He said that Neal Pilson and Ted Shaker had made comments about him getting old. Pilson had made comments about him not returning the next season because he would be too ill. Shaker said to Jimmy on several occasions, "Greek, you're getting too old." In fact, at one time, Jimmy came in with letters from his doctors proving he was in good enough health to work for them. When someone suggested Jimmy do something extra for the show or outside of the show, Shaker would say, "He's [Jimmy the Greek] too old to do that." Court papers contended that as soon as he was fired, he was replaced with Dick Butkus, who was much younger than Jimmy the Greek. He believed this helped substantiate his claim that CBS thought he was too old.

His biggest obstacle with the lawsuit was overcoming the timeliness issue for not filing more promptly. As a result, he was unable to file an Age Discrimination in Employment Act claim because there was a 300-day statute-of-limitation period. In addition, he was unable to sue CBS for defamation and other business mishandling because a one-year statute of limitation had expired. Also, through an AFTRA (American Federation of Television and Radio Artists) agreement made solely between CBS and Jimmy the Greek, he was not permitted to bring suit against executives and employees of CBS, NBC, and Ed Hotaling.

Jimmy was left with only a suit for breach of contract against CBS. CBS fought to have arbitration stopped because of the period of time elapsed between the incident and the claim, but the request was denied.

Jimmy's contentions were that CBS verbally promised to exercise his option to renew his contract prior to the interview. CBS breached the contract when they failed to honor their word. In addition, CBS never gave him written notice of refusal to exercise their option.

His prior experience with CBS was to have a verbal discussion of the contract renewal and paperwork that followed. Barry Frank, his former agent, and he relied so heavily on this practice, they never sought alternative employment. This was corroborated through his past contracts.

On at least five occasions, his contracts were dated after the renewal date. On each of these contracts, the proper date appeared at the top of the contract, but another date existed in the bottom left corner. The date in the corner indicated when the contract was formally prepared and executed. His contract for January 1, 1977, had an execution date of March 8, 1977. Another contract for January 22, 1979, had a completion date on some pages of May 21, 1979, and July 31, 1979, on others. This indicates that paperwork was incomplete up to six months into the original contract date. One contract dated December 10, 1979, has a rendering date of March 18, 1980, but a cover letter to Jimmy the Greek not dated until June 13, 1980. His contract dated February 14, 1982, has an implementation date of July 12, 1982, in the corner and an amendment dated March 31, 1982, with its execution date being June 5, 1982. Even his final contract represented the same pattern. It was scheduled to begin on March 29, 1987, but was still being compiled through the summer. In fact, on June 23, 1987, Jimmy received a letter depicting new inclusions provided in the contract; therefore, this indicated the contracts were still incomplete.

Proceedings were held in November 1994. Jimmy testified that on December 21, 1987, Barry Frank returned from a luncheon with Neal Pilson and said that in regards to his option being renewed, Pilson told Frank, "Tell the Greek not to worry." He also pointed out that several newspaper articles stated that his contract would most likely be renewed. In an article in *USA Today* dated January 12, 1988, Rudy Martke interviewed Brent Musburger. When asked if Jimmy the Greek would return the following season, he replied: "The Greek will be back next year. When you walk into an ad agency they don't ask who the Greek picked — they ask what the ratings are." In another *USA Today* article dated November 30, 1987, George Veras, producer for *The NFL Today* show, said: "There are no possible changes planned . . . Jimmy's had a terrific year, Brent's the best at what he does and no one's had more scoops than Will."

Jimmy believed Pilson would support his testimony of the details of the luncheon with Barry Frank. In addition, on several occasions, Jimmy asked Pilson whether or not the contract would be renewed and Pilson told him, "What have you got to worry about? As long as I'm here, you're here."

CBS argued that Jimmy's agreement clearly stated the decision to exercise his option required written notice. They said CBS had no policy of giving oral notice before any written.

Though Jimmy the Greek's claims were substantial, problems arose from a weak testimony by Barry Frank and a lack of corroboration with the testimony of Neal Pilson. Barry Frank, who has a strong relationship with CBS because he represents several clients under their employ, had a testimony that was less than convincing. One could not help wondering whose best interest was in mind. On at least two occasions he has held high-ranking positions at CBS, and is a personal friend of Neal Pilson. In fact, they golf together and have dinner together socially several times a year. Frank *did* testify that during the luncheon he asked Pilson if Jimmy's contract was going to be renewed and

Pilson responded, "Tell the Greek not to worry." He also stated that it was his "impression" that his contract would be renewed.

Pilson denied having said that. He testified that he told Frank that no decision was made and would not be made until the end of the season. He also denied that CBS had any oral practices of contract renewal.

Because of the lack of timeliness, the weak testimony of Barry Frank, and lack of corroboration of Neal Pilson, Jimmy's claim that CBS breached its contract was denied. His grievance was dismissed on November 11, 1994.

Jimmy was virtually unmoved by the decision. He held no grudges with CBS or any of the people who disappointed him. The end of the lawsuit represented a closure to the CBS chapter in his life. He was allowed to release his feelings and confront individuals with the facts of how deeply affected he was by CBS's mishandling of his future. His attempt for financial compensation put an end to the question of whether or not he should sue them. The judicial system did not work for him. Politics overruled justice, and timeliness governed fairness.

His lingering concerns with the aftermath of CBS consisted of three issues. His first concern was his lack of income. Though financial planning provided for him to live comfortably for the rest of his life, he had no gambling money. That bothered him. His second concern was that he was left with no job. The job provided him with an identity. He no longer had one. His third issue was a fear of being remembered as a racist. He lost his dignity and self-respect. He wanted to clear his name.

Just around the corner was the remedy for these unresolved conflicts. It existed in an idea of a dear friend who had a persistence and drive that matched that of Jimmy the Greek's.

Chapter 24

Making Peace
With the Past

SOMEONE ONCE SAID, "A TRUE friend walks in when the rest
of the world walks out." Through the years, Jimmy the Greek was
blessed with friends. But in his latter years following his expulsion from CBS, he isolated himself from people. It was an unconscious act, one that resulted from severe depression and feelings
of worthlessness. Tommy Manakides nudged his way into his life
in 1988 and played a significant role in his final years. His
encouragement and support guided him toward making peace
with his past while savoring the sweet flavor of his heritage.

Sharing a taste for fine cigars, the two met during a poker
game at the Mirage when Tommy lit a Prince Philip Macanudo
Maduro and Jimmy remarked how much he enjoyed smoking
the same brand. The following day Tommy placed an extra cigar
in his pocket, and when they met again at the poker room he
gave it to Jimmy. Their friendship evolved through this small act
of kindness and was enhanced in the realization that both were
Greek. They were the offspring of Greek immigrants and products of a strong Greek heritage and culture.

But their friendship was cultivated most in Tommy's ability
to see through a thick, hard shell that surrounded Jimmy. Inside
was a frightened child who craved affection and respect. Almost
immediately after they met, Tommy began to see a pattern with
Jimmy. He was warm and caring as long as the relationship was

solely acquaintances. But the minute that it began to develop any form of intimacy, he lashed out. He did not hesitate to tell anyone to "Go fuck yourself." Most people would leave after being told that once or twice, but Tommy stuck around and chipped away fragments of the shell, piece by piece. He recognized the remarks as part of Jimmy's own defense system, one that would not allow anyone to know the *real* Jimmy the Greek and one that would not end in pain and disappointment for him. A wall of intimidation disguised the warm, generous, and vulnerable side of him.

Tommy invited Jimmy to dinner the day after they met. As they moved through the crowded casino, he was puzzled at Jimmy's demeanor. He walked in a stooped position with his feet shuffling the floor. He could not understand why someone with his fame and notoriety exhibited the manner of a common man.

Shortly after they sat down to eat, he hurled a question at his new friend.

"You're Jimmy the Greek — a living legend — so why do you move through the crowds like you're nobody special?"

Jimmy looked at Tommy, not bothering to answer the question.

Then an approaching voice called, "Greek, it's good to see you. You know I used to couldn't wait until Sundays to watch you on the show. How the hell are you?" The stranger spoke as if reunited with a long lost friend.

Jimmy looked up and saw two middle-aged men smiling at him.

"All right," Jimmy said.

"Hey, listen, I just wancha to know if it's any consolation, I think you got screwed."

"Thanks," Jimmy said, offering a half-smile.

The two strangers turned to walk away.

"That's what they always say," Jimmy said to Tommy. "They never say, hey, you sonofabitch, you oughta be ashamed."

Several minutes passed and then Jimmy said, "You know you got a lot of nerve asking me that question."

"What question?"

"You know, the question you asked me when we first sat down — why I walk around like I'm nobody special?"

"Oh, *that*. You're still thinking about that?" Tommy asked.

"What the fuck am I supposed to do — I'm dead," Jimmy said.

"What do you mean, *dead*? Everywhere you go, people stop and stare. They all recognize you. You saw those two guys — they love you, Jimmy," Tommy said. "As long as the public still loves you, there's a demand for your name to be out there. So who handles your promotions, anyway?"

"Nobody."

"Then let me promote you."

"What's in it for you?" Jimmy asked.

"I'll tell you what. You let me promote you, and it won't cost you a dime. If I can turn things around for you and we can make some money together, then I'll take a cut."

"Why the hell would you do that?"

"Because you were given a bad rap and I want the world to see what a legend you are. What have you got to lose?" Tommy asked.

Jimmy looked at him. He was serious. "All right," Jimmy said.

Tommy began working on the production of a major motion picture on the life of Jimmy the Greek. He made numerous calls and trips in an effort to find an interest. To his surprise, he found little. Finally, a producer enlightened him with this information: People were too afraid to get involved with the controversy that hovered around his name.

After exhausting his resources and spending a great deal of money and time, Tommy gave up. He had received little support or encouragement from Jimmy. He seemed too preoccupied with his own problems. Between his poor health, depression, and the stress of a pending lawsuit with CBS, Jimmy was moody and uncooperative with any efforts Tommy made to promote him. Tommy continued to keep in touch with him on a friendly basis, but abandoned the idea of the movie and any promotional efforts.

A turning point came in March 1992, when Vicki, Jimmy's daughter who lives in Las Vegas, called. She told Tommy that Jimmy was in town and wanted to see him. Tommy said he would meet him that evening.

"Tommy," Vicki said, "you know, I'm really worried about Dad. He's in bad shape. When I walked into the card room today, I didn't even recognize him. I thought I'd better prepare you," she said.

"What do you mean, *bad shape?*" Tommy asked.

"It's like he's given up. He needs a haircut, he hasn't shaved. I'm really concerned. I mentioned him getting cleaned up today, but he won't listen to me. You're the only one he'll listen to."

"Don't worry, he'll be all right," Tommy said.

When Tommy walked into the poker room at the Barbary Coast, he saw Jimmy sitting at the end seat of the Pai Gow poker table. They had dinner that night, and every night thereafter, with Vicki joining them as often as she could.

After seeing the condition of his friend, Tommy became even more determined to put Jimmy's name on top again. He was saddened at what CBS had done to him. He vowed to himself to never again abandon his dream for Jimmy.

After a couple of days, Tommy said, "Jimmy, you gotta get cleaned up now so we can put this show on the road. I'm taking you today to get a shave and a haircut." Jimmy did not argue. Tommy took him to a private salon, where he received a haircut and a shave. Then he took him for a facial and a manicure.

Jimmy the Greek was a different person during that trip to Las Vegas. He was more passive and cooperative. It looked like he was ready to make his comeback, so Tommy set out again with diligence to get a movie going. Then it occurred to him that an updated book might be the catalyst. So he made the arrangements. Jimmy seemed encouraged with the idea. Now, when Tommy mentioned new ideas to promote him, he was receptive.

As time passed, Jimmy had a desire to revisit the religion of his childhood and to rediscover the pride of his Greek heritage. One day Tommy told him he was going to church on Sunday at the St. John's Greek Orthodox and asked Jimmy if he wanted to go. Jimmy said he would like to, but when Sunday came around, Tommy could not get Jimmy out of bed.

Several days later, Tommy arranged to have lunch with the priest, Father Katri. He wanted Jimmy to meet him and he liked the idea of Father Katri being present, because it represented a sanctity or blessing in their endeavors.

"I haven't been to a Greek Orthodox Church since I was a little boy," Jimmy said. "My wife was Catholic, so I went to church with her. But I always missed the Greek church," he told Father Katri.

Jimmy found Father Katri to be warm and caring. He told him that day, "I've got three children buried at Palms Cemetery, downtown, and I would like to visit their graves before I leave. Do you think you could bless them for me?"

"I would be honored," Father Katri said.

Father Katri met Tommy and Jimmy at the grave the following day. He blessed the graves of the children with a beautiful, moving ceremony. While Father Katri spoke, Jimmy alternately stared at the graves and the ground. His cane nervously bounced from side to side and his face bore a somber look.

Jimmy talked about the ceremony for several days. It was closure for him — a farewell to the children and a farewell to his own guilt for not spending more time with them when they were alive.

Father Katri invited Tommy and Jimmy to stop by the church the next day. He showed them around and offered a brief liturgy and a prayer. While they were there, the Greek ladies society, known as the *Philoptichos,* had just ended their weekly meeting. Immediately they walked up to say hello, and Jimmy spoke in his native Greek language. He did not introduce himself as James Snyder, or Jimmy the Greek, but rather, as Demetrios Georgios Synodinos. He used his given name, the one that represented his heritage.

Father Katri invited Tommy and Jimmy to dinner that evening at an Italian restaurant near the church. Jimmy ribbed the owner about the food being lousy but had no trouble finishing everything on his plate. When the waiter brought the check, all three men went for their wallets. Jimmy and Tommy insisted on paying, but Father Katri sternly told the waiter, "I'll never come here again if you do not give me the check." How could a waiter show disregard for a priest's request?

On the way home, Tommy said, "We oughta be ashamed letting him pick up the check. I've never seen a priest pay for dinner."

"I haven't either," Jimmy said. "Come to think of it, I've never seen *anyone* pick up the tab. It's always you and me."

About a week later, something began to happen to Jimmy's health. He got out of bed later and later and began to forget things. One night while they were waiting for dinner to be served, Jimmy turned to Tommy and asked, "What did I order?"

Tommy was aware that Jimmy was diabetic and immediately became concerned. He went to his room and saw he had insulin, but apparently was not taking it. It was vital for Jimmy to take his insulin. He was eating dessert every night, drinking a glass of wine with dinner, and eating candy and fruit. That is like suicide to a diabetic.

The next day, Jimmy announced he was going to New York.

Tommy said, "Jimmy, I don't think you need to go by yourself. New York is not the place to be walking around alone. You'll get yourself killed."

When Jimmy would not budge in his decision, Tommy said, "Okay, you win. You can go to New York, but I'm going with you." They made reservations for the next day. Tommy told Jimmy they would ride together to the airport. Then he made sure they left with inadequate time to make the flight because he was concerned about Jimmy's health.

He got Jimmy a room at the Rio Hotel and Casino for two weeks. Then his friend's health worsened. Jimmy would not get out of bed at all. Tommy convinced him to go to the Miami Heart Institute, where Jimmy had been treated through the years. Tommy accompanied him.

As soon as they arrived in Miami, Tommy took him to the institute and Jimmy was immediately hospitalized. Dr. Cassis, the young doctor who cared for Jimmy, came in to report that Jimmy was in bad shape. His blood pressure was dangerously high, causing him to have an enlarged heart, and his sugar-count level was also extremely high. His whole system was in disarray. Dr. Cassis turned to Tommy and said, "It's a good thing you brought him in today. One day later and he would've been dead."

He paused for a few seconds, realizing his bedside manners might have been a little too harsh. Then he said, "Okay, now that we got that out of the way, tell me, Greek, who do you like for the basketball game this weekend?"

Suddenly, Jimmy the Greek came to life. Before, he was disoriented, lethargic, and quiet. Now he sat up on the side of the bed and began jabbering away at upcoming games with the clarity of someone in perfect health. It was as if Dr. Cassis, through his blunt approach, had rendered him a shock treatment that temporarily healed him.

About that time, a nurse walked into the room. She looked at Tommy and then at Jimmy and asked, "Is this your son?"

"Yeah, he is," Jimmy replied sincerely.

Tommy said, musingly, "No, I'm not the son, I'm the enemy."

"What do you mean, the enemy?" she asked.

"I'm the enemy because I make him do everything that's healthy — so I'm the bad guy."

They all laughed. From then on, Jimmy often referred to Tommy as "the enemy" whenever he made him eat a salad, skip dessert, or do anything healthy.

While Jimmy was in the hospital receiving treatment, their friendship deepened. Tommy treated Jimmy with the same love and respect as he did his own father. There was so much more to Jimmy the Greek than most people ever knew.

It was not long before Jimmy regressed to his old ways.

One day Tommy said to Jimmy, "As soon as you get out of here, the first thing we're going to do is go to Joe's Stone Crabs."

Jimmy said, "We don't have to wait till then. Give me my green book." (The green book was an old dilapidated address book that listed everyone Jimmy had known through the years — from his gambling buddies, grapevine sources, all the way to celebrities and prominent businessmen. He carried it everywhere he went.)

"I'm going to call Joe, the owner, and have him bring over six or seven buckets for dinner, but you better make sure you're back here tonight to eat them."

Tommy left the hospital for several hours. When he returned, Jimmy was in his hospital gown, sitting on the edge of the bed. He had a bucket of stone crabs in his lap, and was spitting empty shells onto the hospital floor. Shells were scattered everywhere.

Jimmy said, "There's only one more bucket left. If you want some, you better get 'em while you can."

Jimmy had ordered six buckets and had already devoured five of them by the time Tommy returned.

Tommy laughed. It reminded him of another story.

"Jimmy," Tommy said, "do you remember when you checked yourself into that diet clinic [Pritikin] to lose weight?"

Jimmy smiled, already knowing what he was going to say.

"Remember I sent you that *care* package?"

"Yeah, a care package with *baklava* [a Greek pastry rich with assorted nuts and butter] and the nurses ate it all."

They both laughed.

Jimmy was released from the hospital a week later. As they drove away, Jimmy dictated his agenda. "Let's go to the track, to Joe's Stone Crabs, and Mike's Cigar Store."

Tommy said, "No, Jimmy, you're going back to North Carolina to get back your health."

"Well, you're not coming with me," Jimmy said.

"All right, Jimmy, I'll go to North Carolina with you for a few days."

As Tommy drove, he could not resist the temptation to go to Mike's Cigar Store, so they made a detour before catching their flight to North Carolina. There they picked up five boxes of Prince Philip Macanudo Maduro cigars — the cigars that brought them together.

They went to the airport to catch their flight to North Carolina and Tommy arranged for an attendant to have a wheelchair ready for Jimmy. He went ahead to confirm their seating arrangements while the attendant and Jimmy followed. When Tommy was finished, he turned around and saw the attendant wheeling Jimmy out of Burger King. Jimmy had two unopened hamburgers lying in his lap and was alternately taking bites of french fries and another hamburger.

"What are you doing? Don't you know that's the last thing you need to be eating?" Tommy asked.

Jimmy said, "Mind your own business, enemy." He laughed and continued stuffing the food into his mouth.

"I'll tell you what," Tommy said, "you lay off that junk food and I'll arrange for a friend of mine, a chef named Stephan Kasouris out of Cleveland, to cook you the best pasta dinner you've ever eaten."

"No one can top Agnes', my stepmother's," Jimmy said. "She makes the best."

"Well, Kasouris is Greek too. He's cooked for Aristotle Onassis and Frank Sinatra and other famous people. I guess you're right. It wouldn't be good enough for you."

"No," Jimmy said, "I could go for some good pasta. When can he come?"

"Just leave it to me. I'll fly him in to Durham when we get there and you'll see for yourself that this guy knows what he's doing."

"I like your style, kid," Jimmy said.

They took the flight to North Carolina and when they arrived, Jimmy's driver, Mike, was waiting for them. They drove up to his large, cozy home in the woods where no one was home. Joan, Jimmy's wife, was in Washington visiting their daughter, Stephanie.

They walked into the dark, lonely house and Jimmy sat down at the bar. Tommy walked over and said, "I'm gonna have some ouzo."

"Where's mine?" Jimmy asked.

Tommy poured him a shot.

The two toasted "to better days."

After a few minutes, Tommy turned to Jimmy and asked, "What do you *really* want, Jimmy? What would you really like?"

Jimmy was silent for several seconds. "To have horses," he said. "To have racehorses that wear the Greek colors in the winning stretch."

"Blue with white trim — well, here's to your horses in the winning stretch, Jimmy," Tommy said, extending his shot glass into the air.

Off to the side, within purview, was Jimmy's old office. The wall was adorned with CBS memorabilia and pictures of Jimmy the Greek with other famous people. These priceless mementos served to remind him of the "better days" he now toasted.

"We're gonna make it, Jimmy. We're gonna make it," Tommy said with conviction. Tommy's original plan to stay a couple of days was extended to two months, through careful coaxing by Jimmy.

After everything they had been through together in the recent weeks, there was nothing that could come between their friendship. When Tommy left, both of them were saddened.

They frequently called one another, and Tommy visited him often in North Carolina. Jimmy made trips to Las Vegas when he could.

During one of Tommy's visits to North Carolina in January of 1995, Joan mentioned that Anthony, Jimmy and Joan's son, was getting married that following May.

"Now promise you'll be back for the wedding," she said. "After all, we'll be having the reception at Cafe Parizade and George Bakatsias would not forgive you if you missed that."

Bakatsias, a fellow Greek, who owned Cafe Parizade, was Tommy's good friend, and Joan knew Tommy could not resist dining there when he visited North Carolina.

"Don't worry," Tommy said. "I'll be back in May."

Jimmy and he attended the wedding together. When it was time for Tommy to leave, Jimmy asked, "Where ya going?"

"I'm going back to Las Vegas to wrap up things for the book. The sooner things are finished, the sooner you'll have your two racehorses on a ranch in California."

"Ah, you'll leave and forget about the Greek," Jimmy said.

"Well," Tommy said, "you don't wanna go back with me. Every time I come out here, I ask you to come and you never want to."

"You didn't ask me now," Jimmy said.

Tommy asked him if he wanted to come along, and to his surprise, this time Jimmy said yes.

They made arrangements to leave together. Having been surrounded by family during the wedding made Jimmy long to see Agnes, his stepmother, John, his half brother, his sister Marika and half sister Angela in Steubenville, and his sister Mary in Athens, Greece. He told Tommy how much he missed them. "They love me, really love me. There's nothing they wouldn't do for me."

"Do you want to drive to Steubenville before we go to Las Vegas and see everyone?"

"Yeah," Jimmy said. "I'd like that."

Tommy tried to arrange for the driver and Jimmy's personal nurse, Anthony, to go along. Anthony had an illness in the family and could not go, so they were unable to make the trip to Steubenville.

The day they left for Las Vegas, Jimmy was not himself. He complained of aches and pains and was grumpy. Tommy had Anthony check his insulin and blood pressure and everything seemed normal, so they went ahead and made their flight.

Jimmy's maid, Marion, stood at the door as they left, crying. She told Anthony she was crying because she knew she was never going to see Jimmy again. Tommy told her that was ridiculous. Little did he know that her intuition was right.

Jimmy continued to complain that his back hurt throughout the flight. They finally arrived in Las Vegas and settled into the hotel room at 1:00 A.M. Tommy unpacked Jimmy's clothes, gave him his medicine, and got him settled into bed. Tommy had not been home in a month, so he told Jimmy he was going to sleep at home and would call him first thing in the morning. He left the bathroom light on and said goodbye.

Coming to Las Vegas was a big step for Jimmy the Greek. He wanted to return to gambling. He realized that he would be happier in Las Vegas than he would in Durham, because he did little to stimulate his mind there. He hardly even got out of bed. It was a new beginning for him, and with Tommy close by, he felt confident in his decision.

Chapter 25

A Fight for Life

SOMEWHERE IN JIMMY THE GREEK'S determination to overcome his battles, he was swallowed up into the greatest one of all: a fight for life.

Fate would not permit him to make a comeback. The time ran out on his hourglass shortly after he resolved his inner conflicts. When he felt peace of mind to start anew, he was given a new beginning somewhere else.

Tommy tried to call Jimmy the next morning in his hotel room at 10:00 A.M. There was no answer. Tommy continued calling and got no answer. Finally, he went over to check on him. He had an extra key to the room and let himself in.

Jimmy was not in the bed. He was lying on the floor with a pillow under his head.

Tommy said, "Jimmy, what are you doing on the floor — are you okay?"

Jimmy was groggy.

Tommy tried to help him up, unsuccessfully. Then he tried to lift him to sit him in a chair, but he was too heavy. He called hotel security to assist him. They lifted him to his feet and realized he was in pain and unable to stand on his own. They called an ambulance and he was taken to Valley Hospital, where he was diagnosed with a broken hip. Dr. Rucker ordered immediate surgery to insert a hip replacement. The operation was a success.

After the hip began to heal, Jimmy was put in Las Vegas Rehabilitation Clinic, the finest rehabilitation facility in Nevada. He was slow, however, in making progress because of his excess weight and age.

While he was recovering, Bob Stupak, the famous Las Vegas hotel owner, was also recovering from his well-publicized motorcycle accident. Because Stupak made a miraculous recovery, Tommy used him as an example to give Jimmy the incentive to get better.

One day Tommy introduced them.

He said, "Jimmy, this is the guy who built the Stratosphere Tower. He was in a horrible motorcycle accident and almost died. Look at him now, and you're still in a wheelchair."

Jimmy turned and looked at Stupak and said, "Anybody who rides a motorcycle oughta be dead."

Stupak laughed.

Then Stupak informed Tommy that growth hormones had saved his life. He said, "You need to give them to Jimmy. If you don't, he's never going to get out of that wheelchair." Because the growth hormones were so new and Tommy was unsure how it would affect Jimmy, he never pursued making an appointment with the doctor. But Stupak was right: Jimmy never got out of the wheelchair.

Tommy teased Jimmy, "If you don't get up and start getting active, they're going to kick us out of here."

Jimmy said, "That's all right, you'll find another place for me."

Jimmy was still unable to walk on his own. Soon they moved him to a semi-rehabilitation center. There he was not as active, but he was content.

One day Tommy said to him, "Jimmy, what are you going to do when the book is out and they want you to do a book-signing tour? Are we going to have to wheel you around in this bed?"

Jimmy smiled and said, "Yeah, that's okay."

"Welcome to *Larry King Live* and today our guest is Jimmy the Greek, here to promote his new book in the comfort of his own bed," Tommy jested.

"He'd understand," Jimmy said. "You know, I knew him way back in Miami and he's a nice guy."

"How'd you know him?"

"We used to see each other at the tracks. We even bet each other a couple of times. That kid came a long way. I always knew he'd make it."

"Yeah, he made it all right, straight to the top. How is it that everyone you knew made it big?"

"They kept the right company, kid. That's how," Jimmy said.

One afternoon in August of 1995, before leaving for a trip to California, Tommy and his son, Thomas, stopped by to see Jimmy. He was in great spirits, and as soon as they walked in, he asked, "What did you bring me? Did you bring my lemon yogurt?" He had become accustomed to them bringing him the sugar-free, fat-free frozen yogurt, and lemon was his favorite flavor. Thomas brought his hands from behind his back and produced the yogurt. They stayed for a little over an hour that day and Jimmy sang and laughed.

When Tommy returned the next week, he got a call from the rehabilitation center. "We've got a problem with Jimmy," the nurse said. "It's not serious, but give us a call."

The nurse said he was disoriented and they wanted to take him to Valley Hospital to have a brain scan. The brain scan explained the disorientation: he had a minor stroke. The stroke left him partially paralyzed on the left side of his body. His speech was slurred, and it was difficult for him to write and converse.

From the beginning, when Jimmy was admitted to the hospital, Tommy took extreme precautions in seeing that no media was permitted to see him and no information was leaked to the press. He wanted to make certain Jimmy the Greek maintained his dignity. Doctors, nurses, and staff had specific instructions to let no one visit except for the names designated on a list he provided.

Tommy received a message one day that there was a visitor at the rehabilitation center.

"Someone here to see Mr. Snyder. It's Al Davis of the Oakland Raiders."

Tommy told them he would be right down. When he arrived, Al Davis and David Humm, a former Oakland Raiders player, were waiting. Tommy prepared them for what to expect because Jimmy had just suffered the stroke and was disoriented. When Davis walked in, Jimmy took his right hand and reached out to him. Davis held his composure, but pain and sympathy showed on his face. Jimmy loved Al Davis.

Davis wanted to announce on a broadcast his concern for Jimmy. Tommy asked him not to. "Well," Davis asked, "what can I do? Do you need the doctor from the team, money . . . ?"

Tommy assured him there was nothing he could do, that his presence was more than enough help for Jimmy.

In the beginning of January, shortly after the Christmas holidays, Tommy visited Jimmy. As he walked into the room, he felt an instant warmth. Icons of religious saints were selectively placed in his room, and beautiful Christmas cards adorned the walls. Tommy looked at the cards and saw they were from his Steubenville and North Carolina family. Angela, Marika, Johnny, Joan, Stephanie, and Anthony had been in to spend several days with him and left tokens of their affection all over the room.

As Tommy looked at the cards, tears came to his eyes. He felt peace in the fact that Jimmy had seen all his family. Their planned trip to Steubenville had not worked out. But his family came to him, instead — a characteristic that mirrored the Greek culture's love for family.

In time, Jimmy began to make progress. He was talking to Tommy again and writing notes whenever he did not feel like talking. But the inactivity began to affect his lungs. Pneumonia set in and would not leave.

In February 1996, Jimmy was taken to the Intensive Care Unit at Valley Hospital. His breathing became irregular.

The doctor told Tommy, "Jimmy's very sick."

In March, he was moved to a private hospital, where his pneumonia worsened. He was placed in a special unit that was quarantined for germs for his own protection. Visitors had to wear masks and jackets. Because of this special procedure, Tommy limited his visits to fifteen or twenty minutes.

Between Tommy and Vicki, Jimmy saw someone every day. Jimmy and Vicki's relationship was strengthened as he saw her so often by his side. The three became like a family.

On Friday night, April 19, 1996, Tommy stopped by to see him and noticed that the television was turned off. He turned it on for him. Jimmy was unresponsive. Tommy went to the nurse's station and inquired about Jimmy's condition. The nurse said he was okay, probably just tired.

Something urged Tommy to stay longer than usual. He dampened a towel and wiped Jimmy's eyes and face and said to Jimmy, in Greek, "Jimmy, open your eyes." Jimmy opened his eyes briefly. Then Tommy told him, "Jimmy, you know I'm never gonna let anybody fuck you." He often told him this. Then he said, "You know I love you, don't you?" Tommy did not tell him he loved him often but felt compelled to tell him then.

He was unable to visit Jimmy the next day, but Vicki went over at 7:00 P.M. She brought him a red, pink, yellow and white rose that her friend's neighbor, who had a multitude of rose bushes, encouraged her to take to her father. On her way in, she saw the respiratory therapist and he remarked on how much better Jimmy was. Vicki walked in and placed the roses by his bed.

She tried to awaken him with no success. After seeing that he would not open his eyes for her and was snoring heavily, Vicki said, "Dad, I hope everything's all right. I hope you're okay." She stayed for a while, holding his hand, but Jimmy never awoke. Finally, she said, "Well, Dad, I'll see you tomorrow. I love you."

Tomorrow was shortened for Jimmy the Greek. He barely made it through to the next day.

Very early on Sunday morning, Tommy noticed that his answering machine light was blinking, indicating there was a message. As he played the message, these words rang out, "Tommy, it's Vicki . . . the hospital called. Dad just died." Jimmy had died from a massive coronary and pulmonary arrest. His heart and lungs had completely shut down. The stress of what his body had endured was too great on his vital organs.

Tommy and Vicki were in shock. They never anticipated he would die so soon. They comforted each other over the phone.

Tommy handled the press entirely for the family. He called Father Katri and asked him to do a private ceremony at Palm Mortuary the next day, before the body was taken to Steubenville, where Jimmy had requested to be buried.

The next day, Father Katri offered a brief Greek Orthodox liturgy and prayer at Palm Mortuary while Vicki, Joan, Stephanie, and Tommy looked on. Ironically, his body was temporarily held at the Palm Mortuary downtown, where his three children's bodies were buried. There, a couple of years before, Father Katri had blessed their graves at the request of Jimmy.

Following the small private service, his body was taken to Mosti Funeral Home in Steubenville, Ohio. Tommy, who had become Jimmy the Greek's caretaker out of love for his friend, felt lost. It had been part of his routine to call the hospital to inquire on Jimmy's health and drop by to see him. He even called the funeral home to ensure that Jimmy's body had safely arrived. In fact, the day after Jimmy died, Tommy awoke and reached for the telephone. It was hard to get used to the fact that Jimmy was dead.

During the viewing at Mosti Funeral Home that following Wednesday, a small, thin, African-American man walked into the room. He looked at Jimmy in the casket and sobbed incoherently. He quickly rushed out of the room.

Vicki and her cousin noticed him and immediately ran outside after him. Vicki said to him, "I don't know who you are, but you musta known and loved my dad. I just want you to know you are welcome here."

The little man looked up at her with tears streaming down his cheeks and said, "I loved your dad. He was good to me and my family. He used to give us meat and bread from the store because we didn't have any food. He wouldn't let us starve, you know. He kept us alive, and I'll never forget him."

In some small way, Jimmy's fear of being remembered as a racist was quieted by this stranger's presence.

At the funeral on Thursday, Father Dean Dimon delivered a eulogy at Holy Trinity Greek Orthodox Temple. He said, "A football team doesn't have all day to score — it only has one hour. A baseball player only gets three strikes. The Ultimate Umpire has set a time limit on life and has called on Jimmy."

Jimmy's body lay in an open casket under the roof of the church he generously contributed to through the years for its construction and renovations. It was in this same church that his daughter, Vicki, was baptized. His casket was surrounded by icons of Christ and holy saints. The liturgy bore the language of his people — Greek. He rested in peace covered with white and deep blue carnations — his colors, the Greek colors.

At Union Cemetery mausoleum, the graveside eulogy was delivered by Frank Deford, chairman of the Cystic Fibrosis Foundation, writer for *Newsweek* and commentator for Home Box Office and National Public Radio. Deford was a long-time friend of Jimmy the Greek, and they shared a common pain. Deford had lost a child to cystic fibrosis.

Deford opened by immediately noting an erroneously designed floral arrangement. It was a horseshoe, with the open end facing down. He said, "Our friend, Jimmy, would have noticed that. Anyone who has spent time around the track knows if the horseshoe has the open end down, all the luck runs out." He asked a family member to reverse the arrangement.

Then he delivered the following eulogy:

. . . Whatever, except for those curiously dainty little hands of his, this man was large in every way — huge of heart and spirit and so possessing a great bundle of humanity.

. . . Jimmy always knew he was lucky. Even when he wasn't lucky, he knew he was going to *get* lucky again, soon enough. . . .

How happy to have had such great love about you [Jimmy the Greek] in your family. How happy to have had such wonderful friends to share along the way, laughing and joking and lying together. How happy to have had such amazing experiences in your seventy-seven years upon this earth. How happy was Jimmy the Greek!

And make no mistake. This man: Demetrios — Jimmy — The Greek — this man carved out one of the unique lives of our time. It was a huge, genuine, grand life.

Jimmy the Greek was an original — a wonderful, complicated, cantankerous, caring, generous, stupendous, original human being who marked these days of ours with his singular self, so we will not forget his presence — not any of us blessed to know him.

I remember once he told me: "All the best guys are dead and gone. The only reason I'm still around is because I started so early."

Well, on this spring day in the place where he started, the early is finally late now, and we are gathered here today to celebrate and lay to rest one more of the very best of the guys.

And today, friends, it is *not*: who do you like, Greek? But rather, who do *we* like? And we like the Greek. We like you, Greek. We all love you, Jimmy.

Jimmy was laid to rest in the north side of the mausoleum, on top overlooking Steubenville, the town that had molded him into who he was; near to the place where his mother and father are buried. Directly across the alley is the old home he grew up in after returning from Kios, Greece — the house he lived in when he began gambling. That was the home where he was surrounded with the love of his father; Agnes, his stepmother; his sisters, Mary and Marika; his half sister, Angela; and his half brother, Johnny. That love still radiates, for most of them live nearby.

Only blocks away is a mural on the side of a building, a dedication of the White Star Market, painted in the mid-1980s. It depicts his father's store that provided his family a comfortable living; the same store where little Jimmy had given a black boy food for his family. Sixty years later, that boy, now a man, cries over his generosity. That final act screams out, "I was not racist. How can a four-minute interview take precedence over a lifetime that proved otherwise?"

In the heavens above, perhaps a soothing voice says, "Demetrios, you don't have to worry about fumbling over your words here. I know your heart and that's all that matters. May your soul now rest in peace . . ."

Bell, Nynex complete $23 billion merger WORLD & NATION / **PAGE 1B**

LAS VEGAS SUN

Vol. 46 / No. 308 © LAS VEGAS SUN a P.M. STREET Monday, April 22, 1996 / 50 CENTS

'Greek' legacy remembered

Personality, not picks, led to fame

SUN STAFF AND WIRE REPORTS

Jimmy "The Greek" Snyder may not have been the best oddsmaker to come out of Las Vegas.

The joke often was that gamblers in need of a big win would tune into CBS' Sunday football pregame show, get Snyder's hottest pick, then bet the other side.

Snyder

Nevertheless, the colorful tout with the gift of gab was responsible for making sports betting one of the most popular forms of mainstream entertainment.

Snyder's death Sunday at a Las Vegas convalescent center brings to an end the life of a man who climbed to the top by espousing knowledge he took a lifetime to learn, only to crash and burn in an instant by commenting on an issue far out of his realm -- the genetics of black athletes.

Snyder died of heart failure after a long illness. He was 76.

"Jimmy was a colorful guy," said legendary professional gambler Lem Banker, who met Snyder in 1957. "People who got to know him found he was a really great person. He rubbed elbows with many of the biggest people in the world and across the country."

Banker said he plans to nominate Snyder for the Gamblers' Hall of Fame.

Services for Snyder – an on-again-off-again Las Vegas resident since the 1950s – will be Thursday at Holy Trinity Greek Orthodox Church in Steubenville, Ohio. Burial will be in Union Cemetery there.

Snyder first penned his sports betting column for the Las Vegas SUN in the early 1960s, long before such information was legal to use in other states.

Though sports betting still is illegal in most communities, such information to assist gamblers now is printed in

SEE **SNYDER, 6A**

6A LAS VEGAS SUN Monday, April 22, 1996 a

FROM PAGE ONE

Snyder

CONTINUED FROM **1A**

practically every newspaper in the country and sports betting today is a multibillion-dollar business.

By 1975, Snyder had written his first book, appropriately titled "Jimmy The Greek," and a year later became a CBS sports commentator, where, at his peak he earned $500,000 a year for what amounted to his opinion on the outcome of pro football games.

All that ended in 1988, when he was fired from "NFL Today" for saying that black athletes were superior to whites.

The incident occurred during an interview for WRC-TV in Washington. The station was seeking comment in connection with Martin Luther King's birthday, asking about the progress blacks had made in society.

During the Civil War, "the slave owner would breed his big black with his big woman so that he would have a big black kid," Snyder said during the interview. "That's where it all started."

Snyder also said a black athlete was better than a white one because "he's been bred to be that way because of his thigh size and big size."

Snyder lived out the remainder of his life in virtual obscurity. He alternated between his homes in Durham, N.C., and Las Vegas.

Local sports commentators and oddsmakers praised Snyder not so much for his prognostications but for his colorful image.

For a while in the 1960s, Snyder owned the Vegas Turf and Sportsroom, where "he was generous to anybody," said Banker, who saw Snyder last year at Valley Hospital Medical Center and noted he was not looking well then.

In 1962, Attorney General Bobby Kennedy shut down Snyder's betting parlor and fined him $50,000 after he was caught giving odds to a friend over the phone. President Ford later pardoned him.

A longtime friend, Tommy Manakides, said Snyder's autobiography, "Wizard of Odds," is to be published next month.

Snyder, born Emetrios Synodinos in Steubenville, correctly predicted the winner of 18 of 21 Super Bowls.

Snyder moved to Las Vegas in the 1950s. Not knowing what else to do after losing his betting parlor, he started an odds column for the SUN that propelled him to national attention.

The Snyders lost three children to cystic fibrosis.

Snyder is survived by his wife, Joan; a son, Anthony Snyder; daughters Vicki Snyder and Stephanie Snyder, all of Steubenville; John Synodinos of Wintersville, Ohio; sisters Mary Papalios of Athens, Marika Berris of Steubenville, and Angela Kayafas of Wintersville, and one grandson.

Family said donations can be made in Snyder's memory to the Cystic Fibrosis Foundation.

SUN REPORTERS Tim Graham, Bob Cloud and Ed Koch contributed to this report.

Sunny, high 81, low 56

LAS VEGAS REVIEW-JOURNAL

NEVADA'S LARGEST AND MOST COMPLETE NEWSPAPER

April 22, 1996 ★ ★ a A Donrey Media Group Newspaper Sunrise Edition

Jimmy 'The Greek' Snyder dies in Las Vegas

☐ The frequent LV visitor turned odds-making into mainstream entertainment in the 'NFL Today' shows.

By Tim Dahlberg
Associated Press

Jimmy "The Greek" Snyder, who parlayed odds-making skills and a gift for gab into national prominence before his television career crashed over ill-advised remarks about black athletes, died Sunday.

Snyder, 76, died of heart failure at a local hospital after a long illness, longtime friend Tommy Mannkides said.

SNYDER

■ **THE BETTOR:** Most would agree that Jimmy "The Greek" Snyder's work with CBS had a positive effect on sports betting in Las Vegas.

Page 1E

Snyder, who at his peak was a colorful and often-quoted CBS Sports commentator, lived his late years in virtual obscurity after being fired by the network in 1988 for saying that black athletes were superior to whites.

"He really just went downhill after that," said longtime Las Vegas gambler Lem Banker. "It was a shame. He was real bitter. He got a bum deal from them."

Snyder turned odds-making into mainstream entertainment in his 12 years as part of CBS TV's Sunday afternoon "NFL Today" pre-game shows, and became a popular personality whose predictions were followed closely by his fans.

His career abruptly ended, however, after he ignited a firestorm in an interview with WRC-TV in Washington. The station was seeking comment in connection with Martin Luther King Jr.'s birthday, asking about the progress blacks had made in society.

During the Civil War, "the slave owner would breed his big black with his big woman so that he would have a big black kid," Snyder said during the interview. "That's where it all started."

Snyder also said that if blacks "take over coaching jobs like everybody wants them to, there's not to be anything left for the white people."

Please see GREEK/2A

2A/Las Vegas Review-Journal/Monday, April 22, 1996

Greek

From 1A

Snyder also said a black athlete was better than a white one because "he's been bred to be that way because of his thigh size and big size."

CBS Sports fired Snyder the next day, and he issued an apology saying, "I am truly sorry for my remarks, and once again I offer my heartfelt apology to all I may have offended."

"CBS Evening News" anchor Dan Rather read an apology on the air the night after Snyder's remarks were made public. Snyder later sued the network, claiming CBS used the remarks as an excuse to fire him because of his age.

"He took the firing personally," his brother, John Synodinos, told The Associated Press on Sunday in a telephone interview from Wintersville, Ohio. "He felt he was falsely accused. He was praising the blacks actually.

"It bothered him that they thought ill of him. The accusations that they made were wrong and mistaken and that bothered him.

"Some things he said were history, but not the proper thing to say at the time — not politically correct."

Despite the nature of their parting, CBS had kind words for Snyder.

"Jimmy The Greek was a good friend to CBS for many years," said network spokeswoman LeslieAnne Wade. "He was an original who helped make the 'NFL Today' the premier pre-game show of its time. He'll be missed."

Snyder, who lived in Durham, N.C., but often visited Las Vegas, had been in and out of hospitals for several months.

An autobiography, "Wizard of Odds," is to be published next month. An earlier book, "Jimmy The Greek," was published in 1975.

Snyder, born Emetrios Syncdinos in Steubenville, Ohio, regularly talked about upcoming games and made predictions on the "NFL Today." His biggest claim to fame was picking the winner in 18 of 21 Super Bowls.

His reputed odds-making skills earned Snyder a reputation beyond the sports arena. When he wrote a newspaper column syndicated to 240 papers across the country, he often forecast presidential and other political races.

"His objective was to get national recognition, and he did," said longtime friend Jack Franzi, an odds maker for the Barbary Coast. "Jimmy knew how to market himself. He absolutely became the most noted and famous odds maker in the country."

Franzi said Snyder was an innovator as a sports book operator and credited him with helping the sports betting industry explode to the multibillion-dollar business it is today.

"He helped the betting industry immensely," Franzi said. "Ninety percent of the people would turn on the TV to hear Jimmy give the prices. They would wait for his odds for the games."

Former Secretary of State George P. Schultz once drew chuckles and headlines when he was asked the odds on a possible U.S.-Soviet summit.

"If you were in a statistical frame of mind, and if Jimmy the Greek was here, maybe the probability would be something between 2 and 4 (out of 10)," Schultz said.

Snyder also spoke frequently to business groups and corporations, and did television commercials.

He made headlines eight years before his dismissal by CBS when he and "NFL Today" host Brent Musburger got into a brief fistfight at a midtown New York bar. They reportedly argued over the amount of airtime Snyder was getting from Musburger, who also was the show's managing editor.

In 1988, six days after his January firing by CBS, the heavyset Snyder spent several days in the Duke University Medical Center, where examinations revealed that one of the three arteries to his heart was blocked.

"The interns were laying 15-1 odds that I would make it," he said at the time.

Snyder was a 10th-grade dropout who dealt craps growing up in Steubenville. His mother was shot to death in front of her house by her brother-in-law when Jimmy was 10.

Snyder moved to Las Vegas in the 1950s, where he was an odds maker and gambler before starting his own betting parlor in the downtown area.

In 1962, Attorney General Bobby Kennedy shut down his Vegas Turf and Sportsroom and fined him $50,000 after he was caught giving odds to a friend over the phone. President Ford later pardoned him for gambling violations.

Not knowing what else to do, he started an odds column for a Las Vegas newspaper that propelled him to national attention.

Snyder and his wife, Joan, lost three children to cystic fibrosis: Tina died at 2½; Florence at 30 days; and son Jamie at 27.

In addition to his widow and brother, survivors include his stepmother, Agnes, of Wintersville; daughters Vicki and Stephanie, and a son, Anthony, all of Steubenville; sisters Mary Papalios of Athens, Greece; Marika Berris of Steubenville, and Angela Kayafas of Wintersville, and one grandson.

The funeral will be Thursday at Holy Trinity Greek Orthodox Church in Steubenville. Burial will be in Union Cemetery.

The family requested that contributions be sent to the Cystic Fibrosis Foundation.

Obituaries of Jimmy the Greek . . .

B10   z   THE NEW YORK TIMES **OBITUARIES** MONDAY, APRIL

Jimmy (the Greek) Snyder, 76; Sports Oddsmaker and Analyst

By ERIC PACE

Jimmy Snyder, known as "Jimmy the Greek," an oddsmaker and football personality who brought gambling to the forefront of televised sports but was fired by CBS Sports for saying that black Americans were better athletes than whites because of physical traits dating back to slavery, died yesterday in a Las Vegas, Nev., hospital. He was 76.

He had spent the last year in a hotel or hospital room in Las Vegas or in Durham, N.C., where he and his wife, Joan, had lived.

A friend, Tommy Manakides, said that Mr. Snyder had suffered from diabetes and had been in declining health and died of a coronary at Transitional Hospitals.

Mr. Snyder was born Emetrios Synodinos in Ohio, and his family's roots are in the Greek island of Chios in the Aegean Sea. He was raised in Steubenville, Ohio.

"He got involved in sports at a young age," Mr. Manakides said of the high school dropout, "and he would follow all the newspapers and all the sporting events going on" and he began compiling sports data.

As a teen-ager in Steubenville, Mr. Snyder kept company with bookmakers, laying bets chiefly on college basketball and football games. Later he took money he had won by gambling and invested it in oil-drilling and coal strip-mining ventures.

But after some bad luck as an investor — "22 dry wells" is how he once described it — he made his way to Las Vegas in 1956, and there he became known as an oddsmaker on the weekly pro football betting line. In 1968, he gave this terse summary of his analytical techniques in football: "Overall team speed is the biggest factor. Then the front four on defense. Then the back defense, especially the cornerbacks. Then the quarterbacks, and then I have to consider the intangibles."

Mr. Snyder went on to spend 12 years as the betting analyst, specializing in forecasts intended to help bettors, on the CBS Sports program, "The N.F.L. Today," — aired each Sunday in the pro football season — to mixed reviews. Mr. Snyder often spoke vaguely or indecisively in appraising games, which gave rise to another, lesser-known nickname, "Nick the Meek."

But he was not meek when he remarked — among other things — in a videotaped luncheon interview with Ed Hotaling of WRC, a Washington television station: "During the slave period, the slave owner would breed his big black with his big woman so that he could have a big black kid — that's where it all started."

Mr. Snyder made his statement, which was broadcast on Dr. Martin Luther King Jr. Day in a WRC report about blacks' progress in society.

Mr. Snyder was swiftly fired by CBS Sports, which issued a statement saying, "In no way do these comments reflect the view of CBS Sports."

Reuters, 1985

Jimmy (the Greek) Snyder

Afterward, Mr. Snyder observed, with regard to his remarks, "What a foolish thing to say." He also complained of chest pains and spent a few days in a Durham hospital.

For his part, Floyd H. Flake, a Democratic Congressman from Queens, wrote that Mr. Snyder made "racially offensive statements and racial slurs more acceptable" with such comments.

Jesse Jackson, who was then a presidential candidate, criticized Mr. Snyder's remarks but said that he should not be a scapegoat for the sports world's failure to hire more black managers. The Miami Herald published an editorial on what it called the ignorance reflected in Mr. Snyder's remarks. And The New York Times sports columnist George Vecsey derided what he called "the Jimmy the Greek Television Bookie School of Genetics."

After the 1988 uproar, Mr. Snyder lived relatively quietly and wrote a betting column for a Las Vegas newspaper. But on one summer morning in 1992 at the old Saratoga Race Course, he mused to a reporter: "The 3-year-old colts? The division is wide open."

The Snyders lost three children to cystic fibrosis. Tina died at 2½; Florence at 30 days, and son Jamie at 27.

In addition to his wife, Mr. Snyder is survived by a son, Anthony Snyder; daughters Vicki Snyder and Stephanie Snyder, all of Steubenville; John Synodinos of Wintersville, Ohio; sisters Mary Papalios of Athens, Marika Berris of Steubenville, and Angela Knyafas of Wintersville, and one grandson.

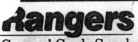

Rangers | Fire | Deal
Graves' Goals Spark Crucial Win / **Sports** | Blaze Probe Shows Deep Flaws / **Page A3** | Telephone Giants Try to Merge / **Page A4**

SPORTS FINAL

Newsday

QUEENS • MONDAY, APRIL 22, 1996 • 50¢

He Fought Odds

THE ASSOCIATED PRESS

Las Vegas — Jimmy (the Greek) Snyder, a self-styled oddsmaker and expert on sports who was fired as a CBS Sports commentator after making controversial remarks about black athletes, died yesterday at age 77.

He died of heart failure at Transitional Hospital Corp. after a long illness, longtime friend Tommy Manakides said.

"He fought like a champ. He tried to beat the odds of his life," Manakides said in a telephone interview.

Snyder turned oddsmaking into mainstream entertainment as part of CBS-TV's Sunday afternoon "NFL Today" pregame shows, and became a popular personality.

That position fell apart, however, in 1988 when he said in a television interview that black athletes were bred to be superior to whites.

During the Civil War "the slave owner would breed his big black with his big

Jimmy 'The Greek' Snyder dies at 77

woman so that he would have a big black kid," Snyder said. "That's where it all started."

Snyder also said that if blacks "take over coaching jobs like everybody wants them to, there's not to be anything left for the white people."

Later, Snyder said a black athlete was better than a white one because "he's been bred to be that way because of his thigh size and big size."

CBS Sports fired Snyder the next day. "I am truly sorry for my remarks and once again I offer my heartfelt apology to all I may have offended," Snyder subsequently said.

Snyder, who spent 12 years on television, made headlines several years before his dismissal when he and "NFL

Today" host Brent Musburger got into a brief fistfight at a midtown New York bar. They reportedly argued over the amount of airtime Snyder was getting from Musburger, who also was the show's managing editor.

Jimmy (The Greek) Snyder

An autobiography, "Wizard of Odds," is to be published next month, Manakides said.

Snyder, born Emetrios Synodinos in Steubenville, Ohio, is survived by his wife, Joan Snyder; two daughters, a son, a brother, two sisters and a grandson.

LORDS OF THE RING
Bell Atlantic, NYNEX in mega-merger
SEE PAGE 2 & BUSINESS

DAILY◉NEWS
QUEENS EDITION

50¢   NEW YORK'S HOMETOWN NEWSPAPER   Monday, April 22, 1996

JIMMY THE GREEK LOSES FIGHT FOR LIFE

SEE PAGE 3

The Greek dies at 76

Oddsmaker's career rocky

By CORKY SIEMASZKO
Daily News Staff Writer

Tart-tongued television oddsmaker Jimmy (The Greek) Snyder, who capsized his controversial career by saying blacks were bred to be better athletes, died yesterday of heart failure. He was 76.

Snyder, whose biggest claim to fame until then was picking the winner in 18 of 21 Super Bowls, was already battling heart disease when he was fired by CBS Sports in 1988.

A year before that, Snyder joked that the interns "were laying 15-to-1 odds that I wouldn't make it" when he was hospitalized with a blocked artery.

But Snyder beat the spread by living almost another decade — disgraced and in exile from the medium that made him famous.

He was recovering from a broken hip when he died yesterday morning at Transitional Hospital in Las Vegas.

Snyder's career-ending comment came in 1988 on the Rev. Martin Luther King's birthday, when a reporter asked him about the progress blacks have made in American society.

"The slave owner would breed his big black with his big woman so that he would have a big black kid," Snyder replied. "That's where it all started."

Snyder also said that if blacks "take over coaching jobs like everybody wants them to, there's not going to be anything left for the white people."

CBS Sports fired Snyder the next day. Snyder later apologized.

Born Emetrios Synodinos in Steubenville, Ohio, Snyder started out as a kid betting on horses.

Then he discovered that he could

make money by studying out-of-town newspapers and cultivating coaches before placing bets on sports teams.

He made his first big score in 1945 when he won $54,000 by picking a Navy football team to upset mighty Notre Dame.

Walter Winchell wrote about Snyder's score, and The Greek's career took off.

Snyder moved his operation to Las Vegas in 1956 but stopped gambling six years later when he was convicted and fined $5,000 for illegally sending gambling information across state lines.

But soon Snyder was raking in the bucks as a syndicated columnist.

And in 1976 he turned oddsmaking into mainstream entertainment as part of CBS-TV's popular Sunday afternoon "NFL Today" pregame show.

Snyder claimed to be right about 75% of the time.

But he made the Baltimore Colts 18-point favorites to trounce Joe Namath and the Jets in the 1969 Super Bowl.

The Jets won, 16-7.

Snyder also picked the 1969 Baltimore Orioles to beat the "Amazing" Mets in the World Series.

The Mets won in five games.

Snyder was a hit with sports fans. But during his 12-year television career, he didn't always get along with his colleagues.

He and co-host Brent Musburger got into a brief fistfight at a midtown bar over the amount of airtime Snyder was getting.

Snyder is survived by his wife, Joan; two daughters; a son; a brother; two sisters, and a grandson. He lived in North Carolina, but the funeral will be in Steubenville, a friend said.

Jimmy (The Greek) Snyder

San Francisco Chronicle

HOME DELIVERED **EAST BAY** EDITION

NORTHERN CALIFORNIA'S LARGEST NEWSPAPER

★★★★

MONDAY, APRIL 22, 1996

AIR EDIT $1

415-777-1111   50 CENTS

A20 San Francisco Chronicle ★★★★   MONDAY, APRIL 22,

OBITUARIES

JIMMY 'THE GREEK' SNYDER
Controversial commentator

Jimmy 'The Greek,' CBS Commentator, Veteran Oddsmaker

Jimmy "The Greek" Snyder, a self-styled oddsmaker and expert on sports who was fired as a CBS Sports commentator after making controversial remarks about black athletes, died yesterday. He was 76.

Mr. Snyder died of heart failure at Transitional Hospital Corp. after a long illness, longtime friend Tommy Manakides said.

"He fought like a champ. He tried to beat the odds of his life," Manakides said in a telephone interview.

Mr. Snyder, born Demetrios Georgios Synodinos in Steubenville, Ohio, was a 10th-grade dropout who dealt craps while growing up in the town.

He moved to Las Vegas in the 1950s, where he was an oddsmaker and gambler before starting his own betting parlor downtown.

In 1962, Attorney General Robert Kennedy shut down Mr. Snyder's Vegas Turf and Sportsroom and fined him $50,000 after he was caught giving odds to a friend over the phone. President Gerald Ford later pardoned him for gambling violations.

Not knowing what else to do, he started an odds column for a Las Vegas newspaper that propelled him to national attention.

Mr. Snyder turned odds-making into mainstream entertainment as part of CBS-TV's Sunday afternoon "NFL Today" pregame shows, and he became a popular personality.

That position fell apart, however, in 1988, when he said in a television interview that black athletes were superior to whites because of breeding.

"The slave owner would breed his big black with his big woman so that he would have a big black kid," Mr. Snyder said. "That's where it all started."

Mr. Snyder also said that if blacks "take over coaching jobs like everybody wants them to, there's not going to be anything left for the white people."

CBS Sports fired Mr. Snyder the next day.

"I am truly sorry for my remarks, and once again I offer my heartfelt apology to all I may have offended," Mr. Snyder subsequently said.

An autobiography, "Wizard of Odds," is to be published next month, Manakides said.

A funeral will be held in Steubenville, Manakides said.

The family requests that contributions be sent to the Cystic Fibrosis Foundation.

Associated Press

Los Angeles Times

CIRCULATION:
1,058,498 DAILY / 1,457,50 SUNDAY

MONDAY, APRIL 22, 1996
COPYRIGHT 1996 / THE TIMES MIRROR COMPANY / CC1 / 52 PAGES

DAILY
DESIGNATED AREAS HIGH

GAMES / EVENTS / PEOPLE

SPORTS

SECTION **C**   MONDAY   APRIL 22, 1996   CC1

Los Angeles Time

HIGHLIGHTS

Jimmy "the Greek" Snyder

GREEK DIES: Jimmy "the Greek" Snyder, arguably the most famous oddsmaker in the betting world, died of heart failure at age 77. C4

C4   MONDAY, APRIL 22, 1996 ★

Heart Failure Claims Jimmy 'the Greek'

■ **Television:** Oddsmaker known as for his work on CBS' 'NFL Today' was 77.

By J. MICHAEL KENNEDY
TIMES STAFF WRITER

Jimmy "the Greek" Snyder, the blustery oddsmaker and sports commentator whose career came to an end because of controversial comments he made about black athletes, died Sunday in Las Vegas. He was 77.

Snyder, who had been in poor health for some time, died of heart failure after being hospitalized for the last month and a half in Las Vegas, according to a long-time friend, Tommy Manakides.

He was arguably the most famous oddsmaker in the betting world, much of that notoriety coming from his uncanny knack at self-promotion. And that reputation was enhanced in 1976 when he became a regular on CBS' "NFL Today" pregame show.

All that ended, however, after an off-hand television interview in 1988, given while he was eating lunch in Washington. Snyder said that black athletes were superior to whites because of breeding and that the only thing whites continue to control are coaching jobs.

The comments ignited a major protest from black leaders and Snyder was fired from his CBS job the next day. Part of the problem, coming only a short time after Dodger executive Al Campanis said blacks lacked the "necessities" to be major league managers and front-office executives.

"The black is a better athlete to begin with because he has been bred to be that way," Snyder said in the interview. "This goes all the way back to the Civil War, when the slave owner would breed his big black to his big black woman so that he could have a big black kid, see."

And on the prospects of more blacks in coaching, he said, "There is not going to be anything left for the white people."

Manakides, Snyder's friend who was acting as the family spokesman Sunday, said "the Greek" was haunted by the possibility that he would only be remembered only for those remarks.

After Snyder was fired, his health almost immediately began to fail him. Less than a week after he was dismissed by CBS, he was admitted to Duke Medical Center with complaints of chest pains.

In the years after his firing, Snyder lived in semi-isolation at his home in Durham, N.C. Manakides said he convinced Snyder to return to Las Vegas—"where the action is"—last year.

Snyder, born Emetrico Synodinos in Steubenville, Ohio, never made it past the ninth grade. But he became a part of the Las Vegas scene as the town grew into the gambling capital of the world. At one point, his syndicated column ran in more than 240 newspapers around the nation.

Services will be in Steubenville. Snyder is survived by his wife, Joan; daughters Vicki and Stephanie Snyder; son Anthony; a brother, sister and grandson. In lieu of flowers, the family asks that contributions be sent to the Cystic Fibrosis Foundation, the disease that claimed three of his children.

OBITUARIES

Jimmy 'The Greek' Snyder Dies at 77

By Leonard Shapiro
Washington Post Staff Writer

Jimmy "The Greek" Snyder, 77, the flamboyant oddsmaker who was fired as a CBS Sports commentator for making controversial statements about black athletes, died April 21 at a hospital in Las Vegas, where he was being treated for a broken hip.

over coaching jobs like everybody wants them to, there's not going to be anything left for the white people." During the interview, all recorded by a WRC camera crew, Mr. Snyder said a black athlete was better that a white one because "he's been bred to be that way because of his thigh size and big size."

His remarks came less than a year

managing editor. The two patched up their differences and remained colleagues until Mr. Snyder was dismissed.

Mr. Snyder made odds on all sports. He almost always carried a huge wad of $100 bills in his pocket and had a particular penchant for the racetrack. He attended most of the major events, and, at one point, his syndicated column and daily odds were picked up by more than 200 newspapers. He liked to boast that he had picked the winners in 18 of first 21 Super Bowls. After CBS fired him, however, many papers dropped his service, and he essentially retired to his home in Durham,

JIMMY "THE GREEK" SNYDER

1979 PHOTO

THE NEW YORK TIMES

Jimmy (the Greek) Snyder, 76, Is Dead; a Sports Oddsmaker

By ERIC PACE

Jimmy Snyder, known as "Jimmy the Greek," an oddsmaker and football personality who brought gambling to the forefront of televised sports but was fired by CBS Sports for saying that black Americans were better athletes than whites because of physical traits dating back to slavery, died yesterday in a Las Vegas, Nev., hospital. He was 76.

He had spent the last year in a hotel or hospital room in Las Vegas or in Durham, N.C., where he and his wife, Joan, had lived.

A friend, Tommy Manakides, said that Mr. Snyder had suffered from diabetes and had been in declining health and died of a coronary at Transitional Hospitals.

Mr. Snyder was born Demetrios Georgios Synodinos in Ohio, and his family's roots are in the Greek island of Chios in the Aegean Sea. He was raised in Steubenville, Ohio.

"He got involved in sports at a young age," Mr. Manakides said of the high school dropout, "and he would follow all the newspapers and all the sporting events going on" and he began compiling sports data.

As a teen-ager in Steubenville, Mr. Snyder kept company with bookmakers, laying bets chiefly on college basketball and football games. Later he took money he had won by gambling and invested it in oil-drilling and coal strip-mining ventures.

But after some bad luck as an investor — "22 dry wells" is how he

once described it — he made his way to Las Vegas in 1968, and there he became known as an oddsmaker on the weekly pro football betting line. In 1968, he gave this terse summary of his analytical techniques in football: "Overall team speed is the biggest factor. Then the front four on defense. Then the back defense, especially the cornerbacks. Then the quarterbacks, and then I have to consider the intangibles."

Mr. Snyder went on to spend 12 years as the betting analyst, specializing in forecasts intended to help bettors, on the CBS Sports program, "The N.F.L. Today," — aired each Sunday in the pro football season — to mixed reviews. Mr. Snyder often spoke vaguely or indecisively in appraising games, which gave rise to another, lesser-known nickname, "Jimmy the Meek."

But he was not meek when he remarked — among other things — in a videotaped luncheon interview with Ed Hotaling of WRC, a Washington television station: "During the slave period, the slave owner would breed his big black with his big woman so that he could have a big black kid — that's where it all started."

Mr. Snyder made his statement, which was broadcast on Martin Luther King Jr. Day in a 1988 WRC report about blacks' progress in society.

Mr. Snyder was swiftly fired by CBS Sports, which issued a statement saying, "In no way do these comments reflect the view of CBS

Jimmy (the Greek) Snyder   Reuters, 1985

Sports."

Afterward, Mr. Snyder observed, with regard to his remarks, "What a foolish thing to say." He also complained of chest pains and spent a few days in a Durham hospital.

For his part, Floyd H. Flake, a Democratic Congressman from Queens, wrote that Mr. Snyder made "racially offensive statements and racial slurs more acceptable" with such comments.

Jesse Jackson, who was then a presidential candidate, criticized Mr. Snyder's remarks but said that he should not be a scapegoat for the sports world's failure to hire more black managers. The Miami Herald published an editorial on what it

a longtime fund-raiser to help cure the disease.

"The man had a heart of gold," said Gil Brandt, former personnel director of the Dallas Cowboys and one of Snyder's closer friends. "I think he did a lot of good things for the NFL, even though there was always that stigma of gambling attached to him. He got the league a lot of attention just by talking about it."

An autobiography, "Wizard of Odds," is to be published next month. An earlier book, "Jimmy The Greek," was published in 1975. Mr. Snyder also spoke frequently to business groups and corporations and appeared in television commercials.

Survivors include his wife, a son, two daughters, his mother, a brother, three sisters and a grandson.

Mr. Snyder was the son of a Greek immigrant grocer. After World War II, he moved to Las Vegas and began making his reputation in public relations, at one point representing Howard Hughes. Before the 1948 presidential election, he polled 1,900 women and found that most of them did not like men with mustaches. As a result, he made Harry S. Truman a 17-to-1 favorite to beat the mustachioed Thomas E. Dewey. When Truman won, Snyder reportedly made $1,000,000 and was on his way.

He took "The Greek" moniker from a renowned horseplayer of the 1950s, known as Nick The Greek. Snyder moved to South Florida in the 1970s and often was a regular at Hialeah, Gulfstream and Calder tracks. His life also was touched by tragedy. Two of his daughters died from cystic fibrosis, and he was

Snyder handicaps the races at the Belmont Track in New York.

Final farewell at the Steubenville Greek Orthodox Church on April 25, 1996.
— Eric Ayars, The Intelligencer

Herald-Star

VOL. 190, NO. 325   FRIDAY, APRIL 26, 1996

GOODBYE TO A WINNER

GOING HOME — The funeral motorcade for Steubenville native Jimmy "The Greek" Snyder crosses the Washington Street overpass on its way to Union Cemetery where Snyder was laid to rest Thursday. Snyder always maintained ties with his hometown.

Friends, family remember Jimmy 'The Greek' Snyder

By MATZ MALONE
Business editor

STEUBENVILLE — Jimmy "The Greek" Snyder went out a winner, said one of his long time associates after the funeral for the famous odds-maker who got his career off to a start when Steubenville was a rough and tumble town.

Snyder's public life was centered around sports activities, posting odds and booking bets on football, basketball and baseball games.

This theme was to continue through his life and into his funeral as the Rev. Dean Dimon, of Holy Trinity Greek Orthodox Church, said during a eulogy "a football team doesn't have all day to score — it only has one hour.

"A baseball player only gets three strikes. The Ultimate Umpire has set a time limit on life and has called time on Jimmy."

The funeral was attended by about 100 of Snyder's family members and close friends.

Frank Deford, chairman of the Cystic Fibrosis Foundation, a writer for Newsweek and commentator for Home Box Office and National Public Radio, was a long-time friend of Snyder. Snyder was very active in the Cystic Fibrosis Foundation, after three of his children died from the disease. Snyder lost three children to the disease and Deford had one child die from it.

"It was a sad connection in a way," Deford said. "Jimmy was often difficult to know. He didn't let a lot of people get close to him, but we were at that same place (because of their family losses).

"Probably the fondest memory of Jimmy was one time in the back of a limo when he broke up (over the loss of his children). He was a tough guy, but he broke up. He leaned on me and cried.

"That was so 'un-Jimmy-like.'

"I have a lot of happy memories, too," Deford said. "Like being at the race track with Jim. To join that was to join the aura of 'The Greek.'"

Before the funeral service began,

CONSOLED — Jimmy "The Greek" Snyder's stepmother, Agnes Synodinos of Steubenville, is consoled by family members at the funeral of the famous odds-maker Thursday.

Snyder's daughter, Vicki Snyder, was talking with Deford and Tommy Manakides, "The Greek's" personal and close friend.

"Jimmy died very peacefully. He never suffered," Manakides said.

Snyder's daughter, who was born in Steubenville and now lives in Las Vegas, looked at the massive stone columns in front of the church. "I was baptized in this church. I was about 3."

She said her father made many donations to the church for its building and renovation projects over the years.

"He was a wonderful, kind, loving and the sweetest father. He was the best to me," she said.

At the funeral Mass, Snyder's open casket was at the front of the ornate altar with icons of Jesus Christ and the church's saints. The liturgy was mostly in Greek with the priests intoning the message and the cantors replying.

The lower half of Snyder's casket had a floral blanket of white and deep blue carnations.

At the end of the Mass, Snyder's friends and family members paid their last

farewell to the Steubenville native who became known as "The Wizard of Odds.

As the funeral service concluded, Darrel Neilson of Richmond, Va., a long-time friend and former business associate of Snyder's said, "Just say Jimmy was a winner. I learned so much from him. He was tremendously giving."

Deford delivered the eulogy at the cemetery, saying he was the surrogate for all of "The Greek's" friends.

Deford noticed one of the flower arrangements, a horseshoe, was technically upside-down. The open end of the horseshoe was down.

"Jimmy would have noticed that. Anyone who has spent time around a track knows that if the horseshoe has the open end down all the luck leaks out."

Deford asked one of Snyder's grandsons to make sure the flower arrangement was turned right side up before he left the funeral.

"This man carried out one of the unique lives of our time. He was an original," Deford told the people who gathered at the Union Cemetery mausoleum Thursday.

Herald-Star
obituary by
Matz Malone.
— Mike Bordo

Index